C.2

Fashion
Production Terms

Language of Fashion Series

Fashion Production Terms

Debbie Ann Gioello
Adjunct Associate Professor: Fashion Design Department
Fashion Institute of Technology

Beverly Berke
Adjunct Assistant Professor: Fashion Design Department
Fashion Institute of Technology

Fairchild Publications
New York

Book Design by: Janet Solgaard
Photographed by: Debbie Ann Gioello
                 Staff of Fairchild Publications Photo Department

Standard Book Number: 87005-200-4

Library of Congress Catalog Card Number: 78-62284

Printed in the United States of America

Contents

Foreword **vii**
Preface **ix**
Acknowledgments **xi**
1 Shape & Design Control **1**
2 Aids, Tools & Equipment for Draping, Drafting, Measuring & Marking **14**
3 Drafting Terminology **30**
4 Draping Terminology **37**
5 Terminology Common to Drafting & Draping **44**
6 Tracing & Marking Terminology **51**
7 Types of Patterns **54**
8 Fabric Structure **58**
9 Fabric Terminology **67**
10 Spreading and/or Folding Fabric **71**
11 Pattern Layout **75**
12 Aids, Tools & Equipment for Cutting **84**
13 Cutting Terminology **101**
14 Hand Sewing Needles **106**
15 Sewing Machine Needles **111**
16 Thread **121**
17 Aids & Tools for Garment Construction **139**
18 Basting **160**
19 Bias **164**
20 Casing **171**
21 Elastic **174**
22 Facings **179**
23 Fasteners **182**
24 Buttons **198**
25 Buttonholes & Openings **203**
26 Zippers **211**
27 Hems **222**
28 Plackets **234**
29 Seams **238**
30 Seam Finishes **250**
31 Seam Terminology **258**
32 Hand Stitches **262**
33 Machine Stitches **272**
34 Waistline Treatments **281**
35 Various Construction Details **290**
36 Related Construction Terminology **301**
37 Aids, Tools & Equipment for Pressing **312**
38 Pressing Terminology **322**
39 Listing of Notions & Findings **323**
Bibliography **327**
Index **329**

In order to maintain an intimate involvement during more than thirty years in the "rag business," communication with my superiors, co-workers, and subordinates has been an absolute necessity. In the early stages of my career, I believed I could speak and, when necessary, write in a manner that could be clearly understood in the day-to-day dialogue of the Industry. How soon I learned my error in judgment! Investigation led me to conclude that it was not my command of the English language that was the barrier to complete comprehension, but rather the complexity of a multifaceted Industry.

Each segment of the trade has had its own history during which time specialized methods and equipment have led to trade jargon peculiar to that segment alone. Because management was reluctant to risk employing a person "unfamiliar with the Industry," as shown by a lack of understanding during an interview, individuals bred in a specific segment of the Industry tended to stay in that segment thus perpetuating the closed nature of its language.

The faculty of the Management Engineering Technology Department at the Fashion Institute of Technology long ago recognized this situation and, over the years, has attempted to standardize the language taught to students both within the department and out. When Professors Debbie Gioello and Beverly Berke, of the Fashion Design Department, first approached me with their idea regarding this book, I jumped at the chance to volunteer whatever assistance in the form of information or guidance I could contribute.

The reader must realize that *The Language of Fashion* is not a "how-to" book, but a true reference for those in and trying to enter the Industry who are in need of a more precise understanding of the terms used in the Industry.

There have been other dictionaries and glossaries, but none have presented the material in such depth and with such clarity, precision and logic—and with photos to illustrate *each item listed.* At an early stage in the development of *The Language of Fashion,* Professors Gioello and Berke realized what a tremendous task it would be to compile into one volume all of the information from an industry of such broad scope. Thus, *Language* will appear in its final form as a seven-volume illustrated encyclopedia.

I want to thank them for allowing me to have a small part in this monumental undertaking and for their confidence in me to have accepted my offer of assistance. It has been an exhilarating experience working with two such knowledgeable, warm, and vivacious professionals of the Fashion Industry. I look forward to a continuing alliance on future volumes.

Jack Walfish, Associate Professor, PE, CCE
Management Engineering
Technology Department
Fashion Institute of Technology

ꝰreface ―――――――――――――――――――――――――――

The language of fashion stems from a group of widely diversified trades, whose combined efforts constitute the garment industry. An understanding of the language of fashion, as used in these diverse trades, provides a means of communicating facts and ideas.

The growth and development of the garment industry is reflected in the new methods of manufacturing, the changes in clothing production, and the advances in machinery. These advances and changes produced an increased vocabulary which necessitated new definitions and revisions of existing terms.

Our research has shown that:

• Various applications for garment construction, with regard to seams, stitches and details, are referred to by more than one term
• Trade sources often identify different stitches, finishes, and construction applications by the same name
• Terms well known in one segment of the industry are not always familiar in others

The purpose of this illustrated encyclopedia is to resolve the inconsistencies and discrepancies in terminology in the trade; and to help clarify the meaning and identify items, processes, and equipment used in the apparel industry.

This book, *Fashion Production Terms*, is the first in a series entitled *The Language of Fashion*. It is intended to be used as a source of reference for materials and terms relating to the design room professional, production room technician, apparel trade manufacturer, retail merchandiser, educator, student, as well as the consumer and layman.

Information has been compiled from our experience as designers and educators; through research of trade journals and publications; by communication with suppliers and manufacturers; through personal contact with technicians, educators, and individuals knowledgeable in their respective fields. Accuracy has been of greatest importance. But new works are rarely free from error. We hope that the reader will call attention to errors of commission or omission.

The chapters are presented in a progression that relates to the flow of the production process or the route of the garment from its origin through development to completion.

The terms are grouped according to the subject in which they may be used or applied. *Each* chapter is preceded by a list of terms within the chapter and an introduction. The terms are listed alphabetically or, in some cases, alphabetically under general headings. There is also an alphabetical cross-referenced index at the end of the book.

Each term is defined and illustrated with photographs and/or drawings for identification. Photographs, illustrations, and charts have been positioned with relationship to the definitions and uses of the term so that full visual and written information may be utilized. For the purpose of illustration and clarity of presentation, samples have been assembled and prepared in exaggerated proportions or contrasting texture and color. Drawings are also exaggerated for a clearer representation of the term.

For most terms a bulleted listing of uses follows the definition and offers quick assimilation of facts. Where necessary, special comments are included to expand initial information.

Due to lack of space, some judgment regarding information to be included within each chapter was required. Subjects too expansive to be incorporated into this volume will be covered in detail in subsequent volumes. Books to follow will cover:

• *Figure types and size ranges* including commercial pattern sizes
• *Fabrics* including type, hand and drapeability qualities; use, care, pressing and sewing techniques involved
• *Silhouette* including parts of the garment and design details
• *Trimmings* including embroidery, decorative stitches, and buttons
• *Fitting* including fitting problems, figure types and styles for different figures
• *Machinery* including attachments, parts and accessories

1979

Debbie Ann Gioello
Beverly Berke
New York

Acknowledgments ———————————————

The authors wish to acknowledge the following people and various companies for their cooperation and aid in making available information and many of the sample products, charts, photographs, and illustrations used throughout this book: George B. Armstead Jr., The Merrow Machine Company; Harry Bard, Cutting Room Appliances; John Bloch Jr., The Wolf Machine Company; Charles H. Brody, Fairgate Rule Company, Inc.; Brookfield Inc.; Arnold Burton, Tex-O-Graph Corporation; Robert Calabro, Joan Carron, and Mr. Finn, J.P. Stevens; F.M. Cottrell, The Singer Company; Richard DeVitto, Delbon & Company; E.I. du Pont de Nemours & Co. Inc.; William Fioravanti Inc.; James J. Flaherty and H.W. Kunhardt, Scoville; Teresa Gramuglia, Successful Creations; Gary E. Graves, American Thread Company; Charles Grecco, W.T. Gensheimer, Inc.; Sharon Hart, B. Blumenthal & Company, Inc.; Herb Jaggi, G. Braf Company, Inc.; Edward R. Johnson, Lever Manufacturing Corporation; Janet Klaer, Coats and Clark; Irving Lederich, Truemart Fabrics Corporation; Gary Lee Pesa, The Perfection Table Company; Joseph G. Maimin, H. Maimin Company, Inc.; Frank Masi, Rheem Textile Systems, Inc.; Senta C. Mead, Fashionetics, Inc.; Jonathan Meyers, A. Meyers & Sons Corporation; F.E. Morris Jr., The Reece Corporation; Barbara Narhadian, William E. Wright & Company; Seymour Ossam, Hoffritz for Cutlery, Inc.; Rae Pantalone, Butterick Fashion Marketing Company; June P. Reep, Belding Lily Company; W.T. Rowles, Talon/Textron (Universal Fasteners); Robin Sanders, McCall Pattern Company; Kenneth L. Sandow, Union Special Corporation; Paul Schepis, U.S. Blindstitch Machine Corporation; Herman Schwabe Inc.; G.L. Scott, Velcro Corporation; Spreading Machine Exchange; Superior Sewing Machine Supply Corp.; M. Sweeney, Sears, Roebuck and Company; Mitsue Toriumi, Y K K (U.S.A.) Inc.; Vinson Ulke, Vin-Max Company; Norman F. Vandervoort, Belding Heminway Company, Inc.; George Waldes, Waldes Kohinoor Inc.; Betty Watts, National Home Sewing Association; Wallace L. Wilson, The Torrington Company; The Wolf Form Company.

We wish to thank and extend our appreciation to the following members of the faculty and staff at the Fashion Institute of Technology for their invaluable assistance: Jack Walfish, Management Engineering Technology Department; Marjorie Miller, Peter Smith, Lorraine Weberg, and staff of the Library Media Service; Robert Riley, Tom Drew, Don Petrillo, and staff of the Design Lab; Bernard Zamkoff, Chairman of the Fashion Design Department; Clara Branch, Lotis Mallard, Charles Turner, and staff of the Fabric Room; Robert Cabrera (tailoring), Herbert Ross (fur), Lita Konde (design studio) of the Fashion Design Department; Joseph Ferby, Management Engineering Department; Harry Besserman, Patternmaking Department; Frank Jagusiac, Machine Operations Department. Our appreciation is also extended to Fay Mammano, formerly of the High School of Fashion Industries, New York City.

Our personal gratitude to David T. Novick and Robert J. Berke, for their time and assistance in the formation and development of this book.

1 ~ Shape & Design Control

Apparel Design Feature
Apparel Silhouette
Cut on the Bias / Bias Cut
Cut of the Garment / Flare
Dart:
  Dart
  Decorative Dart
  Flange Dart
  Dart Slash
  Dart Tuck
  Double Dart / Double-Ended Dart
Ease
Gauging
Pleat:
  Pleat
  Accordion Pleat
  Box Pleat
  Crystal Pleat

Inverted Pleat
Kick Pleat
Knife Pleat
Side Pleat (Single)
Side Pleat (Multiple)
Sunburst Pleat
Seams
Shirring:
  Shirring / Gathering
  Elasticized Shirring
  French Shirring / French Gathering
  Waffle Shirring
Smocking:
  Hand Smocking
  Machine Smocking
Tucks:
  Pin Tucks
  Released Tucks (Outside and Inside)

Fashion trend and styling determine the type and amount of shaping or fullness that becomes the design element of the garment.

Silhouette, style and proportion are achieved through the placement of fabric grainlines and design lines, and the manipulation of excess fabric.

Style is the essential characteristic of a garment with regard to silhouette, design feature, proportion, color, and fabric. Proportion is the harmonious interrelationship of silhouette, design feature, style line, and fabric grainline in a given design with regard to figure type.

Fabric is molded, shaped or released to conform to body contours for functional and/or decorative purposes forming the silhouette and/or style line of the garment.

Seams, darts, and tucks are used as a means of shaping fabric to fit the figure. Fullness is introduced to clothing through the use of pleats, released tucks, and shirring. Fullness may be drawn to a desired width by elastic or drawstring enclosed in a casing, or by elastic stitched directly to the garment. Bias-cut fabric, or the cut of the garment, may be molded over the body contour to fit and/or add fullness to the garment.

Pleats are folds in fabric used as a means of adding fullness and motion to a garment. They create a vertical line design and facilitate ease of body movement and action.

Pleats are designated as *flat* or *dimensional*. *Flat* pleats may be folded and left unpressed, creased, or stitched to a designated length. They may be planned singly, in groups, or in evenly spaced series. *Dimensional* pleats are permanently set into a pattern of creased ridges or fluting. Flat and dimensional pleats may be shaped and/or controlled to fit body measurements and body contour.

Crease lines of pleats are parallel and follow fabric grainline with the exception of sunburst pleats which have radiating lines. Firm and closely woven fabrics hold creases better than soft or loosely woven fabrics.

Professional pleaters, utilizing specific pleating machines, permanently set pleats on prepared panels of predetermined length and width with regard to design and/or manufacturers' specifications.

The functional and decorative features used for design control and shaping may be planned vertically, horizontally, or diagonally according to the design of the garment or the effect desired. These features are planned as part of the draped or drafted pattern pieces.

The type of shape or design control selected depends on:
• Silhouette effect desired
• Design and style of garment
• Type of garment
• Use of garment
• Care of garment
• Figure type and size range
• Type and weight of fabric

Apparel Design Feature

Style lines and/or design features within the silhouette of the garment including:

Necklines
Collars
Pockets
Closures
Trimmings
Yokes and/or Sleeves

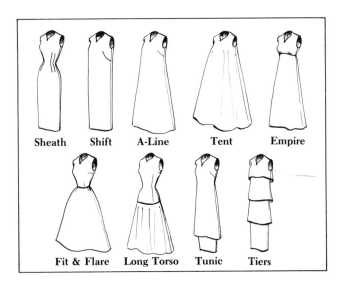

Apparel Silhouette

The shape or outline of a garment, not including design detail, identified as:

Form Fitted to Full
Sheath
Shift
A-Line
Tent

Horizontal Division—Seams
Empire (under bustline)
Fit and Flare (natural waistline)
Long Torso (hipline)

Horizontal Division—Overlays
Tunic
Tiers

Cut on the Bias / Bias Cut

Manipulation of the bias or true bias of fabrics, to conform to the body curve and affecting the controlled fullness of the garment.

- On garments made of soft, lightweight and loosely woven fabrics to achieve body clinging silhouettes.
- On heavyweight or closely woven fabrics to produce crisp silhouettes which stand away from the body.
- For lingerie, slips and petticoats.
- To emphasize geometric fabrics; sheen, light refraction or glitter of novelty fabrics.

Bias-cut garments utilize seams for fitting, emphasing design detail, or extending fabric width.

Bias Flare

Cut of the Garment / Flare

The result achieved by manipulating fabric, without darts, pleats or gathers, to conform to a body contour, seam or style lines affecting the controlled fullness at the lower edge of the garment.

- To produce flared silhouette.
- To develop a flared skirt, tent top or cape.
- To develop a topper or swagger coat.
- To develop a bell or caplet sleeve.
- To develop Palazzo pants.
- On geometric fabrics to achieve chevrons at seam lines.
- On garments made of lightweight and loosely woven fabrics to achieve softer silhouettes at lower edges.
- On garments made of heavyweight and closely woven fabrics to produce crisp silhouettes which stand away from the body.

Pleats or gathers may be introduced into a flared garment section for added fullness, design emphasis, or style variation.

Fullness at lower edge may be minimal or exaggerated depending on the fabric used, silhouette or design effect desired.

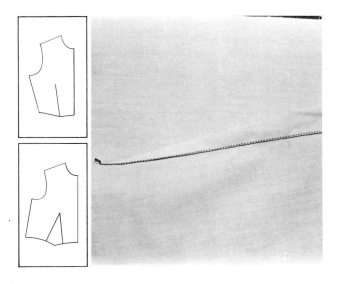

Dart

The take-up of excess fabric, of a determined amount, at the edge of the garment and converging to a diminishing point.

- To fit pattern section to contour of body.
- On front bodice section, from any perimeter point, towards apex to shape fabric over bust.
- At back neck or at back shoulder seam to shape fabric over upper shoulder and allow ease over shoulder blade.
- At back bodice waist to fit fabric to waistline.
- At elbow of a long, fitted sleeve to allow for elbow movement.
- On skirt front and back sections to shape fabric to waistline and allow ease over hips.
- On side front and side back panels of gored skirt to shape fabric to waistline and allow ease over hips.

Darts formed to fit body contour vary in shape and size and may result in straight, concave or convex converging pattern lines. Shape of dart is indicated by convergent lines on finished garment.

French darts are diagonal darts tapering to the apex; originating from any point between the hipline to two inches above the waist along the side seam.

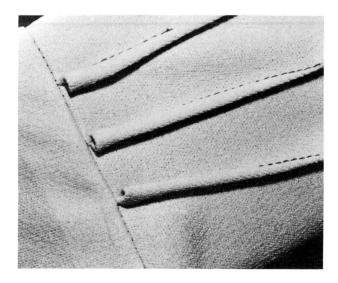

Decorative Dart

The take-up in a pattern piece of excess fabric constructed so that the excess fabric forming the dart is on the *face* of the garment.

- To create a design effect.
- To emphasize a style line.

The decorative dart may be stitched with the same, contrasting or buttonhole twist thread; emphasized with cording insert or stiffening.

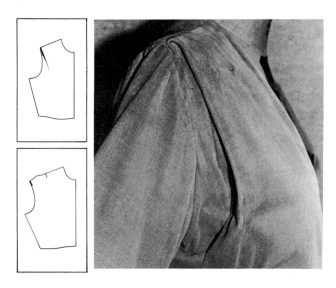

Flange Dart

The take-up of excess fabric, of a determined amount in the form of a pleat, on a front pattern piece, at the intersection of the shoulder and armhole seam.

- To create an illusion of wider shoulders.
- To create ease across the chest and upper armhole.
- To maintain symmetry of a geometric fabric design.

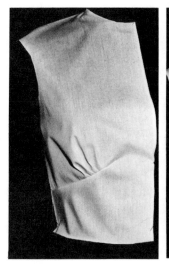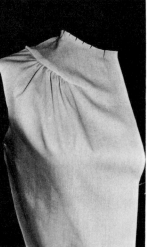

Dart Slash

A fitted dart constructed as a seam, designed so that one convergent line introducing gathers, dart tucks or pleats is of greater measure than the other.

- To release fullness to fit contour of bust, shoulder or hip.
- To introduce design fullness for style effect.
- Horizontally for yoke effect at hip or shoulder.
- Horizontally to create midriff or band effect.
- To create variation in sleeve silhouette.

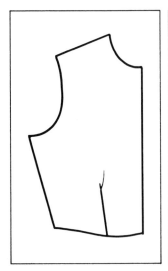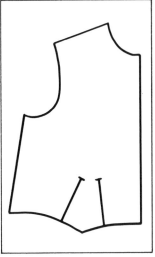

Dart Tuck

The take-up of excess fabric, of a determined amount, at the edge of the garment and converging towards a point or points of release.

- On front bodice at waistline, shoulder or center front releasing fabric to conform to bust shape.
- On back bodice at waistline or shoulder releasing fabric to conform to body contour.
- At waistline of skirts, pants or shorts allowing ease over hip and abdomen.
- On one-piece garments at waistline releasing fullness above and below fitted area.
- On full sleeves to fit wrist.
- Instead of darts to create a softer design effect.

Fabric excess may be distributed into two or more dart tucks.

Dart tuck is formed by the partial stitching of a dart along its convergent lines releasing fullness.

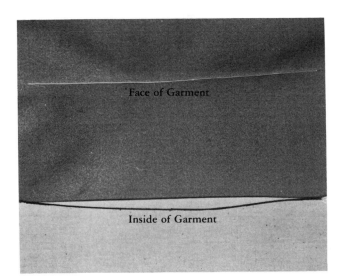

Face of Garment

Inside of Garment

Double Dart / Double-Ended Dart

The take-up of excess fabric spanning the waistline or center front apex level, of a determined amount, at the center and converging to diminishing points at each end.

- On a one-piece dress, coat or long jacket to fit garment at waistline area.
- On bodice at center front apex level of form-fitted garments such as swimwear and evening gowns.
- To remove excess fabric from one-piece gusset.

Double darts formed to fit body contour at waistline area vary in size and length and may result in straight, concave and/or convex converging pattern lines.

Sometimes referred to as *diamond-shaped* or *clam-shaped* darts.

Ease

The even distribution of fullness at a seam or style line controlling a minimal amount of fabric excess without forming gathers, tucks, or darts.

- To enable one section of a garment to be joined to a smaller section.
- On sleeve cap.
- Instead of dart at elbow of fitted sleeve.
- At elbow area of two-piece sleeve.
- To shape seam of princess line bodice over apex area.
- Instead of darts to shape women's tailored skirts.

Knit, stretch, and loosely woven fabrics can be eased and molded more easily than firmly woven fabrics.

Gauging

Two or more parallel rows of evenly spaced running stitches drawn up to a controlled, predetermined fullness which correspond to a smaller adjoining seam, specified body measurement, or garment area.

- Instead of gathers to emphasize the drawing up of the fullness in the garment style.
- On academic and clerical robes.
- As a design effect to emphasize geometric patterns of fabric.

Small, even folds formed by the gauging pattern are visible on the face of the garment.

Running stitches may vary from 1/8 to 3/8 inch (3.175 to 9.525 mm) in length.

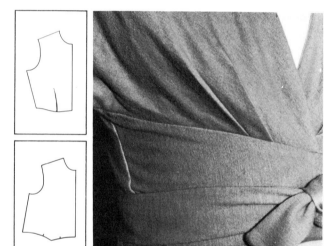

Pleat

The take up of excess fabric at the edge of a garment by means of doubling the fabric ply upon itself, producing a fold and forming an underlay of 5/8 to 2 inches (15.875 to 50.8 mm).

- Singly or in a series.
- At waist, shoulder or hipline.
- Below yoke line.
- To fit lower edge of sleeve into cuff.
- At sleeve cap as a design feature.
- On a blouse, bodice or jacket releasing fullness over apex or across shoulder.

Series may be planned to face in one direction or towards each other.

Creates a softened effect at points of release.

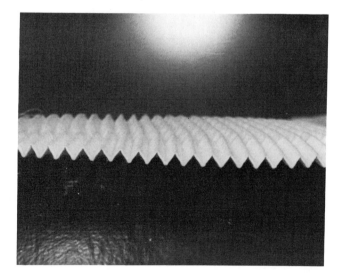

Accordion Pleat

A series of evenly spaced, parallel, alternating creases creating a raised and recessed pattern.

- On garments where a straight or cylindrical silhouette is desired.
- On shifts, skirts, sleeves, and shirtwaist-styled garments.

Pleats are permanently set by an industrial pleating machine.

Panels for garment are cut to a predetermined length and are hemmed prior to pleating.

Unhemmed edge of pleated panel is controlled to fit body circumference and/or style line.

Box Pleat

Evenly spaced folds in a fabric ply doubled over to face away from each other. Appear as inverted pleats on the face of the garment.

- On skirts, blouses, bodices, and one-piece garments.
- Below hip or shoulder yokes.

Depth of underlays producing box pleat need not be equal to width of box.

A box pleat may be unpressed, pressed in place, or partially stitched; grouped or designed to fill circumference of garment.

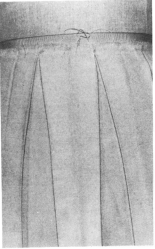

| Face of Garment | Inside of Garment |

Crystal Pleat

A series of evenly spaced, narrow, parallel grooves and ridges.

- On garments where a straight or cylindrical silhouette is desired.
- On evening or bridal wear.
- On shifts, skirts, sleeves and shirtwaist-styled garments.
- On flounces and ruffles.

Pleats can be set into partial length of fabric in a garment section to create a novelty effect.

Panels for garment are cut to a predetermined length and may be hemmed prior to pleating. Garment may be hemmed after pleating for a ruffled effect.

Inverted Pleat

Two folds in a fabric ply, a measured distance apart, doubled under to meet each other at a central point on the face of the fabric.

- At center front, center back or side seam of skirts.
- At side seam of pants.
- At princess line seam of front, back, or both.
- At center back of men's shirts and jackets to allow arm movement.
- At center front and/or center back of garments designed for maternity wear.
- At center front and center back of divided skirts.
- In sportswear garments to provide action room for arm movement.
- On gored skirts and princess line garments to increase circumference.
- At center back of coats and jackets providing sitting ease.

Kick Pleat

An inverted or side pleat released at knee level or below.

- To increase circumference of narrow garment allowing walking ease.
- At side seam, center front, center back, or all three.

A kick pleat may be planned as a single side pleat, double pleat, or with a separate underlay.

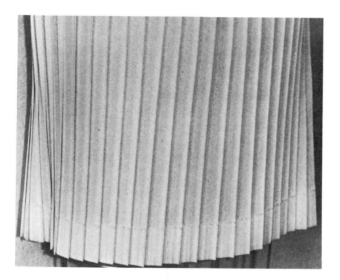

Knife Pleat

A fabric ply doubled upon itself in a series of folds forming underlays of 5/8 inch (15.875 mm) or less; permanently pressed to lie in one direction.

- On skirts, blouses, bodices, and one-piece garments.
- In conjunction with fitted yokes.
- As an insert panel.

A knife pleat is not applicable to stretch, bulky or napped fabrics.

May be planned in groups or as an evenly spaced series filling circumference of garment.

Side Pleat (Single)

A fabric ply folded upon itself producing a fold and forming an underlay of 5/8 to 2 inches (15.875 to 50.8 mm).

- At garment bodice back below yoke allowing arm movement.
- On coats and jackets at princess line to accommodate sitting and walking ease.
- On gored skirts and princess line garments to increase circumference.

A side pleat may be folded and left unpressed, creased or partially stitched to fit body contour.

Side Pleat (Multiple)

A fabric ply folded upon itself producing a fold and forming an underlay of 5/8 to 2 inches (15.875 to 50.8 mm); repeated to form a series of pleats all facing one direction.

- On skirts.
- On one-piece straight silhouette garments.
- At lower edge of sleeves.
- At sleeve cap.
- On blouses or bodices releasing fullness over apex or across shoulder.
- Below shoulder and hip yokes.

Sunburst Pleat

A series of evenly spaced, radiating, alternating creases creating a raised and recessed pattern.

- On garments where a flared or circular silhouette is desired.
- To create a full silhouette without creating bulk at the waistline.
- For tent-style garments.
- On sheer and lightweight fabrics.
- On flounces and ruffles.

Panels for garment are cut to a predetermined size prior to pleating. Pleats are permanently set by an industrial pleating machine.

Hemline and hem finish of garments are established after garment is completed.

Narrow part of pleat formation is used at waist- or shoulder line; or sleeve cap of garment.

Seams

The result of eliminating fabric excess through the manipulation of two or more panels to conform to style line and body contour.

- Instead of darts, dart tucks, or released tucks to fit garment to the body.
- To form princess line bodice; gored garments extending from shoulder to hem such as shifts, tent dresses, capes, coats and jackets; gored skirts.
- To shape one-piece fitted princess line garments.

Style lines of princess line bodice originate and end at any perimeter point on front bodice and cross apex area resulting in two or more panels with corresponding seams.

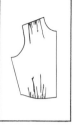

Shirring / Gathering

The control of predetermined fullness drawn up to correspond to a smaller adjoining seamline or specified body measurement.

- Whenever evenly distributed fullness is designed into a garment.
- In a garment section or design detail.
- On garments gathered into a yoke or midriff.
- On dirndl skirts, aprons, and pinafores.
- On necklines of peasant blouses.
- On harem skirts or trousers.
- At sleeve cap to create puff.
- At lower edge of sleeve or pants leg.
- On design elements such as ruffles, ruchings, jabots, and flounces.

Stitches forming gathers are concealed within the seam line and are not visible on the face of the garment.

May be made by drawing in three or less parallel rows of hand running or machine gathering stitches; by a gathering attachment or foot on a home machine; or by specialized industrial machines.

Elasticized Shirring

The control of a predetermined fullness by means of multiple rows of parallel stitching utilizing elastic, cord or thread.

- To produce expansion and contraction in the garment section.
- On garments designed to accommodate more than one size or body configuration.
- To control fullness of entire bodice, partial bodice, midriff or hip area.
- For tube or halter tops.

Shirring forms a decorative design detail visible on the face of the garment. Amount of control is determined by length of stitch, type and expandability of elastic, number and spacing of parallel rows of stitching, and their interrelationship with the fabric.

May be made with elastic thread in the bobbin of a lockstitch or zigzag machine; elastic thread as a chain stitch; or by encasing elastic cord in a zigzag stitch.

Handmade French Shirring

Machine-made French Shirring

French Shirring / French Gathering

The control of a predetermined fullness drawn up to correspond to a smaller adjoining seamline, specified body measurement or area.

- To form a decorative design detail visible on the face of the garment.
- To create yoke effect at shoulder or hip.
- At lower edge of sleeve to create band effect.
- Where fullness is designed to release above and below stitching.

French shirring may be made by drawing up of three or more parallel rows of hand running or machine gathering stitches; produced on multi-needled industrial machines. Number of rows of shirring depends upon location on the garment, body contour and design detail desired.

Stitching may be made with matching, contrasting, buttonhole twist or decorative thread. Stay may be used beneath shirring for reinforcement.

When completed, shirring has no give or elasticity.

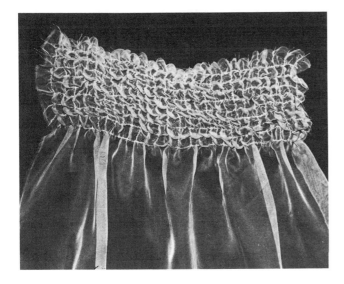

Waffle Shirring

The control of a predetermined fullness by means of a grid of multiple rows of parallel stitching utilizing elastic cord or thread.

- To produce two-way expansion and contraction in the garment section.
- On garments requiring two-way stretch such as body suits, swimwear, and action wear.
- On garments designed to accommodate more than one size or body configuration.
- To control fullness of entire bodice, partial bodice, midriff or hip area.
- For tube or halter tops.
- On small areas as design detail or trim.
- To form decorative design detail visible on the face of the garment.

Amount of control is determined by length of stitch, type and expandability of elastic, number and spacing of grid rows of stitching and their interrelationship with the fabric.

Waffle shirring is made on the length- and crossgrain of the fabric.

Hand Smocking

Drawing a predetermined fullness into a specific amount by alternately stitching together parallel, uniform folds at regular intervals. Fabric folds may vary in size up to 1 1/2 inch (38.1 mm) in depth.

- To create an expandable, decorative-patterned effect.
- To form the effect of yoke, midriff, band or cuff.
- At waistline to release fabric above and below stitching.
- On garment styles and/or areas not subject to strain.

Decorative patterns vary according to stitch or stitch groups used.

Machine Smocking

Drawing a predetermined fullness into a specific amount by means of elastic shirring with additional overlay pattern of decorative stitches applied to the face of the fabric.

- To create an expandable or contractible decorative-patterned effect.
- To simulate handwork in mass-produced garments where *hand* smocking would be expensive.
- To form the effect of yoke, midriff, band or cuff.
- On garments designed to accommodate more than one size or body configuration.
- On waistline of one-piece garments to release fullness above and below stitching.

Decorative patterns vary according to stitch or stitch groups used. Degree of stretchability varies according to type and expandability of elastic thread or cord, length of stitch, and number and spacing of parallel rows of stitching.

Machine smocking is completed on fabric or garment sections prior to construction procedure.

Pin Tucks

The take-up of excess fabric by means of evenly spaced parallel folds, 1/8 inch (3.175 mm) or less, and stitched to be released a designated length from the pattern edge or area to be fitted.

- On the face of a garment.
- To create a limited amount of design fullness.
- On infants' and children's wear.
- To construct a creased fold.

Pin tucks may be evenly spaced either individually or by group; made by machine or hand running stitch; planned to start at a seam line or may be designed within a garment section.

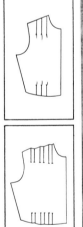

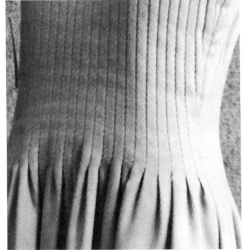

Inside Released Tucks

Released Tucks (Outside and Inside)

The take-up of excess fabric by means of evenly spaced parallel folds, 1/4 to 5/8 inch (6.35 to 15.875 mm) and stitched to be released a designated length from the pattern edge or area to be fitted.

- To create a controlled amount of design fullness in a garment.
- Vertically to form a yoke at shoulder or hip, releasing fullness below stitching line.
- Horizontally to form a yoke releasing fullness into a sleeve.
- To create a midriff in a one-piece garment, releasing fullness above and below stitching.
- At the end of a full sleeve, creating a band.

Folds may be formed to lie on the face or inside of a garment. They may all be turned to face one direction, turned towards or away from the center of a garment, or turned towards or away from each other in groups. Tucks directing fullness may be evenly spaced either individually or in a group. Released tucks may be stitched by hand or machine; with matching, contrasting, or buttonhole twist thread; corded to produce a raised effect. They may be planned as vertical or horizontal design elements; to start at a seam line or designed within a garment section.

2 ~ Aids, Tools & Equipment for Draping, Drafting, Measuring & Marking

Compass
Circle Template
Curve:
    Combination Ruler and Curve
    Hip Curve / Curve Rule / Vary Form Curve
    Irregular Curve / Dietzgen #17 / French Curve
    Neckline Curve
    Sleigh Curve
Eraser
L Square:
    Adjustable L Square
    L Square / Tailor's Square
Model Form
Model Arm Form
Muslin
Notcher
Paper:
    Granite Tag / Fiber Board / Oak Tag
    Graph Paper / Point Paper
    Patternmaking Paper
Pattern Hook / Pattern String
Pattern Punch
Pencil
Pins:
    Push Pins
    Straight Pins

Ruler:
    Center Finding Rule
    Parallel Rule
    Ruler
    Six-Inch Ruler
    Transparent Ruler / Clear Plastic Ruler
    Yardstick / Vertical Rule / Centimeter Stick
Sloper / Foundation / Master / Block /
    Basic Pattern
Style Tape
T Square:
    T Square
    See-Through T Square
Tailor's Chalk
Tailors' Tack Marker
Tailor's Wax
Tape Measure
Tracing Board
Tracing Paper / Dressmaker's Tracing Paper /
    Carbon Paper
Tracing Wheel
Transparent Tape
Triangle
Work Table

Draping tools facilitate the creating of a muslin or fabric pattern. Muslin or fabric is measured, prepared, marked, and molded on a model form or live figure.

Drafting tools are used when developing and making a sloper from measurements and for the development of a pattern from a sloper.

Marking equipment is used in the process of draping and drafting patterns and during procedures for garment construction.

Tools and equipment may be used in a variety of ways. Each tool or piece of equipment has many advantages which serve as a basis for line placement or line transfer, and each suits a particular situation. A combination of two or more tools may be utilized to simplify and accomplish the desired results.

Aids, tools and equipment for draping, drafting, measuring and marking are selected with consideration for:

• Utilization and efficiency
• Type of line or curve
• Placement of line or curve
• Method required for trueing or transfering

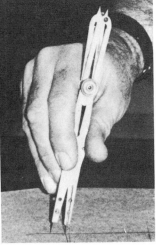

Compass

An instrument consisting of two arms, one sharply pointed the other equipped with a drawing tip, joined at the top by a pivot or center wheel to provide an adjustable movement.

- Instead of a ruler to measure spacing between buttons or buttonholes.
- To establish parallel style and seam lines.
- To duplicate curves such as scallops, cascades, looping, and flounces.
- To duplicate circles for patterns of embroidery, placement of trimming or beading.
- To draw curves and circles.

May be designed with two sharply pointed tips.

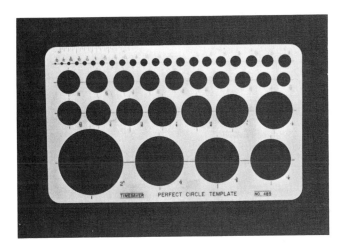

Circle Template

A plastic, wooden or metal form with punched holes. Diameters range in size from 1/16 to 1 inch (1.5875 to 25.4 mm) plus corner radii in inches (and millimeters) of 1/16 (1.5875), 1/8 (3.175), 1/4 (6.35), and 3/8 (9.525).

- To plan the placement and spacing of:
  Buttons or eyelets for draped or drafted designs;
  Circular trimming, appliqué or design on fabric or garment.

Size, arrangement, and shape of template varies with each manufacturer and intended use.
  Form may be in the shape of a square, rectangle or triangle.

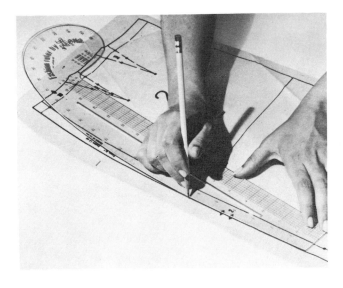

Combination Ruler and Curve

A combination straight-edged ruler, irregular curve, and hip curve marked in both inches and metric terms.

- To measure straight lines.
- To mark and true seam lines; hiplines.
- To establish or alter necklines and armhole curves.
- To true seam lines around gently curved areas such as yokes, waistlines, hiplines, and princess lines.
- To true a line for a curved hem.
- To establish lines of shaped bodices.
- To true darts.
- To form or alter sleeve caps.
- To establish curves of crotch lines.
- To alter commercial patterns.
- To form or draw scallops and stylized lines.

Cutout slot is used to control wheel when tracing seam lines.
  Slot is parallel to straight edge and may be used to form parallel lines.

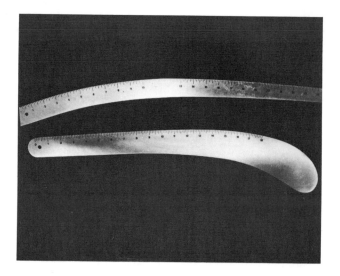

Hip Curve / Curve Rule / Vary Form Curve

A 24-inch (61-cm) ruler shaped as a segment of a catenary curve and marked in inches and/or centimeters and fractional segments.

- To establish curve of revers and lapels.
- To establish and true curved seam lines.
- To establish and true contour hipline of skirts, pants, and trousers.
- On seam lines to establish flares on gored garment panels.
- To establish the curved shape of a godet.
- To true seam line of variable curves such as neckline, armhole, elbow and waistline of bodices; skirts, and pants.
- To true seam lines of princess lines and other gently curving style lines.
- To establish side seams and darts of one-piece garments.
- To true shaped and contoured darts.
- To true hemline of curved, flared or circular garments.

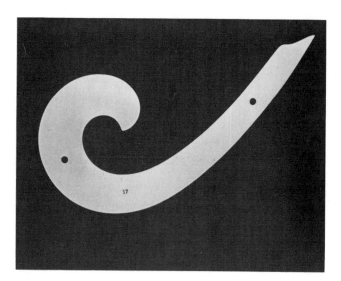

Irregular Curve / Dietzgen #17 / French Curve

A guide, about 10 inches (25.4 cm) long, with an edge describing a spiral curve.

- To shape and true edges of curved collars, necklines and armscyes.
- To true curved part of darts.
- To establish curved lines of crotch.
- To form curved lines of lapels, revers, pockets, collars and cuffs.
- To form body contour lines of skirts and slacks.
- To establish and true variable curves of pattern seams such as necklines, armholes, elbows, waistlines, princess lines.
- To develop the cap and rounded seam of sleeves.
- To alter commercial patterns.

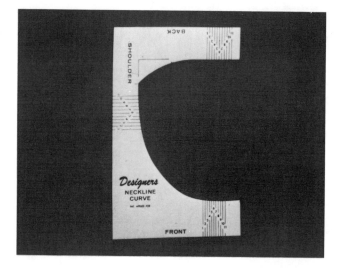

Neckline Curve

A clear, plastic device which includes two curves delineating front and back necklines, each curve being marked in specific segments corresponding to a garment size.

- When drafting to develop the original shape of the neckline on the sloper.

Sleigh Curve

A metal or plastic drawing guide with an edge that includes a variety of curves.

- To establish curves of:
    Revers and lapels;
    Crotch seams.
- To establish and true:
    Shaped and contoured darts;
    Variable curves of pattern seams.
- To shape and true edges of necklines and armscyes.
- To develop the cap and rounded seam of sleeves.

Eraser

Any one of the various types of rubber or rubber-like materials such as gum, kneaded.

- To eliminate unwanted lines and markings on paper or muslin.

Adjustable L Square

A clear plastic rule, with an adjustable slotted arm which can be locked into a variety of desired positions; both arms marked in inches and centimeters, each divided into fractional segments.

As a 90° angle L square:
- To locate straight grain when designing garment section;
- To measure crotch depth;
- To check grainlines on muslin for draping, on paper for drafting, on commercial patterns when adjusting.

As a T square:
- To locate pattern line placement;
- To locate perpendicular lines on muslin, paper or fabric.

As a 45° angle:
- To locate diagonal lines;
- To establish and mark true bias.

As a 36-inch (91.44-cm) rule:
- To mark hem on pattern or figure;
- As a guide for a continued straight line.

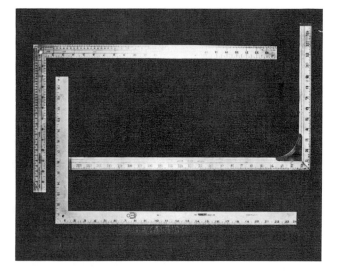

L Square / Tailor's Square

A metal, wooden or plastic rule with two arms of different lengths meeting at right angles; marked in inches and/or centimeters including all fractional measurements.

- To draft slopers or master patterns from measurements.
- To establish length and grainlines on muslin, sloper or pattern.
- To square off corners of muslin, sloper or pattern sections in order to continue subsequent operations of pattern development.
- To establish perpendicular lines, reference points, and levels in the development of an original pattern.
- To measure depth of crotch on pants model form or live model.
- To establish depth and length of crotch for muslin or drafted pattern development.
- To block muslin or fabric.

Scaled to include inch and millimeter segments: 1/32 (0.8 mm), 1/16 (1.6 mm), 1/8 (3.2 mm), 1/4 (6.4 mm), 1/2 (13 mm), 1/12 (2.1 mm), 1/6 (4.2 mm) and 1/3 (8.5 mm).

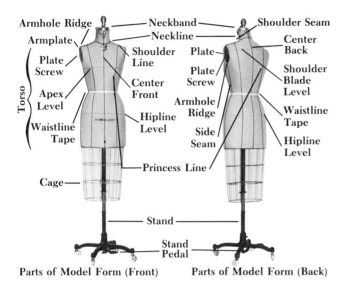

Parts of Model Form (Front)   Parts of Model Form (Back)

Model Form

A standardized duplication of a human torso, cotton-padded and canvas-covered, set on a movable, height-adjustable stand.

- To measure and establish the sloper or master pattern.
- To develop an original pattern.
- To develop a garment from fabric.
- To fit sample garments.
- To alter garments.
- To establish hemline on garments.

Model form is available in a range of standard sizes, height and figure types; according to measurements of a particular size and type of figure for a manufacturer's line; customized to specifications of individuals or manufacturers. The model form is designed and shaped according to the type and category of garment to be made for current idealized fashion figures and replaced when silhouettes change.

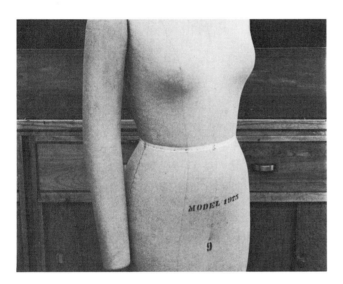

Model Arm Form

A padded, canvas-covered papier mâché or firmly stuffed canvas representation of the human arm made with straps for attaching to model form.

- To drape unmounted or semi-mounted sleeve design.
- To develop drop shoulder style.
- To develop an off-the-shoulder style.
- To drape capes.

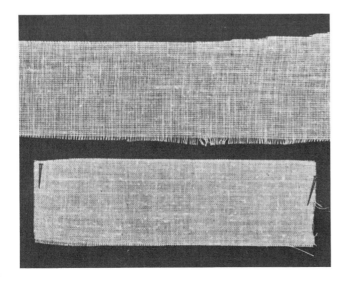

Muslin

A plain weave fabric made from bleached or unbleached carded yarns which varies in weight, from fine to heavy, and in texture, from soft to coarse.

- To drape original patterns or designs on the model form or figure.
- To experiment and develop design concept.

Quality and hand of muslin is chosen according to the texture and characteristics of the fabric to be used for the garment.

Soft Muslin—Simulates draping quality of natural and synthetic silk, woven lingerie, and fine cotton fabrics.
Medium Muslin—Simulates draping quality of wool and medium weight cotton.
Coarse Muslin—Simulates draping quality of heavyweight wool and heavy cotton.
Canvas Muslin—Translates draping of heavyweight fabric, fur and imitation fur garments.

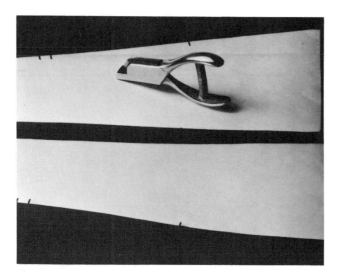

Notcher

A punching tool which produces a 1/4 inch (6.35 mm) narrow V-shaped cut.

- To make notches on the edge of a sloper or paper pattern.

Granite Tag / Fiber Board / Oak Tag

A strong, firm, pliable paper, lighter than cardboard.

- To make:
  Slopers;
  Master, foundation or block patterns;
  Patterns that will be repeatedly copied;
  Templates or guides.

Manila-colored or prepared with a tone on one or both sides. Available in rolls of various widths and in thicknesses from 1X (thin) to 2X (heavy) for patternmaking; and 3X for pleating patterns.

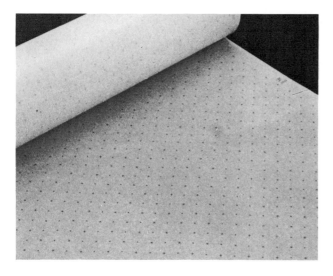

Graph Paper / Point Paper

A strong, white paper printed with a grid pattern of dots or points at one inch intervals, available in rolls of various widths.

- To develop and make patterns.
- To position pattern pieces for grain placement.
- To lay out pattern pieces that will be placed on plaid, stripe, checkered, or border print fabrics.
- To plan and lay out bias.
- As a basis to form a grid pattern.
- Between separate colors of a lay-up when spreading fabric.
- As the top ply of fabric lay-up before marker is positioned.

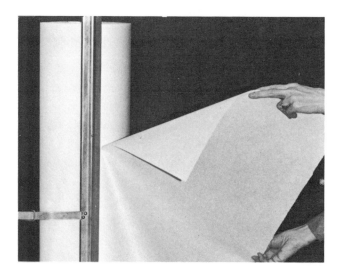

Patternmaking Paper

A strong, white paper in a variety of widths and weights, available in rolls.

- Preliminary pattern drafting.
- The development of the final pattern.
- As a clean surface under dress forms to prevent the garment and fabric from soiling.
- On work tables to provide a clean, smooth work surface.

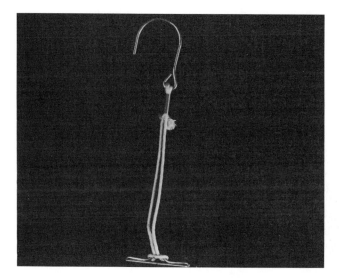

Pattern Hook / Pattern String

A braided nylon cord, approximately 6 inches (15.24 cm) long, to which a metal hook is affixed at one end and a short T-bar at the other.

- To hang slopers.
- To hang a set of trade block or standard block patterns for filing.
- To hang production patterns for filing.

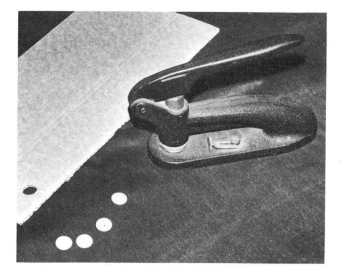

Pattern Punch

A metal hand tool designed with a lever and a circular die-cutter.

- To make a hole in pattern or sloper to facilitate hanging.

Tool can make holes from 3/4 to 3/16 inch (1.92 to .48 cm).

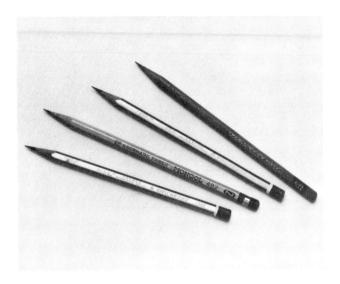

Pencil

A wooden or metal rod-shaped instrument with a center core of graphite or crayon.

- To mark lines in developing the muslin, pattern or sloper:
    4H and 5H—Developing pattern;
    B, 1B, or 2B—Developing muslin pattern;
    Colored crayon—Correcting muslin or pattern lines.

Push Pins

A coarse pin approximately 1/2 inch (12.7 mm) long, with a plastic or metal drum-shaped head.

- To hold Oak tag sloper or pattern pieces to paper on cork top table.
- To hold pattern pieces in place when slashing or spreading in developing a pattern.
- To hold pivot points of sloper or pattern in place when designing.

Straight Pins

A size #17 satin straight pin.

- To anchor muslin or fabric to model form while draping.
- To hold muslin sections together for balancing and trueing.
- To fasten muslin or fabric sections to test accuracy of completed pattern.
- During slash and spread pattern development to fasten parts and pieces to pattern paper.
- To hold parts of the pattern draft together to test shape on model form.

Center Finding Rule

A metal, wooden or plastic ruler marked in inches and fractional segments, with the zero point at the center and the numbers increasing towards both ends of the rule.

- To measure from the center out to either edge.
- To determine the placement of:
    Buttons and buttonholes;
    Multiple fasteners;
    Appliqué, trimming, and inserts;
    Pockets and cuffs;
    Fasteners on double-breasted garments.

For various problems of division, such as finding centers of darts, pleats, and cuffs.

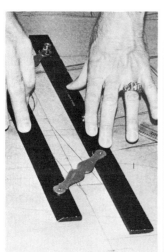

Open and in use parallel rule   Closed parallel rule

Parallel Rule

A pair of straight edges held in parallel juxtaposition by swivel-hinged bars, which also allow varying the distance between the two bars.

- To space the transfer of parallel pattern marks.
- To locate a design detail with respect to the collar, lapel or front closure position of a pattern.
- To locate pocket and flap line on pattern section.

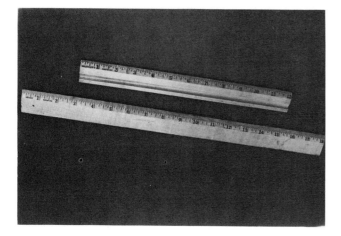

Ruler

A straight-edged strip of metal, wood or plastic, marked with measurements indicating both inches and metric terms.

- To mark a straight line.
- To measure a straight line.
- To establish seam allowances on final patterns.
- To mark 1/8 and 1/16 inch (3.2 and 1.6 mm) measurements in patternmaking, draping, and garment construction.

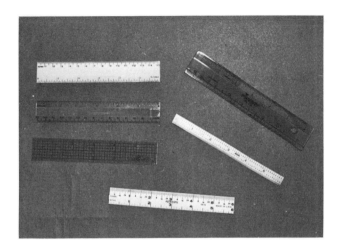

Six-Inch Ruler

A six-inch long, straight-edged strip of metal, wood or plastic, marked with measurements indicating both inches and metric terms.

- When larger measuring tools would be cumbersome.
- To measure small garment sections.
- To properly place grainlines and style lines on small pattern pieces.

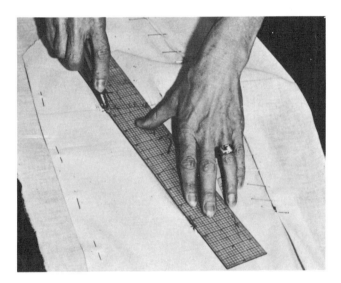

Transparent Ruler / Clear Plastic Ruler

A 1- or 2-inch (2.5 to 5 cm) wide, clear plastic straight edge; 6 (15 cm), 12 (30 cm), or 18 inches (46 cm) long; imprinted with a grid in inches and fractions of inches or millimeters the length and width of the ruler.

When guide lines and marks must be seen through the ruler while establishing a line for:
- Marking parallel lines of seams and such details as pleats and tucks;
- Marking style lines;
- Establishing or correcting seam allowances on garment sections;
- Establishing and marking the position of bound buttonholes and set-in pockets;
- Establishing, marking or measuring bias strips.

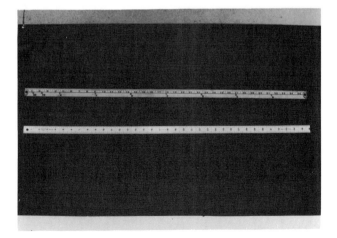

Yardstick / Vertical Rule / Centimeter Stick

A 36- (92 cm), 40- (102 cm), or 45- (115 cm) inch wooden or metal straight-edged rule with measurements marked in inches and/or metric terms.

- To check and establish garment lengths from the floor.
- To establish a uniform length and an even edge on skirts, jackets and peplums.
- To establish the placement of trimmings.
- To establish the placement of grainlines from pattern to muslin.
- To establish the length of bodices, sleeves, skirts and trousers.
- To check grainlines when laying out pattern.
- To measure yardage of fabric.
- To mark long straight lines.
- To measure and establish hemlines on the dress form or live figure.

Numbers are arranged to be read vertically on a *vertical rule.*

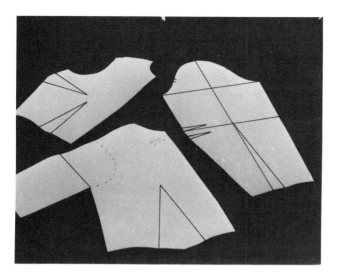

Sloper / Foundation / Master / Block / Basic Pattern

A pattern of a garment component, without style lines or seam allowances, developed from specific measurements of a given size, model forms, or live models.

- As a template or tool from which other patterns may be developed.
- To facilitate the development of original styles.
- To develop various bodice, skirt, dress, pants, or sleeve designs.

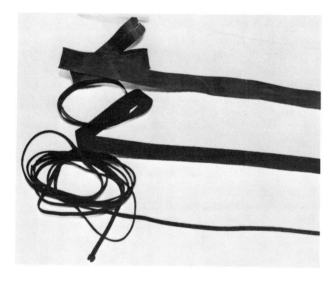

Style Tape

A narrow, woven or plastic tape which has a smooth or adhesive back.

- To delineate style lines on the model form or muslin while draping.
- To hold or control fabric excess while establishing gathers or fullness.

Style tape can be improvised by using commercial bias, seam binding, ribbon, yarn, or the selvage cut from yard goods.

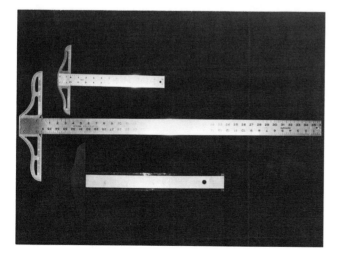

T Square

A straight-edged rule having a short crossbar centered and fixed perpendicularly at one end of a long bar. Both inches and metric terms are indicated on the long bar or on both long and short bars.

- To locate grainlines on patterns, slopers, or fabrics.
- To locate true intersecting grainlines.

Available in metal, wooden or clear plastic, or combination.

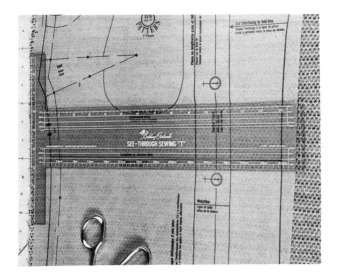

See-Through T Square

A clear plastic, straight-edged rule having a narrow, 9-inch (22.86 cm) crossbar centered and fixed perpendicularly at one end to a 3-inch (7.62 cm) wide by 14-inch (35.56 cm) long rule. Both inches and metric terms are indicated on the long bar or on both long and short bars.

- As a perpendicular measure.
- To determine parallel lines accurately.
- To locate grainlines on muslin, patterns, or fabrics.
- To mark or adjust lines on muslin or paper patterns.
- To establish and mark bias strips.

Transparent, clear plastic allows for unhampered view of object.

Tailor's Chalk

A square, approximately 1 1/2 inch by 1 1/2 inch, of white or colored clay chalk, tapered to a fine edge on two sides.

- To facilitate drawing lines on garments made of silk, cotton, linen, wool or synthetic fabrics.
- To mark fabric which is to be constructed soon after it is marked since the chalk will rub off.
- When the fabric will not take the markings of carbon paper.
- To fit or alter garments.
- To mark wrong side of fabric or garment pieces for identification.
- To develop a draft.
- To transfer draft pattern on fabric.
- To trace a sloper onto paper or fabric.

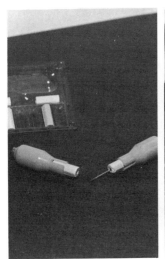

Tailor's Tack Marker

A device for marking with chalk simultaneously on the opposite faces of two plies of fabric.

- To transfer pattern construction markings to fabric.
- When a tracing wheel would mar the fabric.
- Instead of thread tack marks.

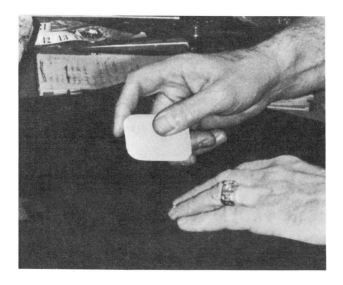

Tailor's Wax

A square, approximately 1 1/2 inch by 1 1/2 inch, of white or colored wax, tapered to a fine edge on two sides.

- To facilitate drawing lines on muslin or wool fabric.
- Only on wool fabrics as it leaves a grease mark on other fabrics.
- To mark fabric which is to be constructed soon after it is marked since the wax will melt into the fabric.
- When the fabric will not take the markings of carbon paper.
- To fit or alter garments.
- To mark wrong side of fabric or garment pieces for identification.
- To develop a draft.
- To transfer draft pattern to wool fabric.
- To trace a sloper onto paper.
- To mark wool fabric for patterns.

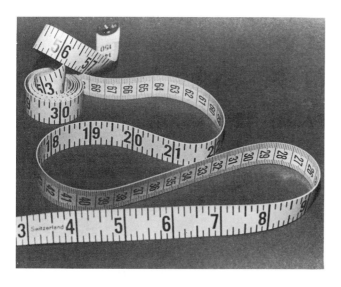

Tape Measure

A narrow, firmly woven durable tape, usually 60 inches (1.524 meters) long, marked with measurements indicating both inches and metric terms.

- To measure circumference, length and width of model form; parts of the body; sections of garments, muslin or fabric.
- To measure length of pants, trousers and skirts.
- To measure length of garments from shoulder to hemline.
- To transfer body measurements to muslin, or paper.

Tracing Board

A self-prepared wallboard or heavy, firm cardboard which has been treated with a layer of builder's chalk and then covered with a net.

With a tracing wheel:
- To transfer pattern markings onto fabric;
- For temporary markings;
- When carbon wax would mar the fabric;
- To mark lightweight, white, or pastel fabrics.

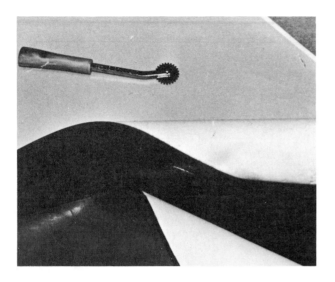

Tracing Paper / Dressmaker's Tracing Paper / Carbon Paper

Paper which has been coated on one or both sides with white or colored wax or chalk.

In conjunction with the tracing wheel to:
• Transfer pattern lines to corresponding or balanced pattern sections when draping or drafting;
• Transfer pattern markings to muslin when marking test pattern;
• Transfer pattern marks to fabric.
• *Only* on tightly woven fabrics where the carbon from the tracing will not show on the face of the fabric.

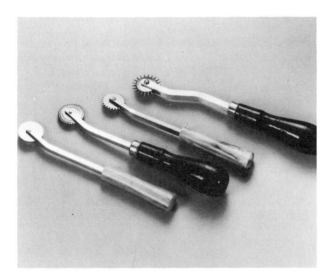

Tracing Wheel

An instrument with a smooth-edged, small serrated, or needle-pointed wheel mounted on one end of a handle.
With tracing paper:
• To transfer markings onto paper or fabric;
• To transfer marks from one muslin pattern piece to another.
With or without tracing paper:
• To transfer balanced seam line of one pattern piece to another.
Without tracing paper:
• On sheer, white, and/or lightweight fabrics (leaving imprint only).
Smooth-Edged Wheel—Used on fine and lightweight fabrics.
Small Serrated Wheel—Used on woven and nonwoven fabrics.
Needle-Pointed Wheel—Used to transfer trued areas of entire pattern markings onto paper or Oak tag.

Transparent Tape

A clear paper or plastic strip with an adhesive surface.

• To hold slashed style lines in place when designing flat patterns.
• To extend paper size.
• To mend tears in pattern.

Triangle

A three-sided tool with two sides of equal length, meeting at an angle of 90°, each joining the third side, or hypotenuse, at a 45° angle.

- To establish true bias lines on patterns.
- To mark and cut true bias.
- In patternmaking, to square a corner.
- To form right angle lines.

Work Table

A flat rectangular, waist-height table, surfaced with wood, vinyl or cork.

As a work surface:
- To prepare, mark, and make muslin patterns or fabric draped garments;
- To cut muslin or fabric.

Portable Work Table

3 ~ Drafting Terminology

Apex of Dart
Balance / Balancing Patternmaking Lines
Break Point Line
Cutting Guide Line
Draft
Equalize / Compromise
Final Pattern
Grainline Indicator
Pattern Identification

Pivot / Pivoting
Pivot Point
Roll Line
Slash and Spread
Sloper
Squared Line / Right Angle Line
Stand
Temporary Dart / Working Dart

Drafting, or flat pattern design, is the technique of manipulating the sloper to achieve an original design.

A set of slopers is drafted from measurements taken from a model form, a live model, or according to standardized or individual manufacturer's specifications.

Using the sloper, pattern paper, and tools, a draft is prepared to be translated into a *final pattern*.

The pattern is developed through the slash and spread method, through the pivot method, or by a combination of both.

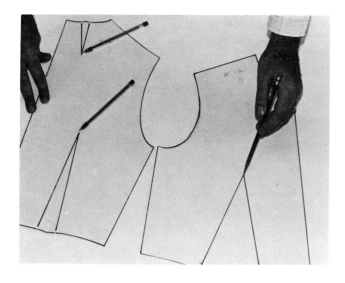

Apex of Dart

The point at which a dart tapers to an end.

- As a pivot point on the sloper for shifting and developing new patterns.
- As a term when establishing or foreshortening new darts.

All front bodice darts converge towards the apex area. All temporary darts are planned towards the apex area. The style line of a princess line is planned through the apex area.

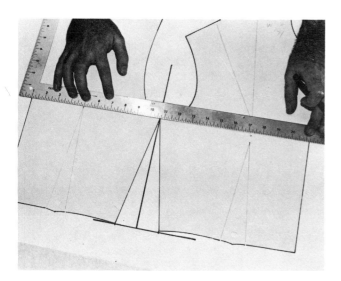

Balance / Balancing Patternmaking Lines

The process of matching or establishing grainlines and/or a common seam line on adjacent pattern sections.

- To true pattern.
- To shape seams of princess line or gored garments.
- To shape side seams on skirts, pants, torso, and bodice.
- To transfer common grainlines or guide lines.

To maintain balance, common seam lines are extended or reduced an equal amount from related guide, seam or fitting lines.

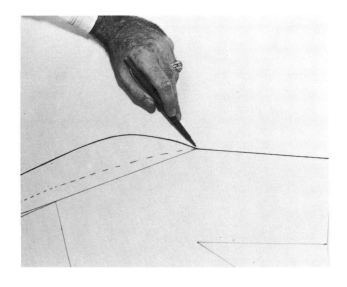

Break Point Line

Strategic markings or drawn lines placed on a pattern.

- To indicate the point of change in the direction on a controlled turn, roll, or flare planned on the finished garment.

Break point occurs on shawl collars; two-piece notched collars; lapels and revers; flares of gored skirts.

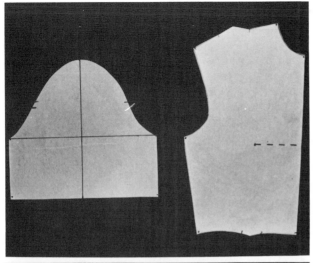

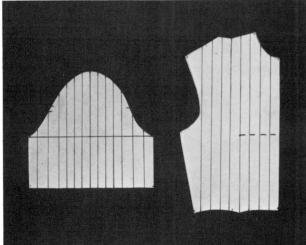

Cutting Guide Line

A drawn line, on the traced sloper or draft.

- A guide for slashing.
- Calculated on the sloper to facilitate specific pattern change and/or development.

As applied to slash and spread method, cutting the line facilitates separating the traced sloper into spreadable and workable pieces.

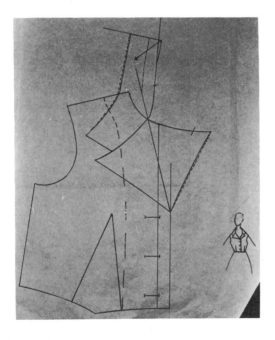

Draft

The intervening step in the development of a pattern by measurements or through the slash and spread or pivot method, which includes all pertinent marks, lines and information for the completion of the final pattern.

- A base to establish style lines, roll lines, break points and design features.

Draft does not include seam allowances.

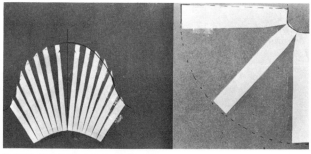
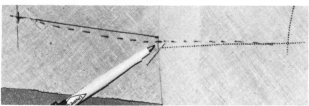

Equalize / Compromise

Forming a continuous line by the correction of discrepancies in a seam or style line resulting from the slash and spread or pivot method of patternmaking.

- To preserve the symmetrical contour of a pattern line.
- To eliminate irregularities while trueing corresponding seam or style lines of necklines; side seams of bodices, skirts and pants; sleeve underarms; inseams of pants; midriffs and yokes.

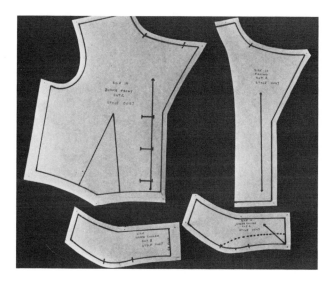

Final Pattern

The paper pattern of individual sections drawn from the draft which includes trued seam lines, seam allowances, notches, grainlines and pattern identification.

- A pattern for the muslin proof.
- A pattern for cutting out a trial or sample garment.

Final pattern is tested in muslin or fabric. Corrected after muslin proof for the development of the sample or production pattern.

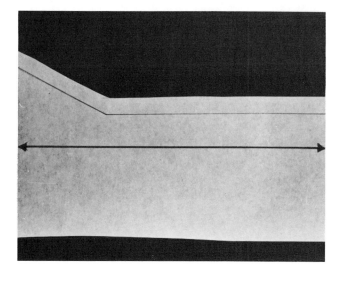

Grainline Indicator

A straight line with an arrow on each end drawn on the draft and final pattern pieces indicating the direction of lengthgrain.

- To determine placement of pattern piece on corresponding grain of fabric.
- To align pattern on corresponding fabric grain.

Length of line made with regard to size of pattern piece. Grainline arrows on the pattern pieces are placed parallel to the selvage of the fabric.

Bracketed grainline with instruction *"Place on Line of Fold"* is indicated on the pattern edge; pattern is placed on the on-grain fold of the fabric. Instruction applies to center front or center back.

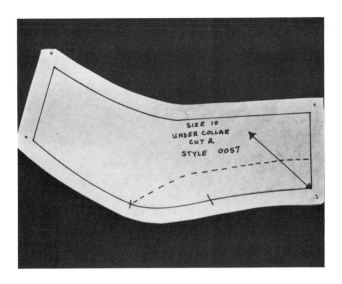

Pattern Identification

Words, numbers, and symbols placed on the individual sections of the final pattern.

- To identify the pattern section.
- To indicate the pattern size and style number.
- To indicate the quantity of individual pattern pieces required to complete the garment.

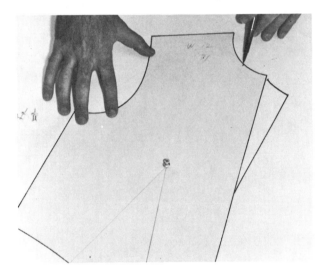

Pivot / Pivoting

The shifting or moving of a sloper on pattern paper from a marked position towards a designated guide line.

- As part of the process of developing a new design.
- An alternative to or in conjunction with the slash and spread method to manipulate the sloper.

Pivoting is controlled from apex, point or points on the perimeter, or from a given point within the sloper.

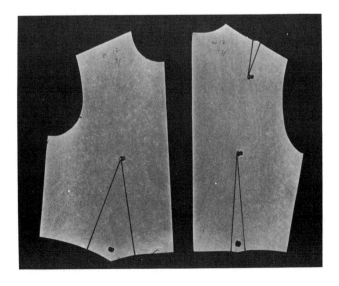

Pivot Point

A designated position on the sloper calculated to facilitate manipulation in the development of the desired design. Predetermined by the design element of a garment section.

- A control factor in the shifting, moving and/or marking for the development of new patterns.

Pivot point may occur at the apex, on the perimeter or from a given point within the sloper.

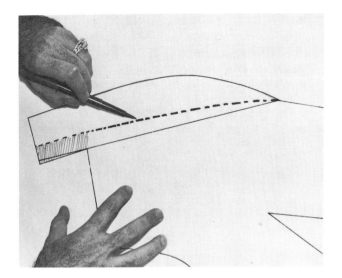

Roll Line

A strategic line placed while developing a pattern.

• To designate the stand and the turn or roll of a finished collar and/or lapel; a cuff at sleeve or pants edge.

Roll line occurs where the exposed part of a collar turns under towards the portion fastened to the neckline of the garment.

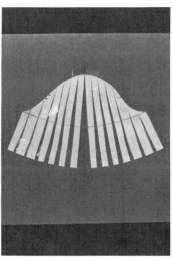

Slash and Spread

Part of a process for developing a new design and/or introducing fullness to a design, by cutting a traced sloper along predetermined guide lines and opening or spreading apart the pieces to a designated measurement.

• An alternative to or in conjunction with the pivot method to manipulate the sloper.

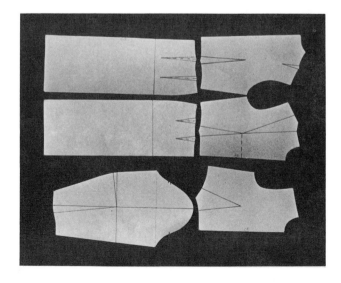

Sloper

A pattern of a garment section, without style lines or seam allowances; developed from specific measurements, model form, live model, or manufacturer's specifications.

• A template or tool in the development of original patterns.
• A tool to create new designs.

Also known as *standard pattern, foundation pattern,* or *block pattern.*

Slopers conform to current fashion, shape, and silhouette.

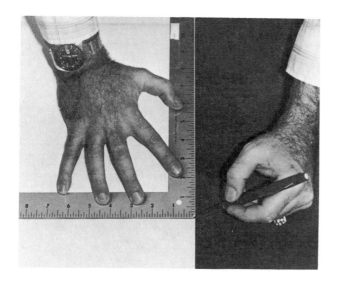

Squared Line / Right Angle Line

A line drawn perpendicular to another line or pattern fold.

- To establish perpendicular lines in the development of a sloper, draft or pattern.
- To establish lower edge of sleeve when developing sleeve variations from sloper.
- To establish crotch lines of pants.

L-square, T-square, or see-through ruler facilitate drawing of squared lines.

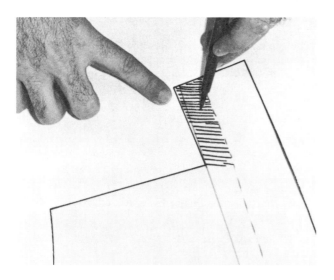

Stand

The area of the collar, close to the neck seam, which determines the height and establishes the roll of the collar.

Stand may be planned for a portion of the collar front or back, or may be part of the entire collar.

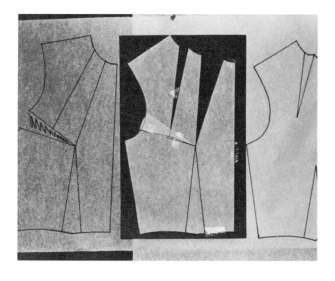

Temporary Dart / Working Dart

The relocation of all or partial dart pick-up, placed at a right angle to the style detail being developed.

- To develop a style featuring two or more parallel darts or dart substitute.
- To extend an area for gathers, tucks, or released tucks.

In the process of developing a new style line or controlled fullness, temporary dart is absorbed and is *not* part of the finished pattern.

Apex
Balance / Balancing of Muslin
Break Point
Crease
Crossmarks
Dots
Drape / Draping
Ease

Fabric Excess
Fold
Grainlines
Guide Lines on Muslin
Panels
Slash
Slash for Design Detail

Draping is the technique of manipulating cloth to fit and conform to one or more curves of the feminine or masculine model form, or live model, in order to form a pattern.

Using appropriate tools, muslin or chosen fabric is prepared, pinned, cut, and shaped to achieve a desired look or pattern.

Excess fabric may be absorbed or controlled by the use of darts, dart tucks, gathers, seams, or manipulation into flares.

When draping, the lengthgrain of the fabric usually hangs vertically from the shoulder to the hem of a garment, and from the shoulder to the hem of the sleeve. The lengthgrain allows the fabric to fall subtly on the body.

The crossgrain usually appears in the circumference of a garment.

A garment designed on the bias molds when draped, allowing the fabric to cling to the body.

Pattern pieces for symmetrical designs are developed representing only the right half of the garment and are marked with bracketed symbols at the center front or back to indicate alignment with the grainline fold of the fabric.

Pattern pieces for asymmetrical and bias cut designs are developed in their entirety and are marked with grainline symbols to indicate alignment with the grainline of the fabric.

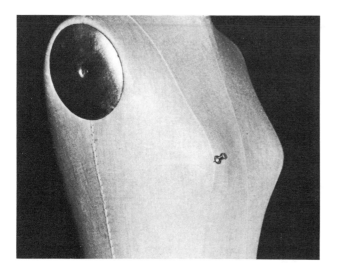

Apex

Highest point of the bust on model form or live model.

- As a guide when establishing crossgrain position on front bodice muslin.

All front bodice darts converge towards the apex area.
  The style line of the princess line garment is planned through the apex area.

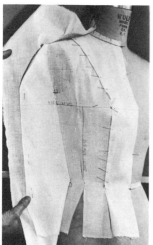

Balancing of muslin while draping   **Shaping a common seam line**

Balance / Balancing of Muslin

A term applied to the matching of grains on adjacent pattern sections.

- Before draping to prepare muslin sections, panels, or blocks.
- During draping procedure to match adjacent pattern sections.
- During trueing to match and/or shape a common seam.
- While draping to balance two sections of a garment.
- To drape torso and shift.
- Before draping the back of flare skirt.
- To develop side seams of skirt, pants, bodice or jacket.
- To true side seams and princess lines.

To maintain balance, common seam lines are extended or reduced equal amounts from related guide, fitting or seam lines.

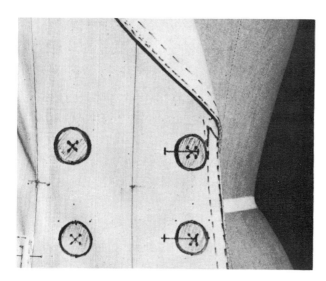

Break Point

The section of a garment where a controlled change in direction occurs producing a roll, turn-back or flare point.

- Where collar folds back to roll on stand or garment.
- Where collar meets at extension.
- Where roll of lapel ends at closures.
- Where lapel folds back from edge of the garment.
- On gored skirt where seam begins to slope or flare outwardly.
- On a garment at a level at which the flare starts to break away from the body to form a cone or to add fullness.

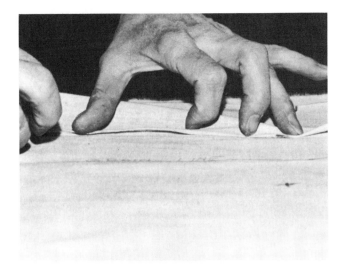

Crease

The setting of a fold along grain or structural lines by pressure or by finger pressing.

- To facilitate pinning muslin or fabric to form.
- To develop darts, dart tucks or folds.
- Along a seam or design detail to facilitate joining of seam lines or darts.

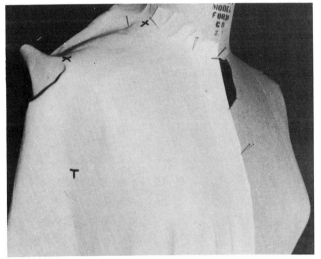

Crossmarks on muslin

Crossmarks

Short lines indicating intersecting and juxtaposition of seam or style lines from the model form to the muslin or fabric.

- When draping an original pattern on a model form or live figure.
- To record seam or style lines on garment sections and pattern details.
- To indicate matching positions where two or more pieces are to be joined.
- As a guide for trueing original seams, darts, and design lines.
- To locate darts, dart tucks, and pleats.
- To indicate position and extent of gathers.
- As an aid to identify various parts of the garment such as front, back or side.
- To assure matching of corresponding pattern sections such as sleeve, collars, cuffs, pockets, and yokes.

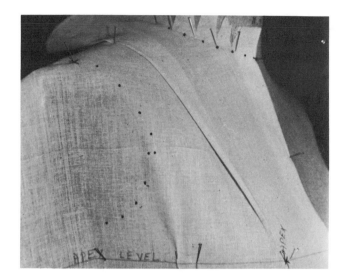

Dots

A mark made with a pencil, marker or chalk on draped muslin or fabric.

- To record the perimeter of seam lines, style lines, and design details.
- A guide for trueing.

Thread tracing, pin line, or a non-marring chalk marker is used in place of dots when draping with *fabric*.

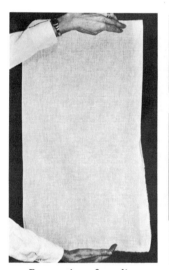
Preparation of muslin

Pinning

Drape / Draping

The process of cutting, pinning, slashing, and marking muslin or fabric in developing a pattern or design on the model form or live figure.

Cutting—The preparation of a determined length and width of muslin or fabric to drape a garment section.

Pinning—The process of anchoring the fabric to the model form on structural, guide and grain lines; the process of securing fabric while developing pattern shape, detail, and perimeter lines.

Slashing—The clipping of muslin or fabric towards the pinned perimeter of the area being draped to relieve fabric tension and facilitate subsequent draping procedure.

Marking—The recording, while on the model form, of the perimeter, intersecting lines, and pattern details in preparation for trueing; using pencil or marker on muslin; or pins, thread tracing, or chalk on fabric.

Slashing

Marking

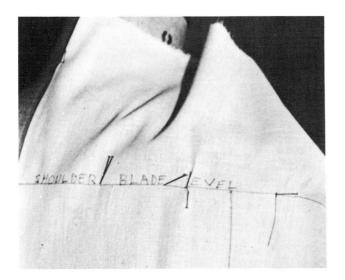

Ease

The amount of fabric allowed in the pattern design to accommodate body movement.

- On back shoulder seam, across shoulder blade, across bustline; at waistline of bodice, pants, and skirt, and across hipline of garment.

Fabric Excess

Portion of fabric which will be shaped or manipulated into darts, or formed into tucks or gathers, to conform to body shape and garment styling.

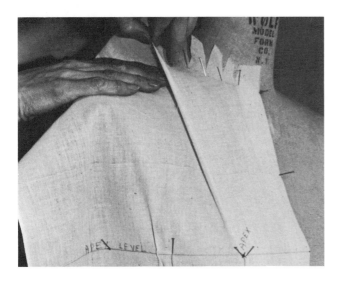

Fold

A fabric ply doubled back upon itself along a creased edge forming an underlay.

- To drape pleats, flange darts, dart tucks, extensions, or self facings.
- To pin or join seam or dart lines.

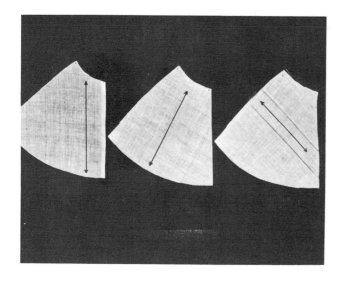

Grainlines

Lines drawn on the length- and crossgrains of muslin which identify grain and guide lines on the finished pattern.

- To facilitate development of original muslin pattern.
- To align pattern on corresponding fabric grain when planning a layout.
- As a grainline indicator when transferring muslin onto paper pattern or sloper.

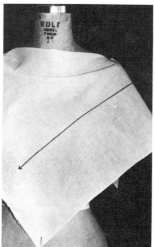

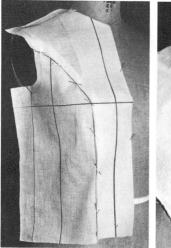

Guide Lines on Muslin

Lines drawn on the prepared muslin.

- To facilitate draping.
- To indicate level of apex, hiplines, shoulder blades, sleeve biceps, sleeve elbow; and center of darts.
- To control grain placement.
- As a structural line to indicate center front, center back, extensions, and fold lines.
- As a structural line to indicate side seams when developing side seams of basic skirt, pants, shift and torso.

Panels

A determined measure of muslin or fabric planned for developing a design which features vertical style lines.

- To produce a multi-seamed or gored garment.

Slash

The cut or cuts made on muslin or fabric, from the perimeter towards the style or seam line, while draping on the model form or live model.

- To relieve tension in muslin or fabric draped around curves.
- To relieve tension in muslin or fabric draped to fit body contour.

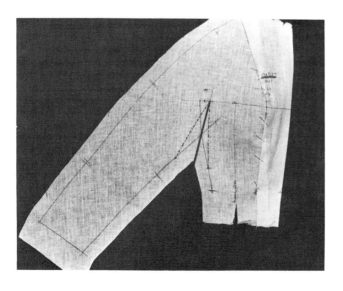

Slash for Design Detail

A straight cut, from a free edge to a designated point, in the body of a draped muslin or fabric garment section.

- To achieve design detail
- To produce sharp corners.
- To allow insertion of gusset or godet.
- To prepare placement of placket.
- To open excess or fold of dart allowing garment section to conform to body contour.
- To drape dart slash design detail.

5 ~ Terminology Common to Drafting & Draping

Blend / Blending
Converge
Cupping
Dart Manipulation
Dart Substitution / Dart Variation
Fold Line
Garment Section
Notches
Seams:
   Seam Allowance

Seam Line
   Directional Seam Line
Style Line
Sweep of the Hem
Transferring
Trueing
Underlay
Verifying the Form

Terminology common to both drafting and draping incorporates procedures and markings that are used in the development of a pattern through both methods.

    The terms relating to establishing and identifying style features, garment sections, seam lines, and seam allowances are applicable to both drafting and draping.

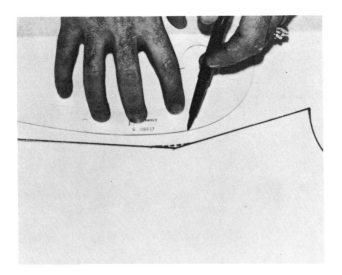

Blend / Blending

The forming of a continuous seam line; the rounding, shaping and smoothing of angular lines; and/or the matching of corresponding style and seam lines.

- On seams of sleeves, armholes, princess lines, waistlines, gored skirts, fitted or contoured side seams and fitted or contoured darts.
- To equalize discrepancies of marks or lines made on muslin or pattern draft.

Process of trueing includes blending lines.

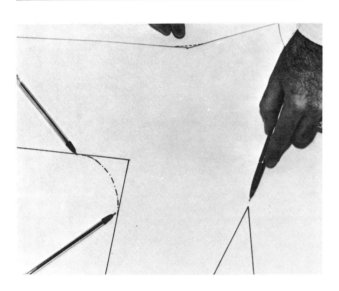

Converge

Lines developed on the paper or muslin pattern which begin from a given point of a calculated measurement and end at their juncture to form a point or points, shaped seam line, or roll line.

- To complete darts, dart tucks, and lapels.
- When planning gusset and/or godet lines on pattern draft.

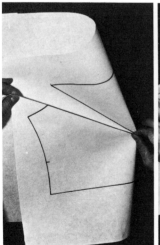

Cupping

The rolling or folding of a pattern section to allow the portion of the pattern being trued or pinned to lay flat.

- To avoid distortion of the line being trued.
- To allow corresponding lines to conform without distortion.

Cupping for trueing   Cupping for pinning muslin

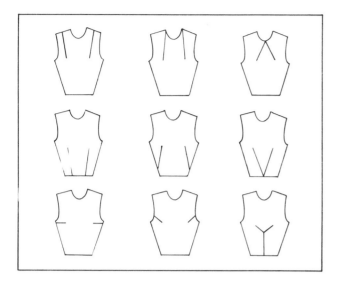

Dart Manipulation

The process of establishing the placement of one or more darts in any one of a variety of dart positions; from a basic one or a two-dart concept to a creative design.

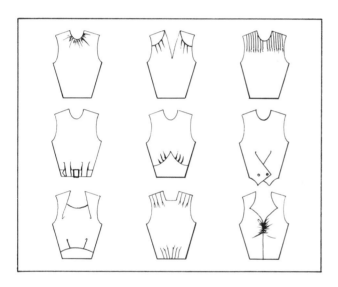

Dart Substitution / Dart Variation

The process of manipulating and distributing dart pick-up from one or two dart concept into flange dart, dart tucks, tucks, released tucks, gathers, seams, or flares.

Additional fullness may be added to garment through fabric planning and draping manipulation.

Additional fullness may be planned to achieve design desired through slash and spread method of drafting.

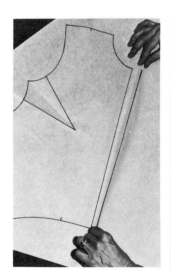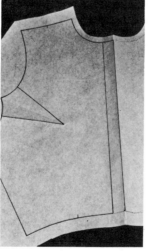

Fold Line

A design line indicating where a fabric ply is to be doubled back upon itself.

- On the finished pattern section to indicate a creased edge which forms a pleat, dart, dart flange, dart tuck, extension, or self facing.
- On the finished pattern to indicate self-facing or self-hem.

Fold line is formed on muslin during draping process and established on paper during development of draft.

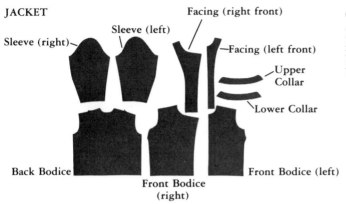

JACKET

Sleeve (right) — Sleeve (left) — Facing (right front) — Facing (left front) — Upper Collar — Lower Collar

Back Bodice — Front Bodice (right) — Front Bodice (left)

DRESS

Facing (back) — Facing (front)

Back — Front

Garment Section

Portion of a garment delineated by seam or style lines forming a pattern piece; identified as front and back bodice, front and back skirt, yoke, midriff, princess panel, band and insert, sleeve, collar, and pocket.

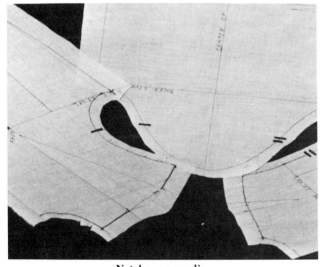

Notches on muslin

Notches

A mark or set of marks placed on the perimeter of a sloper, or across a seam line on the muslin or paper pattern.

- On draped, drafted and test muslin patterns so that the garment seams and sections may be placed in the proper alignment.
- Singly or in groups as an aid to identify various parts of the garment such as front, back, and sides.
- To indicate the position of darts, tucks, gathers, and other design features.
- To indicate the position and extent of ease, gathers, French shirring or smocking.
- To assure matching of corresponding pattern areas such as sleeves, collars, cuffs, pockets, and yokes.
- As an aid to fit a larger drawn-in section to a smaller corresponding one.

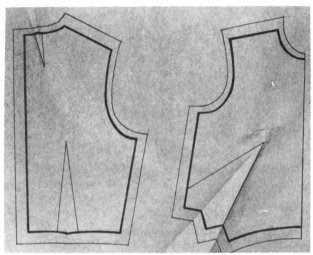

Seam Allowance

Portion of the muslin or paper pattern extending a determined amount from the seam line to the pattern edge.

Seam allowances vary according to development of draft, muslin proof, final pattern, or production pattern; to position and type of seam; weave and type of fabric; type and purpose of garment; specifications of manufacturers; and intended selling price of garment.

Seam allowances on draped patterns and test muslins are planned to be wider for straight and nearly straight seams; and narrow for seams of curves and small details.

Seam allowance on drafted pattern

Seam Line

A line established on a pattern, indicating joining or stitching lines of a garment section.

- To designate the functional or decorative joining or stitching of two or more garment sections.

Seam line may be left unmarked or may be marked by chalk, wax, carbon or thread. Planned according to garment design, a distance from the edge of the ply.

Seam line on drafted pattern

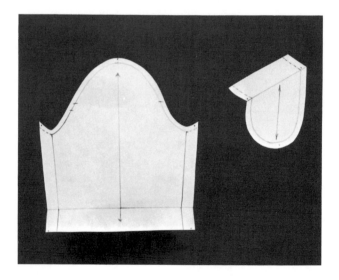

Directional Seam Line

That portion of a seam allowance or hem which when folded back is traced to correspond to the shape or angle of the pattern piece or section.

- To prevent distortion of turned seam when joined to corresponding garment section.
- To allow the turned up hem to fit circumference of the garment section.

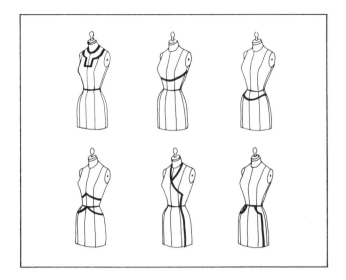

Style Line

A delineation representing a design line, seam line, or finished edge.

Style lines are indicated by a drawn line on pattern draft; with a style tape or pins on model form prior to draping; with a style tape or marking on muslin or fabric pattern during or after draping process.

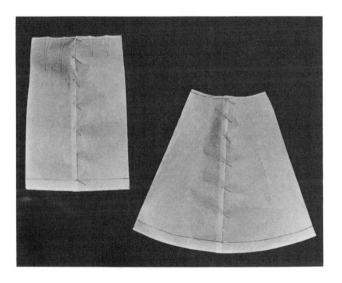

Sweep of the Hem

A term used in conjunction with the measurement of a hem edge of a garment.

- To describe the circumference of a finished garment.
- To describe the hem edge of a finished pattern.
- To describe the hem edge of pattern or garment sections.
- To denote the hem edge of upper and lower torso garments; and sleeves.

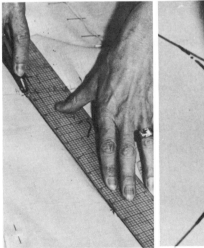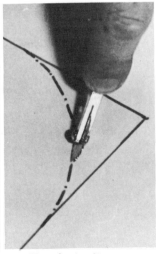

Transferring line on muslin   **Transferring line on pattern paper**

Transferring

The process of tracing a trued seam line or detail marking to another ply of muslin, fabric, or paper.

- To balance grain.
- To duplicate the shape of the pattern section or outline.

Trueing

The process of establishing a corrected seam or style line by blending markings, dots, and/or crossmarks made during pattern development.

- To establish a continuous seam or style line.
- To establish darts, dart variations, and dart substitutions.
- To equalize discrepancies produced in a pattern draft.

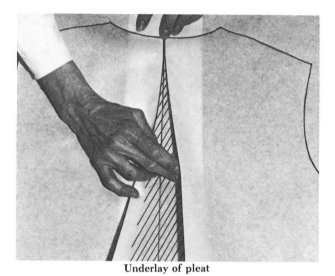

Underlay of pleat

Underlay

Portion of the pattern which constitutes the inside or underside of the design or fold line, or dart pick-up.

Formed when establishing darts, dart tucks, flange darts, pleats, closures, and extensions; fold back directional seam, seam or hem.

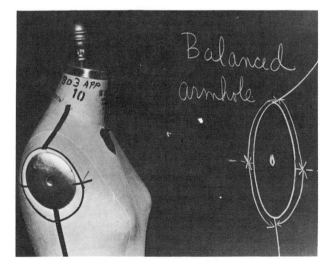

Verifying the Form

Testing the model form for the alignment and balance of shoulder-side seam relationship.

- Prior to draping or measuring form for pattern development.
- To make correction of lower torso side seam.
- To find correct placement of shoulder and underarm side seam.
- To assure proper hang of muslin or drape of fabric.

Alignment may necessitate changing of shoulder and/or underarm seam by establishing new working lines.

6 ~ Tracing & Marking Terminology

Chalked Markings
Chalked Thread
Color Coding

Pin Markings
Tailor's Tacks
Thread Tracing

Markings are the construction symbols transferred from the pattern to the garment section after cutting. Transfer markings may be made on the face, inside or through garment sections.

Markings or tracings indicate the position of points of construction, design detail, grainlines and center lines. Pattern markings on fabric are guides for various means of fitting and sewing.

The method of tracings and transfer markings selected depends on:
- Type and weight of fabric
- Color of fabric
- Placement of marking
- Method of construction
- Methods for fitting
- Methods of production

Chalked Markings

The process of marking one or two fabric plies on the seam, style or detail lines with the use of tailor's wax or chalk or a marking pencil over pin or pins positioned in the fabric.

- Instead of tracing wheel and carbon paper.
- When tracing wheel and carbon paper may mar the fabric.
- On face of fabric for marking details such as pockets, trimmings and pleats.
- On bulky or loosely woven fabrics where carbon marking will not show.
- To mark bonded or laminated fabrics.
- When draping directly with fabric.

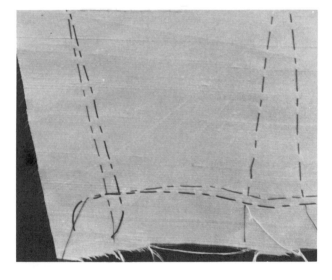

Chalked Thread

Sewing thread impregnated with powdered chalk.

- To mark tightly woven goods where other methods of tracing would damage the fabric.
- To mark silk fabrics where wax would leave a stain and where the imprint of the tracing wheel would damage the fabric.

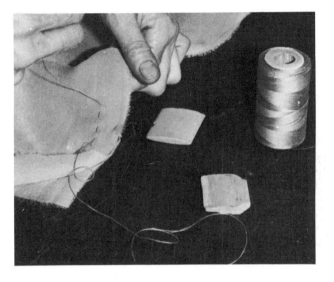

Color Coding

The use of three different color threads to indicate thread tracing, basting, correcting lines after fitting.

- To avoid confusion and clarify commercial pattern marking procedures.
- To differentiate the purpose of pattern markings when transferred to the garment.
- To avoid complications when matching pleat or tuck lines in putting a garment together.

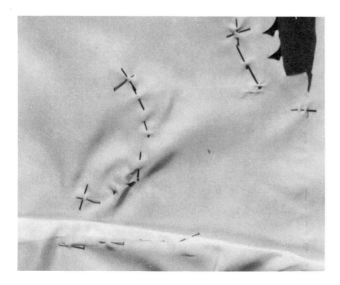

Pin Markings

A line of pins indicating a construction or grainline on a garment section.

- When the garment section part is to be sewn at once.
- When the fit is assured.

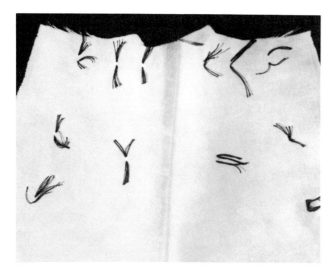

Tailor's Tacks

Temporary small stitches of double thread, with loose un-knotted ends.

- To indicate construction details.
- On the face of the garment to mark construction details such as pockets, trimmings, and pleats.
- To transfer markings for fabrics that are bulky, spongy, sheer, fine, white, or lacy.
- When and where chalk or tracing wheels would mar the fabric.
- When and where fabric will be handled a great deal.
- To mark bonded fabrics.
- An alternative to chalk or tracing paper.
- On fabrics that will not show other types of markings.
- When markings must be seen on both sides of the fabric.

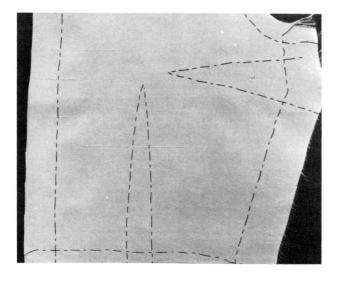

Thread Tracing

A temporary line of alternating long and short hand-sewn stitches through a single layer of fabric.

- To indicate construction of grainlines on each section of a garment.
- To mark the center front and center back folds of a garment.
- To denote grainlines.
- To denote seams, darts, and other construction lines.
- As a guide for basting, sewing, and fitting.

7 ~ Types of Patterns

Commercial Pattern
Drafted Pattern
Draped Pattern
Graded Pattern

Muslin Proof / Test Muslin Pattern
Production Pattern
Trade Block Pattern / Standard Block Pattern

A pattern is a guide for cutting one or more garments. It includes all the pieces needed to make a garment.

Patterns are developed through methods of drafting or draping. They include the processes of checking for accurate fit and interpretation of design; trueing; establishing seam allowances; marking and identification. Style ease, which is part of the design, and wearing ease are included in the development of the pattern pieces.

A pattern for a garment style is graded by the ready-to-wear manufacturer or commercial pattern company to include the size range within a figure type. Patterns conform to standard measurements, but interpretation of the measurements for sizing in the ready-to-wear market vary with each manufacturer and differ from commercial pattern standards.

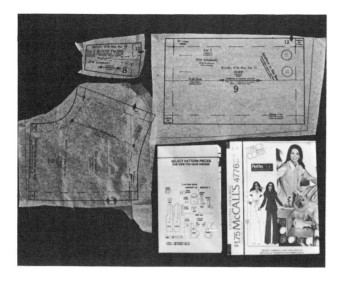

Commercial Pattern

An individually packaged pattern with symbols, markings and instructions printed on each garment section and accompanied by a detailed instruction sheet for pattern layout and garment construction.

Available in retail stores and packaged according to commercial pattern figure type and size range.

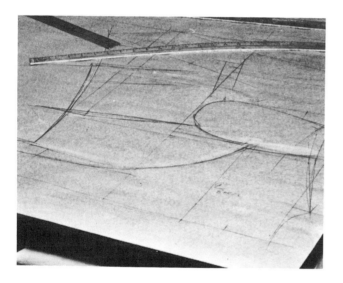

Drafted Pattern

A pattern developed through flat pattern design using measurements taken from the model form or live model from standardized or individual manufacturer's specifications, or through the manipulation of drafted slopers.

• To cut a sample or trial garment.

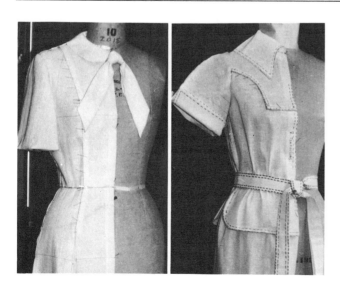

Draped Pattern

A pattern developed through the manipulation of muslin or fabric on the model form or on a live model.

• In sample rooms when cutting sample or trial garments.

Muslin pattern is developed as a half pattern.
For designs utilizing a knit fabric, a knit fabric pattern will be made. Patterns for knits are made of the same knit as the garment to assure proper drape of the garment.

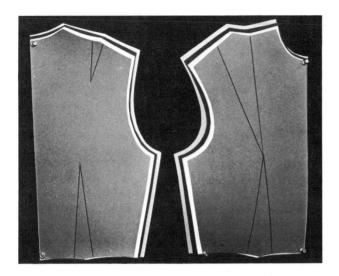

Graded Pattern

Individual patterns of a particular garment or style proportioned to a set of standardized body measurements for each size within a size range.

- To cut duplicate samples.
- To calculate yardage requirements.
- To make a marker.

Production pattern is increased and decreased to form graded patterns. Gradation and methods of grading differ according to manufacturer, garment type and size range.

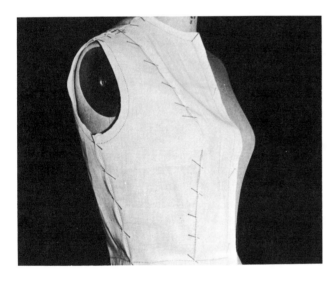

Muslin Proof / Test Muslin Pattern

A muslin reproduction of the finished drafted pattern, pinned or stitched together in the form of the garment.

- To test the fit, balance and proportion of original draft.
- To test fabric potential of drafted design concept.
- To adjust fit of new design or pattern on model form or live model.

Test pattern may be made as right half or complete muslin garment.

Production Pattern

A granite-board copy of the tested and perfected final pattern including the specified seam allowances, perforations, notches, grainlines, and pattern identifications.

- To cut duplicate garments.
- To develop a marker.

Production patterns include pattern pieces for both sides of the garment. Pattern pieces representing half a symmetrical garment section are duplicated to produce both halves, completing one pattern unit. Pattern pieces representing one side of a garment section are duplicated in reverse, producing a pair.

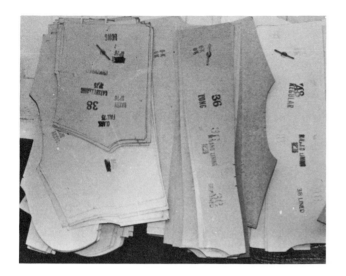

Trade Block Pattern / Standard Block Pattern

A granite-board pattern of a garment section, including seam allowances, notches and details, which represents a basic or recurring fashion silhouette.

- To develop a style variation with the same silhouette.
- To reproduce silhouette of a garment section when incorporating it into another style.

Trade block patterns are adjusted and adapted as current style and fashion demands.

8 ~ Fabric Structure

Animal Skin
Bonded Fabric Structure / Laminated
  Fabric Structure
Felt Fabric Structure
Flocking Fabric Structure
Fused Fabric Structure / Nonwoven
  Fabric Structure

Knit Fabric Structure
Lace Fabric Structure
Napped Fabric Structure
Net Fabric Structure
Pile Fabric Structure
Plastic Fabric Structure
Woven Fabric Structure

Fabric is produced from natural fibers and synthetic filaments which are spun, twisted, cured, shrunk, bulked or manipulated in other ways to achieve yarn for weaving.

Yarns are woven, knitted, knotted or felted in different formations to produce a variety of fabric. Fabric structure is the result of the process by which yarn becomes cloth.

The terms cloth, material, goods and textile are interchangeable with fabric.

Any combination of finishes or treatments whether functional, decorative or permanent may be applied to the fiber, yarn or goods at one or more stages of production. The end result will effect the hand or feel, weight and texture of the finished cloth.

Variations and combinations of fiber, yarn, structure and finish determine the drapeability and design potential of the finished fabric.

The selection of fabric depends on:
• Design and style of garment
• Type of garment
• Purpose of garment
• Use of garment
• Care of garment
• Additions of findings and trimmings
• Method of construction

Animal Skin

The skin of an animal, processed and dressed in one of a variety of surfaces, thicknesses and colors and referred to as smooth leather, suede or split.

Each skin differs in size, color and surface markings. The irregular shape of a finished skin is determined by the animal source.

Skins are available by the length and/or weight. Each skin is marked at the tail end on the wrong side indicating its total length.

The thickness of the skin determines the number of ounces (grams) that one square foot (meter) equals.

Processing and dressing refer to the tanning of leather.

Suede is processed to obtain a soft nap on face side.

Split is processed to obtain rough surface on both sides.

Animal skins include:

Antelope
Buckskin
Calfskin
Cabretta
Chamois
Cowhide
Crocodile
Deerskin
Doeskin
Elk
Frog
Goat
Kidskin
Lizard
Cobra
Ostrich
Pigskin
Pony
Sealskin
Sharkskin
Snake
Python
Elephant
Rabbit
Reptile
Sheepskin

Bonded Fabric Structure / Laminated Fabric Structure

A fabric formed by a process in which an outer or face fabric is joined to a backing or lining ply by an adhesive, bonding, foam fusing, or thermoplastic agent.

Laminated fabric includes foam between face and underply.

Bonded fabric is fused directly to underply.

Bonding or laminating changes the hand of the outer layer, stabilizes an open weave, reinforces a stretch or pliable surface, acts as a backing and gives stability to the face fabric.

Bonded Fabric Structure   Laminated Fabric Structure

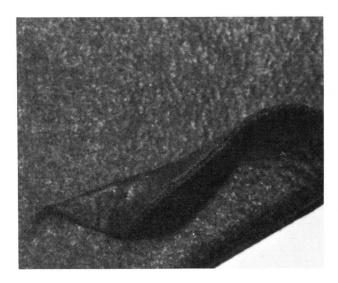

Felt Fabric Structure

A nonwoven fabric structure produced by the application of moisture, heat, agitation and pressure to a web of fibers forming an interlocking, uniform matted layer.

Felt does not have a system of threads such as warp, weft or selvage. It will not fray or ravel.

Felt is produced in a variety of widths, from 60 to 90 inches (1.5 to 2.3 m), depending on the steam box and rollers or specifications of the manufacturers.

Apparel felts are 1/16 to 1/8 inch (1.6 to 3.2 mm).

Fibers used in producing felt are wool, fur or mohair which may be mixed with cotton and/or rayon.

Flocking Fabric Structure

A fabric structure containing synthetic, short staple fibers applied to resin-treated goods by spray or electrostatic methods to produce a napped surface.

Flocking may be applied to any type of fabric as an all-over or patterned design.

Fused Fabric Structure / Nonwoven Fabric Structure

A nonwoven fabric structure produced with bonding agents and the application of moisture, heat, agitation and pressure to a web of fibers forming an interlocking, uniform matted layer.

The method of manufacturing nonwoven fabrics varies with the nature of the fiber, web formation, and bonding agents used.

Depending on the technique employed, the fibers may be laid in a parallel, cross or random web formation and are fused with resin, thermoplastic or stitch-through bonding agents.

Fused fabrics are produced in a variety of widths depending on roller beds and the specifications of manufacturers.

Fused fabrics which may be used for interfacing and underlining include:

Dorron®
Evershape®
Interlon®
Keybak®
Keybak, Hot Iron® (iron on)
Kyrel®
Kyrel, Adheron® (iron on)
Kyrel, Stretch®
Pellon® (regular)
Pellon® (all bias)
Pelomite® (iron on)
Staflex® (iron on)

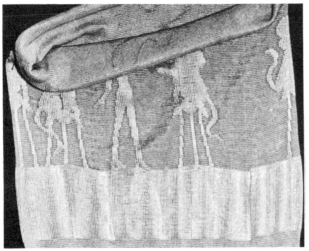

Tubular Knit

Rib Knit

Knit Fabric Structure

A fabric structure constructed through the process of interlocking loops. It is divided into two general types:

1. *Weft Knitting*—Identified by one continuous yarn forming courses across the fabric.
2. *Warp Knitting*—Identified by a series of yarns forming wales in the lengthwise direction of the fabric.

Wales and courses are comparable to the warp and weft in woven goods.

Variations in the pattern of knits are achieved by changing the arrangement of the basic stitch or loop.

The basic structure of knits offers stretchability not found in woven goods. Stretchability of knits varies according to the direction and complexity of loop formation, gauge (size of stitch), and denier (weight of yarn).

Knits can be made to stretch in either the course or wale direction, or both, depending on elasticity desired.

Knitting machines produce either tubular or flat goods in a variety of widths depending on the type of machine and the specifications of manufacturers.

Knit fabric structures include:
Double Knit:
    Bourrelet
    Double Jersey
    Eight Lock
    Pin Tuck
    Piqué, Double
    Piqué, Single
    Plain Interlock
    Ribbed Jacquard
Crochet
Jacquard
Jersey
Interlock
Matte Jersey
Milanese
Plain Knit
Purl
Raschel
    Chain Raschel / Ketten Raschel
Rib
Shell Stitch
Simplex
Single Knit
Terry
Tricot
Tuck
Warp
Weft
Weft Insertion Warp Knit

Venise Lace

Chantilly Lace

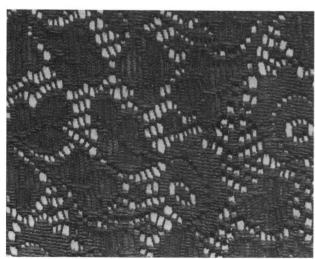

Cluny Lace

Lace Fabric Structure

An openwork fabric structure made by knotting, looping, braiding, twisting, knitting or stitching a network of thread or yarn.

Lace is produced in a wide range of widths, weights, textures and motifs; with or without decoratively finished edges.

Lace fabric structures include:
Alençon
All-over
Aloe
Antique
Argentan
Battenberg
Belgian
Binche
Bobbin
Bobbinet
Bretenne
Brussels
Calais Val
Carrickmacross
Chantilly
Cluny
Crochet
Dresden Point
Filet
Galloon
Guipure
Hardanger
Insertion
Irish Crochet
Irish Lace
Leavers
Macramé
Madagascar
Maline
Milan
Needlepoint
Nottingham
Ratiné
Raschel
Renaissance
Rose Point
Schiffli
Shadow lace
Spanish
Tatting
Torchon
Valenciennes / Val
Venise

Camel Hair

Napped Fabric Structure

A woven or knit fabric structure in which fiber ends have been lifted to the surface by a revolving wire-toothed cylinder, where they are clipped to a uniform length.

Raised surface is brushed to lie in one direction.

Napped fabric structures include:
Alpaca
Angora
Beaver Cloth
Broadcloth
Camel Hair
Cashmere
Chinchilla Cloth
Doeskin
Duvetyn
Flannel
Flannelette
Fleece
Kersey
Mackinaw
Melton
Moleskin
Outing Flannel
Ratiné
Shetland
Suede Cloth
Vicuna
Viyella®
Zibeline

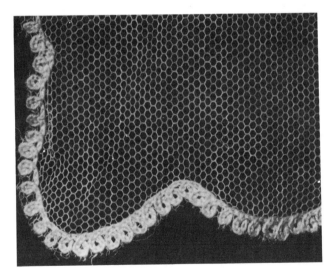

Net Fabric Structure

A fabric construction in which the yarn forming the fabric is twisted or knotted together at each point of intersection producing a geometric, open-mesh formation.

Nets are produced and/or constructed on tricot, raschel, bobbinet or kindle knitting machines in a variation of gauge, denier, and flexibility.

Nets may be made in open hexagonal mesh designs.

Net fabric structures include:
Gossamer
Net
Illusion
Tulle
Bobbinet
Filet
Maline
Point d' Esprit

Wide Wale Corduroy (pile)

Poodle Cloth (uncut pile)

Velveteen (pile)

Pile Fabric Structure

A textured fabric structure produced by interlacing additional yarn into the basic fabric structure producing closely spaced loops which may be cut, sheared or left uncut.

Loops are incorporated into a plain or twill weave or knit base producing a variety of nap surfaces and weights.

Depth of loop, pile or nap may be controlled according to surface finish desired.

Pile fabric structures include:
Bolivia
Chenille
Corduroy:
    Fine Wale
    Pin Wale
    Wide Wale
Frisé
Plush
Karakul
Synthetics imitating furs such as:
    Ashakhan
    Beaver
    Broadtail
    Chinchilla
    Ermine
    Giraffe
    Krimmer
    Leopard
    Mink
    Persian Lamb
    Pony
    Poodle
Terry Cloth
Tufting
Turkish Toweling
Velours
Velvet:
    Bagheera
    Chiffon
    Ciselé
    Crushed
    Cut
    Double
    Façonné
    Lyons
    Nacré
    Panne
    Three pile
    Transparent
    Wire
Velveteen

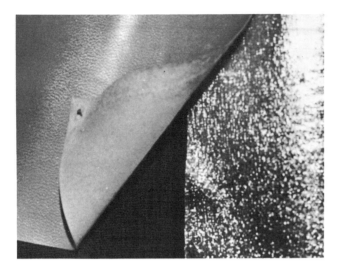

Plastic Fabric Structure

A synthetic, nonwoven fabric formed from thermoplastic and thermosetting resins producing a ply of clear or opaque material.

Plastic fabrics are produced in a variety of surface textures ranging from smooth to rough and in finishes ranging from shiny to matte.

Made to simulate leather, suede or rubber.

Available in various widths; in a single-ply, or fused or laminated to a woven or knit backing.

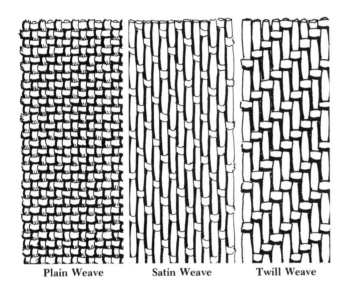

| Plain Weave | Satin Weave | Twill Weave |

Satin Weave

Woven Fabric Structure

Woven fabric structures are produced on a loom by the interlacing and/or intersecting of the warp (length) and weft (cross) yarns.

Plain, twill and satin are the three basic weaves, and the foundation for all other weaves.

Fabric is woven in a variety of widths depending on the size of loom or the specifications of manufacturers.

The number of harnesses determine the construction of woven goods: Two for plain weave; three or more for twill weave; five to twelve for satin weave; as many as forty for jacquard.

Special loop attachments for dobby weaves.

Woven fabric structures include:
Plain Weave
Basket Weave
Rib Weave Filling
Rib Weave Warp
Double Cloth Weave
Twill Weave:
    Right-Hand Twill
    Left-Hand Twill
    Shallow Twill
    Steep Twill
    Broken Twill
    Pointed Twill
    Combination Warp & Filling Twill
Satin Weave:
    Filling-Faced Sateen
    Warp-Faced Satin
Novelty Weave:
    Dobby Weave
    Figure Weave
    Jacquard Weave
    Lappet Weave
    Leno Weave / Doup Weave / Gauze Weave
    Swivel Weave
Piqué Weave:
    Birdseye
    Diamond
    Honeycomb
    Waffle

9 ~ Fabric Terminology

Bias:
  Bias
  True Bias / Forty-Five Degree Bias
Blocking
Face of Fabric / Right Side of Fabric
Grain:
  Crossgrain

Lengthgrain
Off Grain
On Grain
Selvage / Selvedge
Straightening

Grain designates direction of yarn in woven fabric. Grain is a factor that effects designing, draping, patternmaking, and sewing. Fabric grain effects the hang and appearance of a finished garment and is used as a guide in determining handling of fabric during garment construction.

In finished goods, yarns are identified as lengthgrain *(warp)* and crossgrain *(weft* or *filling)*. A diagonal line intersecting length- and crossgrain at an angle is referred to as the *bias* in fabric.

Garments are usually designed with the lengthgrain falling vertically. Lengthgrain is the stronger and more stable grain. Lengthgrain fabrics hang and fall softly on the body and maintain creases and folds better than crossgrain.

Garments are sometimes designed on crossgrain to utilize border designs, geometric fabric patterns or to capture the sheen of a particular weave.

The bias direction of fabrics have give and stretchability. Used in garment design, the bias molds the fabric over the body. Planned in geometric fabric patterns, it produces chevrons along seam lines.

Garments are cut, sewn, fitted, and pressed in relationship to grain and bias. Perpendicular length- and crossgrain are established in the construction of fabric, but they can be distorted or pulled off grain during the printing and finishing process or while rolling, handling or bundling for distribution. Off-grain fabrics can be aligned or put on grain through straightening and blocking.

Straightening and blocking preparations are essential preliminaries to draping, layout, and cutting. Pattern pieces are arranged for cutting on prepared fabric.

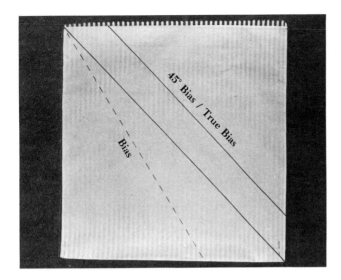

Bias

A direction in the fabric at an angle to the length- or crossgrain.

Bias is the direction in which the woven fabric has give.

Bias conforms to body contour more than length- or crossgrain.

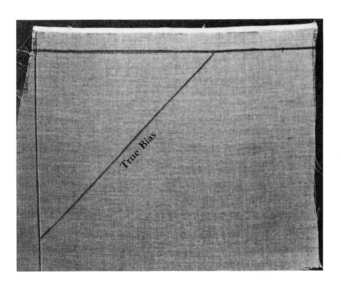

True Bias / Forty-Five Degree Bias

The diagonal line or direction that intersects the length- and crossgrain at a forty-five degree angle.

Fabric cut on the true bias has the maximum give and stretchability of woven fabric.

Bias readily conforms and molds to body contours.

Off-grain fabric

All grains in alignment—properly blocked fabric

Blocking

A process of realignment of length- and crossgrain yarns to a ninety degree angle by pulling on the true bias from the shorter off-grain edge, or by pulling and realigning the fabric on grain while pressing with steam.

Realigned yarns are set by pressing in the direction of the length- and crossgrain.

Permanent-press and heat-set finished fabrics resist blocking.

Face of Fabric / Right Side of Fabric

The surface of fabric designated in the process of weaving, printing or finishing to be used as the outside or face of a finished garment.

Smooth Fabric—More sheen, slick or soft on the face.
Textured Fabric—Slubs or loops are raised and distinct; naps or patterns outstanding.
Twill Fabric—Weave better defined, diagonal pattern distinctly visible.
Printed Design—Color and pattern are sharper and better defined, blurred on the back of goods.

Fabric face and reverse, at times, have no visible difference; either side can be used as the face in garment construction.

Crossgrain

Crossgrain indicates yarn woven across the fabric from selvage to selvage; referred to as weft thread, and is the filling yarn of woven fabric.

Crossgrain has more give under tension than lengthgrain.

Lengthgrain

Lengthgrain indicates yarn paralleling the selvage in woven goods. Referred to as warp thread or warp yarn.

Lengthgrain is firmer, stronger and more stable than crossgrain; has little give under tension.

Lengthgrain is referred to as *straight of goods*.
Yard goods are measured on the lengthgrain.

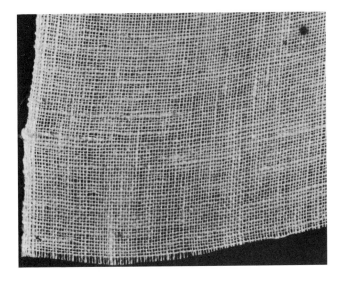

Off Grain

A fabric is referred to as being *off grain* when length- and crossgrain threads have been distorted from a ninety degree alignment, or when crossgrain is not at right angles to selvages or length of goods.

Off-grain fabric can be aligned or put on grain through straightening and blocking.

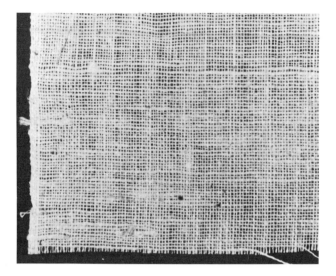

On Grain

A fabric is referred to as being *on grain* when length- and crossgrain threads or yarns intersect each other at right angles.

Perpendicular length- and crossgrain are established in the construction of fabric, but they can be distorted or pulled off grain during the printing and finishing process, or while rolling, handling or bundling for distribution.

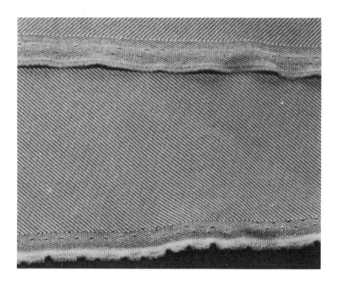

Selvage / Selvedge

The narrow, firmly woven finished edge on both length-grain sides of a woven fabric.

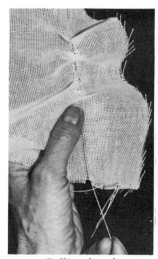 

Pulling thread   Cutting along rib of fabric

Straightening

The cutting of a straight crossgrain across the fabric and from selvage to selvage along the woven crossgrain.

Straightening established by:
1. Tearing of firmly woven fabric after clipping selvage;
2. Drawing, pulling or picking one yarn of loosely woven, stretch or soft fabric from the entire width, selvage to selvage;
3. Cutting on a predominant line of a woven plaid, check or stripe;
4. Cutting on a crossgrain rib.

10 ~ Spreading and/or Folding Fabric

Combination Fold Layout
Crosswise Fold Layout
Lengthwise Fold Layout:
   Lengthwise Fold Layout
   Double Lengthwise Fold Layout /
      Bifold Layout

Partial Lengthwise Fold
Spread:
   Double-Ply Spread Layout /
   Multi-Ply Spread Layout
   Single-Ply Spread Layout /
   Open-Ply Spread Layout

Spreading and/or folding fabric for sample room or non-industrial pattern layout and cutting is planned for maximum utilization of yardage.

The determining factor for the method or manner of folding relates to the type and design of fabric, the style of garment, and the design and size of pattern pieces.

Fabric is folded with right sides together when layout calls for lengthwise, crosswise or partial lengthwise folding of fabric. Napped and laminated fabrics are folded with wrong sides together, with face of fabric outward, to prevent slippage. Pile fabrics are folded with right sides face-to-face to prevent slippage. Plaids, stripes and large print motifs are folded with face of fabric outward when design is to be matched or chevroned.

The method of spreading or folding fabric selected depends on:
- Type of fabric
- Nap or design of fabric
- Width of fabric
- Design and style of garment
- Width of pattern pieces
- Quantity of pattern pieces
- Type of cutting procedures employed

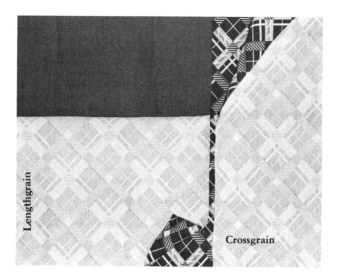

Combination Fold Layout

A layout utilizing fabric folded two different ways for the same layout; one section of the fabric being folded on the lengthgrain or bifolded, and the other folded crossgrain.

- Some pattern pieces are too large for a single lengthgrain or bifolded layout.
- For a nondirectional layout only.

Portion of fabric may be folded first on the lengthgrain, or bifolded, and cut; followed by crossgrain folding procedure to accommodate the remaining pattern pieces.

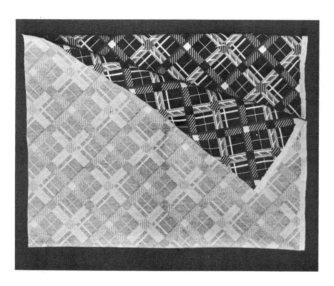

Crosswise Fold Layout

A layout utilizing fabric which is folded on the crossgrain with each selvage aligned over itself.

- To accommodate wide pattern pieces.
- When pattern pieces need not be placed on the lengthgrain fold.
- For a nondirectional layout only.

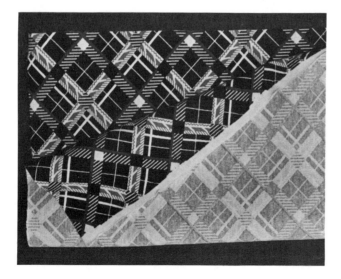

Lengthwise Fold Layout

A layout utilizing fabric which is folded on the lengthgrain with opposite selvages aligned one over the other.

- When garment design balances.
- When fabric design is balanced.
- Half of fabric width will accommodate all pattern pieces.
- For a directional and/or nondirectional layout.

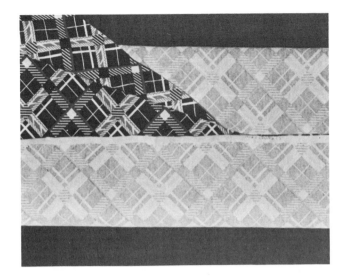

Double Lengthwise Fold Layout / Bifold Layout

A layout utilizing fabric which is folded on the lengthgrain with selvages aligned near or on the center of goods.

- To avoid a nonremovable creaseline of fabric that will detract from the appearance of the garment.
- When pattern design requires many pieces to be placed on the fold.
- For a directional and/or nondirectional layout.

Also may be referred to as *gate fold*.

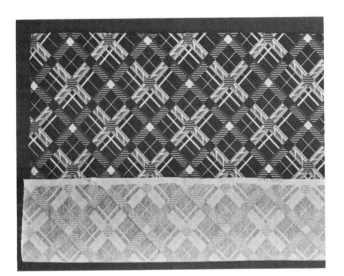

Partial Lengthwise Fold Layout

A layout utilizing fabric which is folded on the lengthgrain with *one* selvage aligned a measured distance from the fold; the balance of the fabric width is a single ply.

- Some pattern pieces are to be cut double ply and others paired or on a single ply.
- For a directional and/or nondirectional layout.

Double-Ply Layout / Multi-Ply Layout

A layout where two or more plies of fabric are spread face-up or face-to-face.

- To cut more than one garment of the same size and style.
- When backing or underlining and face fabric will be cut simultaneously and treated as one ply.
- For a directional and/or nondirectional layout.

Single-Ply Spread Layout /
Open-Ply Spread Layout

A layout utilizing a single ply of fabric.

- On an asymmetrical or bias-cut garment design.
- When pattern pieces representing both halves of a balanced design.
- When cut-out backing or underlining ply is utilized as the pattern.
- For a directional and/or nondirectional layout.
- In commercial cutting.

11 ~ Pattern Layout

Animal Skin
Border Design Fabric
Border Fabric / Finished Border Fabric
Check Fabric / Checkered Fabric
Diagonal Design Fabric / Diagonal Print Fabric
Diagonal Weave Fabric / Twill Type Fabric
Directional Design Fabric / One-Way Design Fabric
Irregular Design Fabric
Knit Fabric
Large Print Fabric / Motif Design Fabric
Light-Reflecting Fabric

Napped Fabric
Pile Fabric
Plaid Fabric:
    Balanced Plaid / Even Plaid
    Unbalanced Plaid
    Uneven Plaid
Plastic Fabric
Stripe Fabric:
    Balanced Stripe
    Even Stripe
    Uneven Stripe / Unbalanced Stripe

A layout is the planned arrangement of pattern pieces on fabric, paper or marker in the preparation for cutting. Pattern layout is planned for maximum utilization of yardage when spreading and/or folding fabric for sample room or non-industrial use.

Factors of garment design affecting the direction of the grain and placement of pattern pieces relating to the layout are

    Balance;
    Direction or pattern in fabric design;
    Direction of raised, brushed or looped nap;
    Light refraction quality of weave or knit fiber.

Pattern layout is planned for maximum utilization of yardage when spreading and/or folding fabric for sample room or non-industrial use.

Lengthgrain as indicated on the pattern pieces is placed on the lengthgrain of goods in preparing a layout. Lengthgrain established on pattern pieces is determined in the initial design and patternmaking. Line and arrow symbols marked on draped muslin, drafted patterns, or commercial pattern pieces indicate the direction of the lengthgrain designed in the original pattern.

Goods with particular weaves, patterns or finishes, known as *directional* fabrics, need special consideration in planning a layout. This group includes knitted, napped, pile, brushed, looped, and satin fabrics. One-way or directional fabric when reversed shows a different color tone and/or design.

All pattern pieces on directional fabrics are placed facing the same or one-way direction; on single- or multi-ply spread, or on lengthwise, partial lengthwise or double lengthwise folded fabric. Directional fabrics require more yardage.

Geometrics such as plaids, stripes, checks, and border designs require matching in planning a pattern layout due to proportion within the design. Motif prints require a special layout so that the motif, after the fabric is cut and seamed, will match. Geometrics and motif print fabrics are oriented to a one-way position and require more yardage.

Commercial pattern instruction sheets include information for the layout of pattern pieces pertaining to the individual design.

The method of pattern layout selected depends on:
* Fabric
    Weave
    Texture
    Surface or Finish
    Pattern or Design
    Width
* Style and design of pattern
* Methods of cutting employed
* Quantity of garments cut
* Methods of construction

For clarity of illustration all fabrics for pattern layout have been folded face out.

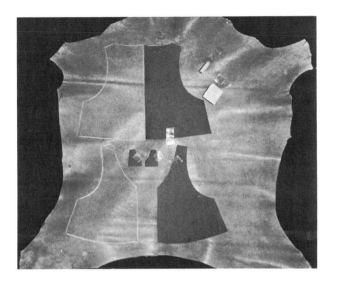

Animal Skin

Animal skins are measured in square feet (square centimeters) and differ individually in shape, size, color, and surface markings. Skins may be enlarged or elongated by piecing to accommodate large pattern pieces. Skins are considered napped fabrics and require a one-way layout on a single-ply spread.

Draped, drafted and commercial pattern pieces are transcribed into complete units or pairs before layout on skins. Pattern pieces representing half of a symmetrical section are duplicated to produce both halves and complete one pattern unit. Pattern pieces representing one side of a garment section are duplicated in reverse and produce a pair.

Border Design Fabric

A fabric design incorporating a woven, printed, painted or embroidered band or pattern along one or both selvages.

Pattern pieces are placed either on the length- or cross-grain direction to utilize or emphasize the border design on the garment.

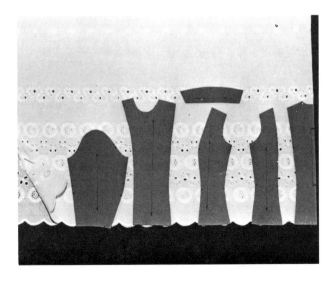

Border Fabric / Finished Border Fabric

A fabric designed with a decorative finish, which may be scalloped, on one or both lengthgrain edges. Group of fabrics include eyelet, schiffli, and lace.

Pattern pieces are placed on either the length- or cross-grain direction to utilize or emphasize the border finish on the garment.

Check Fabric / Checkered Fabric

A two-color design of alternating bands or bars of even width, in both length- and crosswise direction, forming a pattern of boxes.

Pattern pieces arranged in the layout so that checks correspond or produce a chevron at seam line.

Diagonal Design Fabric / Diagonal Print Fabric

A fabric printed with stripes, geometrics or a motif pattern that forms diagonal lines from selvage to selvage.

In the layout, all pattern pieces are placed in the same direction; on a single- or multi-ply spread, on lengthwise, partial lengthwise or double lengthwise folded fabric.

Garment design planned and/or selected so design pattern is continuous, not mitered.

Diagonal Weave Fabric / Twill Type Fabric

Fabric constructed so that a twill or diagonal line of the same or contrasting yarn appears on the face of the fabric.

Pattern pieces are placed on single- or multi-ply spread or on lengthwise, partial lengthwise or double lengthwise folded fabric.

Twill angles appearing in the weave may be imbedded or raised.

Most twills are angles at 45 degrees.

Steep or sharp twills are angled at 63, 70, or 75 degrees.

Reclining or blunt twills are angled at 27, 20, or 15 degrees.

Diagonal weave patterns may appear as right- or left-hand twills.

Fabrics with a diagonal weave are cut in a one-way layout to avoid color tone difference caused by light refraction.

Diagonal weave and twill type fabrics include:

Brocade	Sarah
Canton Flannel	Scotch Tweed
Cassimere	Serge:
Cavalry Twill	Double Serge
Chinchilla Cloth	Filling-Backed Serge
Chino	French Serge
Covert	French-Backed Serge
Elastique	Storm Serge
Denim	Sharkskin
Drill	Silesia
Foulard	Tartan
Gabardine	Tackle Twill
Galatea	Three-Leaf Warp Twill
Herringbone	Tricotine
Hound's Tooth	Tweed
Jean Cloth	Viyella®
Kersey	Whipcord
Pointed Twill	

Twill weaves are found in some drill and twill cloth and in some ticking fabric.

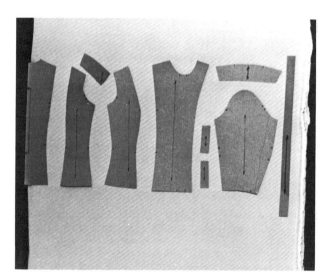

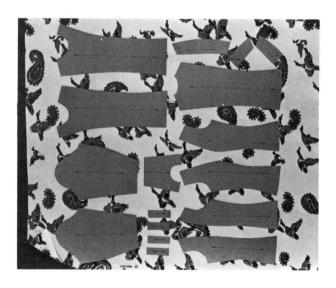

Directional Design Fabric / One-Way Design Fabric

One-way prints or weaves containing a definite design with the motif repeated and facing the same direction. One-way designs are cut according to a recognizable element or effect desired.

In the layout, all pattern pieces are placed facing the same direction; on single- or multi-ply spread, or on lengthwise, partial lengthwise or double lengthwise folded fabric.

Irregular Design Fabric

Hand-loomed, hand-painted, stenciled, silk-screened, block-printed, batik or tie-dyed fabrics with designs which have no repeat, or when repeated may show irregularities in registration or design.

Pattern pieces are placed on fabric according to individual design of fabric or planned arrangement of design on finished garment.

Irregular design fabrics are made in limited yardage or as one-of-a-kind pieces.

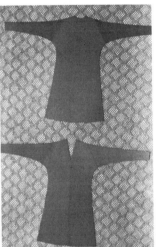

Knit Fabric

Fabric constructed through the process of interlocking loops forming a pattern of wales and/or courses.

Garments are designed to utilize the stretchability of the different knit fabrics.

Pattern pieces are placed on single- or multi-ply spread, or on lengthwise, partial lengthwise or double lengthwise folded fabric.

Tubular, sweater and other knit fabrics are cut in a one-way layout to avoid a difference in color tone.

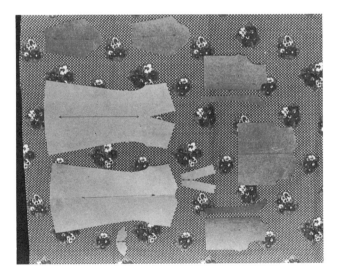

Large Print Fabric / Motif Design Fabric

A fabric with a large repeat pattern or design element.

Layout is planned to assure matching of motifs in garment seams.

Motif arrangement may be asymmetrical, matched or balanced at the center or on either side of the seam.

Moiré

Light-Reflecting Fabric

Fabric with a surface sheen that reflects light in a variety of ways.

Layout is placed on single- or multi-ply spread, or on lengthwise, partial lengthwise or double lengthwise folded fabric.

Weaves and finishes of light-reflecting fabrics cause shading when viewed from different angles and require a one-way layout either lengthwise or crosswise.

Light-reflecting fabrics include:

Antique Satin
Brocade
Brocatelle
Chintz
Cotton Sateen
Crepe Meteor
Damask:
  Single Damask
Moiré
Polished Cotton

Pongee
Satin
Satin Crepe
Slipper Satin / Panne Satin
Taffeta:
  Antique Taffeta
  Faille Taffeta
  Moiré Taffeta
  Paper Taffeta
  Tissue Taffeta

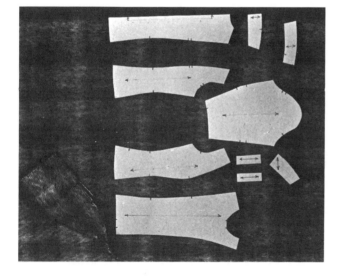

Napped Fabric

A woven or knitted fabric with raised fiber or hair brushed to lie flat, producing a one-way directional surface.

A one-way layout is used in cutting napped fabric with the top of every pattern piece placed in the same direction; on a single- or multi-ply spread; on lengthwise, partial lengthwise or double lengthwise folded fabric.

Garments are designed with the brushed surface oriented downward.

Pile Fabric

Woven or knitted fabric with a high- or low-cut pile, or looped texture on the face producing a one-way directional surface.

A one-way layout is used in cutting napped fabrics with the top of every pattern piece placed in the same direction; on single- or multi-ply spread, or on lengthwise, partial lengthwise or double lengthwise folded fabric.

Downward direction of pile fabric has a smooth texture and color tone of the fabric is lighter with a silver-cast sheen.

Upward direction of pile fabric has an apparently rougher texture and color tone is deeper, richer and darker giving the fabric more depth.

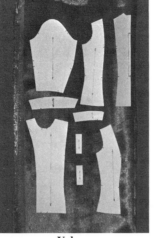

Panne Velvet   Velour

Balanced Plaid / Even Plaid

A design which is the same on both sides of a predominant bar in both the length- and crossgrain of the fabric. The pattern is repeated evenly in both directions.

Pattern pieces are arranged in the layout so that the geometric design corresponds or produces chevrons at seam lines.

Unbalanced Plaid

A design in which the patterns of bars vary on both sides of a predominant colored bar either on the length- or crossgrain, or both, directions of the fabric.

Layout is planned in a one-way direction; on single- or multi-ply spread.

Unbalanced plaids have a one-way repeat horizontally and/or vertically.

Garment is designed so geometrics go around the body in one direction only.

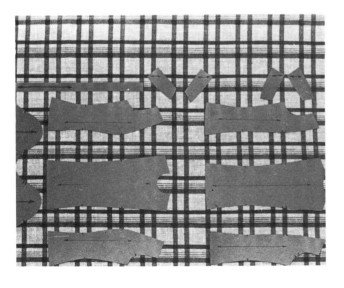

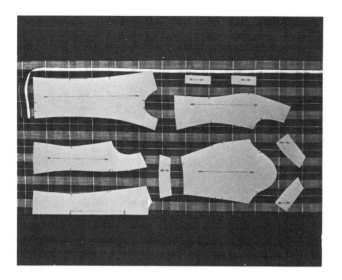

Uneven Plaid

A design in which the pattern of the bars on the length-grain differ from the pattern of the bars on the crossgrain. One-way layout is required in order that the horizontal geometric design can be matched at seam line.

Pattern pieces are placed on single- or multi-ply spread or on lengthwise, partial lengthwise or double lengthwise folded fabric.

Fabric must be reversible with no noticeable face in order to produce chevron from an uneven plaid.

Plastic Fabric

Clear or opaque film manufactured with a smooth or rough surface and a shiny or matte finish which may be bonded or laminated to a knit or woven backing.

Layout is planned as a single-ply spread, or with tissue paper separating layers in a multi-ply spread, or folded with wrong sides together and face of fabric outward.

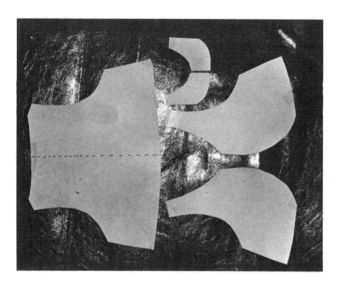

Balanced Stripe

A design with the color and width of a line or series of lines in a mirror repeat to the right and left of a center stripe.

Pattern pieces are arranged in the layout so that the geometric designs correspond or produce a chevron at seam line.

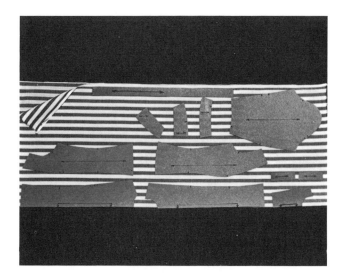

Even Stripe

A two-color design of alternating lines or series of lines, of even width, in either the lengthwise or crosswise direction.

Pattern pieces are arranged in the layout so that the geometric designs correspond or produce a chevron at seam line.

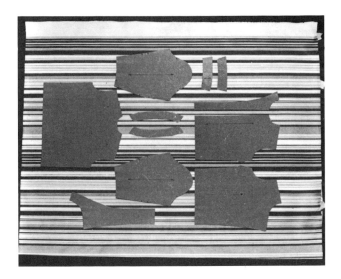

Uneven Stripe / Unbalanced Stripe

A design in which lines of mixed width and color are repeated consecutively forming a one-way directional design.

One-way layout is required to continue stripes in consecutive order at seam line.

Garments are designed so geometrics go around the body in one direction only.

Unevenly striped fabric which is reversible with no noticeable face difference, can be planned to produce a chevron at seam lines.

12 ~ Aids, Tools & Equipment for Cutting

Band Knife
Clamp
Click Press / Die Cutting Press
Cloth Measuring & Inspection Machine
Cloth Notcher:
   Electrical Cloth Notcher
   Manual Cloth Notcher
Cutters:
   Straight Knife Cutter / Straight Cutter
   Circular Knife Cutter / Circular Cutter /
     Rotary Cutter / Round Knife
   Portable Rotary Knife Cutter /
     Portable Rotary Cutter
Cutting Board
Cutting Room Thread Marker
Cutting Table
Cutting Table Triangle
Drill
Pattern Perforator
Razor Blade
Razor Knife
Scissors:
   Buttonhole Scissors
   Embroidery Scissors

Motor-Driven Scissors
Sewing Scissors
Shears:
   Ball-Tipped Shears
   Bent Handle Dressmaker's Shears /
     Bent Trimmers
   Dressmaker's Shears / Straight Trimmers
   Paper Shears
   Patternmaking Shears
   Pinking Shears
   Scalloping Shears
   Serrated Blade Shears / Knife Edge Shears /
     Synthetic Fabric Shears
   Tailor's Shears
Spreader:
   Cut-Off Machine
   End Catcher / End Guide Rail
   Face-to-Face Spreader
   Manual Spreader
   One-Way Spreader
   Tubular Knit Spreader
Thread Clippers / Thread Snips /
   Weaver's Scissors
Weights

In preparation for cutting fabrics, manufacturers employ a variety of machines which include large pieces of equipment and hand-held tools.

Fabric is shipped on rolls, creels, boards, or as flat-folds. The cloth is then measured, examined, and rewound. The wound fabric is placed on a spreading machine that moves back and forth over the cutting table laying plies to a desired length.

Spreading machine and cutting table widths are determined by the width of the goods. Table length is determined by the type of marker and/or its multiples, plus allowance for the fabric stretch factor, and type of machinery.

A marker made of paper, nonwoven cloth or of the fabric itself is placed as the top ply of the plied fabric. Rotary, or reciprocating, electrically driven cutting knives are guided along the perimeter of the pattern outlines on the marker, separating the pattern sections from the body of the lay.

Cutting equipment in a variety of sizes is engineered for heavy duty and general purpose cutting of heavy- to lightweight materials, from work clothes to lingerie. Blades are designed with a serrated, wave, or saw-toothed edge, to accommodate various fabric constructions and heights of lay. In addition, there are knives to cut through synthetic, foam and rubber materials.

Knives are sharpened with smooth, medium or coarse grit stones or belts, considering the edge needed for the type of fabric to be cut. A knife used for synthetic fabric needs lubrication (a stainless liquid automatically dispensed along the blade) to reduce heat build-up which causes fabric fusion. High, low or dual speed motors are available as an alternative means of reducing heat build-up.

Shears and scissors are precision cutting instruments produced by forging, grinding, hardening, polishing, and balancing special grades of iron or steel. They are tools which operate as two opposing sharpened edges of metal pivoting on a pin.

There are three main parts of a shears or scissors:
1. The *blades* which are the cutting part of the instrument;
2. The *shanks* joining the blade with the handles and containing a connecting pin which can be a screw, nut and bolt or rivet;

3. The *bows* or *rings* which are the loops forming the handle.

The shape of the bow differentiates between a shears and scissors.

Shears have two bows of unequal size, one of them accommodating more than one finger. The bow may be contoured to fit or conform to the shape of the hand. Scissors are designed with bows or ring handles of equal size.

Shears and scissors are plated with nickel or chrome and may be made with or without enameled bows. They may also be constructed with aluminum blades and plastic bows.

There are many types and sizes of scissors and shears, all designed to meet particular requirements. In addition, the cutting edge of the blade may be made for a specific cutting purpose or to produce a decorative finishing edge. Blade tips may be made sharply pointed, ball tipped, angled or rounded.

Aids, tools and equipment for cutting are selected with consideration for:
• Cutting capacity needed
• Height of lay
• Type of fabric
• Density of fabric
• Operation intended
• Production methods employed

Rounded blunt point   Angled blunt point   Sharply pointed blade tip

Band Knife

A motor-driven, continuous-action, vertical knife affixed to a cantelevered frame. Table is designed to surround the knife table.

- To cut around acute angles and sharp curves.
- To cut difficult garment sections more accurately.

Equipment is designed so blocked goods are pushed toward moving knife.

Clamp

A gripping device consisting of two opposing metal arms, joined at a central pivot point to form handles and bills; operated through the force of a spring which holds the bills in a closed position.

- To hold cloth lays together.
- To hold marker to lay-up.

Click Press / Die Cutting Press

A single- or double-arm electric, or compressed air, press which houses steel cutting dies made to the exact dimensions of a garment section.

- To cut precisely collars, cuffs, flaps, and pockets.
- To cut small garment parts such as bands, tabs and welts; underlay pieces; shoulder pads.
- When garment parts are duplicated frequently.

Die cutting limited to lay-up of a specific height. Press available in steel rule die for styles that change frequently. Also, available in all steel die for longer life of cutting edge.

Cloth Measuring & Inspection Machine

A motor-driven unit containing a means for supporting a bolt of fabric and a mandrel for rerolling the fabric after it has passed over an inspection board.

- To wind and unwind fabric.
- To measure, examine and rewind goods.
- To package and split rolls.
- To take inventory.

Machine is operated by foot pedal and/or hand control and is available in widths from 48 to 120 inches (1.2 to 3.25 meters). All units have variable speed motors.

Fabric may be wound face-in or face-out as desired. Also, tube-to-tube, board-to-board, tube-to-board, flat fold-to-tube, and other combinations.

Fabrics with much give, such as knits, require units designed to unroll and reroll yardage with a minimum of tension.

Special attachment for handling tubular knit fabrics. Unit may be equipped with an illuminated inspection board.

Electrical Cloth Notcher

A strip-resistant, wire blade connected to a heating unit, housed in a frame with a control switch and handle.

- To produce a slot notch in lays of knitted, soft wool, loosely woven, and bulky fabrics.
- To produce a seared notch limited to the width of the wire blade.

Searing action of the blade produces a limited depth notch resembling a burn mark. Models available for hot and cold notching.

Frame sizes available in 4, 6 and 8 inches (10.16, 15.24 and 20.32 cm). Blade sizes available in 1/8, 1/4, 3/8, 1/2 and 5/8 inch (3.2, 6.4, 9.5, 12.7 and 15.9 mm).

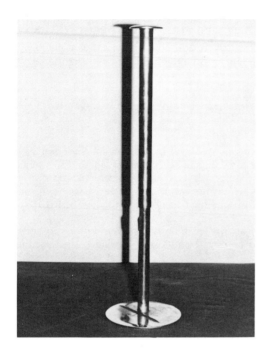

Manual Cloth Notcher

A straight blade fixed to a spring-action recoil piston and affixed to a base.

• To produce slot notches in limited lays of cloth.
• On firmly woven goods.

Frame sizes available in 4, 6 and 8 inches (10.16, 15.24 and 20.32 cm).

   Blade sizes available in 1/8, 1/4, 3/8, 1/2 and 5/8 inch (3.2, 6.4, 9.5, 12.7 and 15.9 mm).

Straight Knife Cutter / Straight Cutter

An electric cutter designed to hold a vertical knife blade which operates with an up-and-down cutting motion or stroke.

• Straight cuts, intricate curves and sharp corners.
• To cut a variety of fabrics, heavy-to-lightweight, according to blade capacity.
• To cut high lays.

Heavy duty motor used for difficult cutting; medium duty motor used for high lays of soft fabric; small motor used for light cutting. Special model offers a heavy duty motor and extra blade length for cutting through high plies of coarse fabrics.

   Machines available in 5, 6, 8, 10 and 14 inch (12.7, 15.24, 20.32, 25.4 and 35.56 cm) sizes with blade length matched to machine size. Available with a wheel or belt sharpener.

   Machines are equipped with a gear reduction unit to slow the blade to half speed preventing fusing while cutting plastic or rubber material.

Circular Knife / Circular Cutter / Rotary Cutter / Round Knife

An electric cutter designed to hold a circular blade which operates with a rotary cutting motion.

- Straight cuts, and wide or gradual curves.
- To cut lays of limited height.

Fabric lay-up in limited to one-half the diameter of the blade.

Heavy duty motor used for difficult cutting; medium duty motor used for lays of soft fabric; small motor used for light cutting. Special featherweight motor offering a 2 1/2 inch (6.35 cm) blade is used for lays under 3/4-inch (1.905 cm).

Machine size ranges from 2 1/2 through 10 inches (6.35 to 25.4 cm) in diameter with blade diameters matched to machine size. Available in different blade sizes and gear ratios to give different cutting speeds for each class of fabrics.

Machines are equipped with a gear reduction unit to slow the blade to half speed preventing fusing while cutting plastic or rubber materials.

Portable Rotary Knife Cutter / Portable Rotary Cutter

A hand-held electric cutter designed with a circular blade and a fabric/table guide, equipped with a recessed safety switch.

- To cut a single ply of leather and heavyweight fabrics.
- To cut two plies of light or medium weight fabrics.
- For cutting sample garments.
- To cut a small quantity of duplicates.

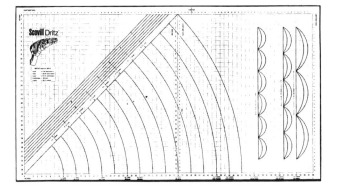

Cutting Board

A coated corregated board, approximately 40 by 72 inches (100 by 183 cm), which is marked in a grid pattern of inches (centimeters) and fractional yards (meters).

• On top of table to enlarge cutting area.
• To lay out fabric and pattern.
• To protect fabrics from soiling and from rough table surfaces.
• As a base to anchor fabric for complex layout; to mark and cut plaids, stripes and border prints.
• As an aid when blocking fabrics.
• To plan pattern and pattern marking.
• To plan curved seams and design details.
• To plan bias strips.
• To check fabric grain for blocking.
• To protect table top from damage by tools.

Available with superimposed patterns of concentric curves and/or 45° diagonal lines.

Designed to fold for storage.

Cutting Room Thread Marker

A large-eyed, long coarse needle housed in a lever and spring operated vertical rod attached to a cantelever frame. Base plate contains a looper mechanism synchronized with needle to complete stitch.

• To mark fabric plies with thread.
• On fabrics where drill holes are not applicable.
• On fabrics where drill holes would not be visible.
• To temporarily mark garment sections for stitching or placement of design detail.

Needles available in different lengths and diameters, and for both natural and synthetic fabrics.

Cutting Table

A flat work area at waist height, with width and length designed according to work room, fabric, spreading machine and/or cutting procedures.

• A base or work surface for layout and cutting operations.

Surface may be polished wood, vinyl, or cork-covered.

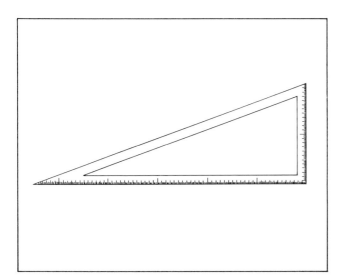

Cutting Table Triangle

A three-sided tool in which two sides, one measuring 5 feet, 6 inches (1.7 meters) and the other 24 inches (0.6 meters), meet at a right angle and are joined by the third side or hypotenuse.

• To square fabric on cutting table.
• In patternmaking for layout work.
• For cutting table layout work.

Drill

An electrically driven metal rod operating with a vertical drilling motion, housed in a frame and base, and provided with a control switch and handle.

• To pierce holes for pattern markings.
• To penetrate through multiple fabric plies to facilitate subsequent sewing procedures.
• To indicate pattern markings such as diminishing points of darts and dart tucks.
• To indicate placement of:
   Pockets and trimmings;
   Buttonholes and buttons;
   Pleats and shirring.
• To indicate point or position of design features such as gussets, godets, and bands.

Some drills are equipped with hollow and hypodermic needles. Drills are available in heavy duty and lightweight models; in models used to eliminate fusing of synthetic fabrics; with adjustable needle heat for permanently setting holes in loosely woven fabrics.

Type of needle used is dictated by the type of fabric. Thinner needles are used for closely woven fabrics. Thicker needles are used for loosely or coarsely woven fabrics.

Marking fluids used may be fluorescent and non-fluorescent.

Machine sizes available in 6, 8 and 10 inches (15.24, 20.32 and 25.4 cm). Needles range from 1/16 to 1/2 inch (1.6 to 12.7 mm) in diameter.

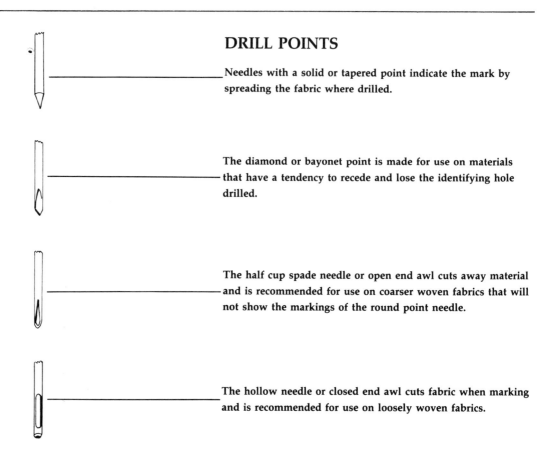

DRILL POINTS

Needles with a solid or tapered point indicate the mark by spreading the fabric where drilled.

The diamond or bayonet point is made for use on materials that have a tendency to recede and lose the identifying hole drilled.

The half cup spade needle or open end awl cuts away material and is recommended for use on coarser woven fabrics that will not show the markings of the round point needle.

The hollow needle or closed end awl cuts fabric when marking and is recommended for use on loosely woven fabrics.

Pattern Perforator

A motor-driven punch housed in a handle-equipped frame, affixed to a stand.

- To punch one or multiple thicknesses of pattern paper or Oak tag when transferring pattern or sloper outline or markings.
- To transfer marks from sloper to pattern and/or nonwoven fabrics.

Disengaging lever allows perforator to be rolled to any point on the pattern without lifting. Perforator punch sizes: 3/64, 1/16, 5/64 and 3/32 of an inch (0.12, 0.16, 0.20 and 0.24 cm).

Perforator is available in heavy duty and lightweight models; in models used to eliminate fusing of synthetic fabrics; with adjustable needle heat for permanently setting holes in loosely woven fabrics.

Machine is available in 6, 8 and 10 inches (15.24, 20.32 and 25.4 cm). Needles range from 1/16 to 1/2 inch (1.6 to 12.7 mm) in diameter.

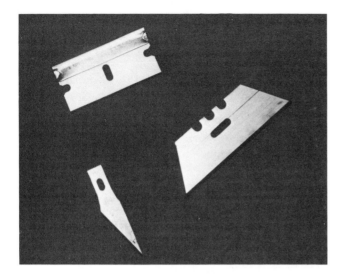

Razor Blade

Any one of a variety of honed-edged blades.

- To rip sewn seams when adjusting or alterating.
- To cut open machine-made buttonholes.
- To cut fur pelts or high pile fabrics.
- To sharpen tailor's wax or tailor's chalk.

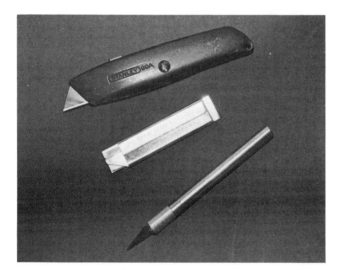

Razor Knife

A metal handle designed to accommodate and secure a removable razor-edged blade.

- To cut fur pelts and high pile fabrics.
- To cut leather and other skins; oilcloth and vinyl.
- To cut seam stitches of garment for repair and correction.

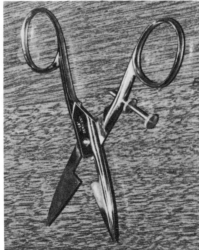

Buttonhole Scissors

A special cutting instrument with a screw and nut arrangement that adjusts the cutting blade to a predetermined length from the shank.

- To incise machine-made buttonholes.

Blade spans all plies of fabric before incising.

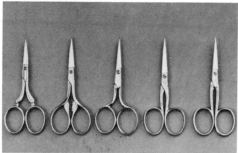

Embroidery Scissors

A lightweight cutting instrument, ranging in size from 3 to 4 inches, (7.5 to 10 cm) with narrow blades tapering into two sharp points. Blades are joined by a pin, screw or rivet and designed with two evenly sized ring handles.

- To cut the intricate work of embroidery and needlework.
- To rip sewn seams.
- To clip machine- or hand-stitches.
- To cut open buttonholes.

Motor-Driven Scissors

A cutting instrument consisting of a pair of short, wide, sharply tapered blades attached to and operated by a hand-held electric motor equipped with a start and stop switch.

- A substitute for shears and scissors.
- Rapid cutting.
- By an individual with restricted hand and thumb dexterity.

Available in battery or electrical plug-in models.

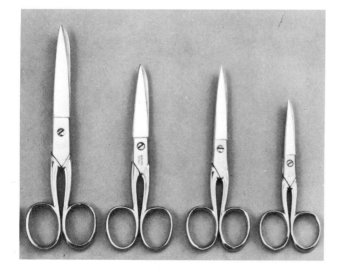

Sewing Scissors

A cutting instrument, ranging in size from 4 to 6 inches (10 to 15 cm), with straight blades. Blades are joined by a rivet, pin, or screw and designed with identical ring handles.

- Light cutting.
- To rip sewn seams.
- To clip threads of hand or machine work.
- To trim seams, corners and detail work.
- Darning and embroidery.

Available with either two sharply tapered points, or with a sharply tapered point and a rounded or blunt point.

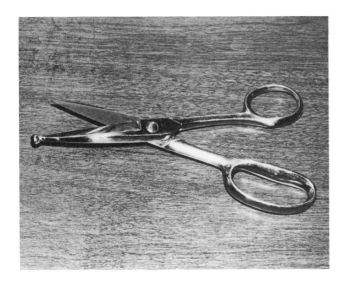

Ball-Tipped Shears

A cutting instrument, ranging in size from 6 to 8 inches (15 to 20 cm), with one blade shaped to a rounded or blunt point and the other tapered to end in a ball. Blades are joined by an adjustable bolt or screw and designed with unequally sized ring handles.

- To cut:
    Loosely woven and open weave fabrics;
    Lace, mesh and net fabrics;
    Knit and lingerie fabrics.

Ball tip end permits tip of blade to glide beneath fabric and eliminates tearing or snarling of fabric.

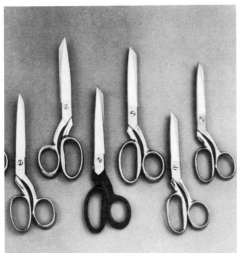

Bent Handle Dressmaker's Shears / Bent Trimmers

A cutting instrument, ranging in size from 7 to 8 inches (18 to 20 cm) with offset blades; one blade is shaped to a sharp point the other to either a rounded or angled blunt point. Blades are joined by an adjustable bolt or screw and designed with equally sized ring handles.

- To prevent work from lifting away from the cutting surface.
- To cut fabrics; skins, paper and vinyl.
- To cut out:
    Drafted or draped patterns;
    Garment from pattern.
- To drape and develop a muslin pattern.

Offset lower blade parallels cutting surface permitting the blade to rest flat on the cutting surface.
    Available in a left-handed model.

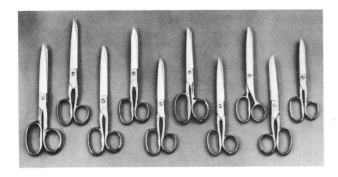

Dressmaker's Shears / Straight Trimmers

A cutting instrument, ranging in size from 7 to 8 inches (18 to 20 cm), with one blade shaped to a sharp point and the other to either a rounded or angled blunt point. Blades are joined by an adjustable bolt or screw and designed with unequally sized ring handles.

- To cut fabric; paper, vinyl and skins.
- To drape and develop a muslin pattern.
- To cut out a drafted pattern.

Available in a left-handed model.

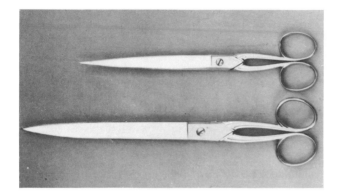

Paper Shears

A cutting instrument, ranging in size from 8 to 12 inches (20 to 30 cm), with two sharply pointed straight blades. Blades are joined by an adjustable bolt and designed with two equally sized ring handles.

- To cut paper and paper patterns.
- To cut slopers from granite board or Oak tag.

In relationship to the handle, the blade length is proportionately greater than that of other shears and scissors.

Because both bows or ring handles are the same size, by definition these should be called scissors, however, they have been traditionally designated as shears.

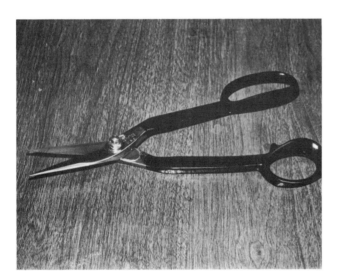

Patternmaking Shears

A cutting instrument, approximately 16 inches (41 cm) in total length, with two wide blades 4 inches (10 cm) long and tapered to rounded points. Blades are joined by an adjustable nut and bolt and designed with contoured handles.

- To cut granite board when making slopers or trade block patterns.

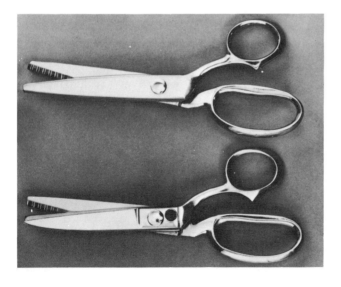

Pinking Shears

A finishing shears, ranging in size from 5 to 10 inches (13 to 25 cm), with precision-matched toothed blades joined by a ball bearing pivot and designed with unevenly sized ring handles.

- To produce an evenly notched edge.
- To notch fabric with a zigzag edge.
- To finish seams and raw edges of garments.
- As a decorative finish for edges of fabrics such as on felt, suede, chamoise, glazed chintz, oilcloth, and vinyl.
- To make decorative trimmings.

Bite varies with length and make of shears.

Smaller shears used for fine fabrics, larger shears for heavier fabrics.

Available in a left-handed model.

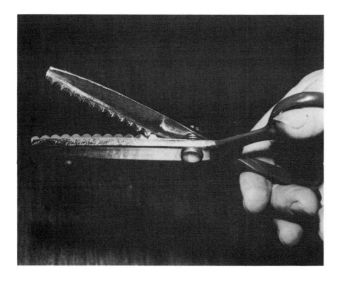

Scalloping Shears

A finishing shears, ranging in size from 5 to 10 inches (13 to 25 cm), with precision matched toothed blades. Blades are joined by a ball bearing pivot and designed with unevenly sized ring handles.

- To produce an evenly scalloped edge.
- To notch the fabric with a scalloped edge.
- To finish seams and raw edges of garments.
- As a decorative finish for edges of fabrics such as on felt, suede, chamoise, glazed chintz, oilcloth, and vinyl.
- To make decorative trimmings.

Bite varies with length and make of shears.
   Smaller shears used for fine fabrics, larger shears for heavier fabrics.
   Available in a left-handed model.

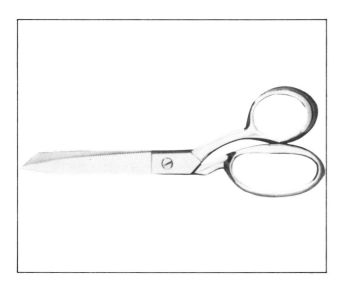

Serrated Blade Shears / Knife Edge Shears / Synthetic Fabric Shears

A cutting instrument, ranging in size from 7 to 8 inches (18 to 20 cm), with offset blunt-shaped blades, one of which is serrated. Blades are joined by an adjustable bolt and designed with equally or unequally sized ring handles.

- To cut:
     Polyester and other synthetic fabrics;
     Knit fabrics;
     Lingerie fabrics such as tricot;
     Supple silk, rayon, or sheer fabrics.

Available in a left-handed model.

Tailor's Shears

A cutting instrument, ranging in size from 12 to 16 inches (30 to 40 cm), with two wide offset blades shaped to rounded points. Blades are joined by an adjustable nut and bolt and designed with unequally sized contoured ring handles.

- To cut heavy fabrics.
- To cut several plies of fabric at one time.

Tension of nut and bolt adjusts the blade to accommodate the variations of fabric thicknesses.

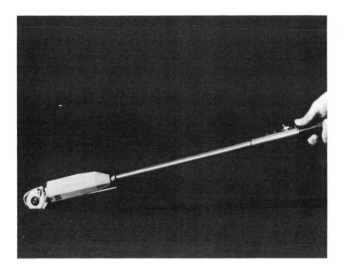

Cut-Off Machine

A magnetically guided electric cutter designed with a long handle and equipped with a circular blade which operates in a grooved cross-table track.

- In conjunction with spreading machine.
- To spread a one-way layup.
- To spread directional or napped fabric.
- To cut square layup of goods precisely.

Machine sizes available in 48 to 78 inches (1.2 to 2 meters).

End Catcher / End Guide Rail

A weighted crossbar hinged to a clamp secured base which spans the cutting table.

- To secure cloth in position when moving spreader back and forth.
- To fold over goods at end.
- To hold fabric ends securely.

Catcher or end rail can be placed and locked at any position on the spreading table. Serrated rubber facing on crossbar eliminates teeth or pin holes in goods. Catcher bar designed to swing out of the way when cutting.

Face-to-Face Spreader

An automatic, motor-driven spreading machine riding on a geared rail; designed to lay and align a ply of fabric with each pass over the cutting table. A catcher actuates a reversing gear at each end of layup.

- A face-to-face layout of multiple plies of goods.

Travel speed of the machine can be set to conform to the type of fabric. Machine widths from 48 to 84 inches (1.2 to 2.1 meters) or wider on special order. Shut-off switch permits machine to ride back "empty" for spreading one-way fabric.

Counts each ply as it spreads. Handles medium and large rolls of fabric.

Manual Spreader

A manually operated spreading machine riding on a rail.

- Permits the operator to maintain alignment of fabric edges while laying multiple plies of fabric face-to-face or one-way spreading of fabric on the cutting table.

Constructed of aluminum for lightweight handling.

One-Way Spreader

An automatic, motor-driven spreading machine riding on a geared rail synchronized to work with an end guide rail and cut-off machine at either end of the layup.

- To lay and align multiple plies of fabric in one direction on the cutting table.
- To spread one-way design or napped goods.
- To conserve fabric as use of cut-off rail eliminates fabric fold buildup.

Travel speed of the machine can be set to conform to the type of fabric. Machine widths from 48 to 84 inches (1.2 to 2.1 meters), or wider on special order.

Counts each ply as it spreads. Spreading machine handles medium and large rolls of fabric.

Tubular Knit Spreader

An automatic, motor-driven spreading machine riding on a geared rail, equipped with an adjustable electromagnet to hold assorted widths of tubular fabrics in place; and actuated by the catchers to reverse direction of spreading at each end of layup.

- To lay and align tubular fabrics with each pass over the cutting table.
- To insure efficiency and accuracy in layout of different widths of tubular fabrics.

Travel speed of the machine can be set to conform to the type of fabric. Machines widths up to 66 inches (1.7 meters) or wider on special order. Shut-off switch permits machine to ride back "empty" for spreading one-way fabric.

Handles different weights and types of tubular knits either in rolls or flat folds.

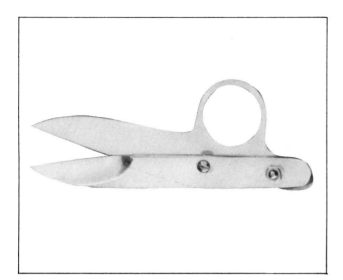

Thread Clippers / Thread Snips / Weaver's Scissors

A specialized cutting tool, approximately 4 1/2 inches (11.4 cm) long, consisting of two pointed blades which operate by a permanent self-opening spring. Blades are joined at one end by a screw.

- To snip threads.
- To clip seam edges.
- To rip sewn seams.

Available without a ring or designed with a single ring for a non-slip grip.

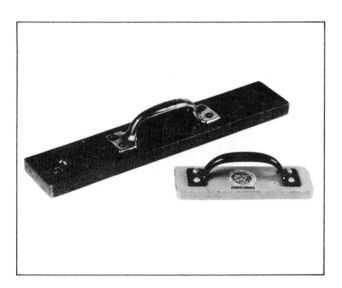

Weights

Metal slabs or bars with or without a handle attached.

- To hold:
  Marker in place on top of fabric plies;
  Section of marker when cutting;
  Sloper, paper or muslin pattern in place for outlining, tracing and cutting;
  Pattern pieces on fabric when cutting garment.

Available in a variety of shapes, sizes and weights.

Industrial Cutting Procedure Guide for
   Fabric Spreading
Bundle
Interlocking of Pattern Pieces
Layout of Pattern Pieces
Marker

Notching
Perimeter of Pattern / Cutting Line
Ply
Plies / Multi-Plies
Spread / Lay / Layup
Spreading Fabric / Spreading of Goods

Cutting terms describe techniques and preparations that are part of the industrial cutting procedure. They include processes for spreading fabric, planning and using markers, and cutting multiple garments.

In preparation for cutting, draped or drafted patterns or slopers are transcribed to make a marker. A completed marker is placed as the top ply on a lay-up.

Design elements and fabric type determine how a marker is planned and how fabric plies are spread.

Industrial Cutting Procedure Guide
for Fabric Spreading

FABRIC		GARMENT		SPREAD
Asymmetrical (directional)	⬅	Asymmetrical		Face One Way—Nap One Way
Symmetrical	⇄	Asymmetrical		Face One Way—Nap Up and Down
Asymmetrical	⬅	Symmetrical		Face-to-Face—Nap One Way
Symmetrical	⇄	Symmetrical		Face-to-Face—Nap Up and Down

Bundle

A stack of cut-out garment sections; separated from the lay, folded and/or tied.

Bundles are sorted and grouped according to pattern size.

Interlocking of Pattern Pieces

The juxtaposition of pattern pieces or slopers of similar outline and the optimum arrangement of dissimilar pieces.

- To achieve fabric economy for pattern layout.
- When planning a marker.

Pattern pieces are placed in relationship to pattern and fabric grainlines; planned according to width and spread of fabric.

Pattern pieces interlock according to the design characteristic of fabric.

Referred to as *laying in* of pattern pieces in some production rooms.

Layout of Pattern Pieces

The planned arrangement of interlocking pattern pieces on paper or fabric in preparation for cutting.

- To estimate yardage requirement for garment made from drafted or draped pattern.
- When preparing to cut a test muslin.
- When preparing to cut sample or single garment.

Pattern pieces are arranged with regard to the structure, design, and width of fabric.

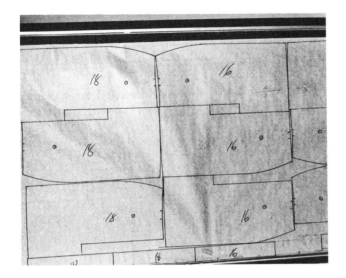

Marker

A cutting guide comprising the outline of all production pattern pieces for one style in one or more sizes. Pattern pieces are arranged or interlocked for fabric economy with regard to width and type of fabric, and design characteristics. Made of paper, nonwoven cloth or on same fabric as layup.

- On the top of a layup or spread.
- When many garments must be cut.
- To determine the length of all plies in a spread.

Planned for various fabric widths.

Notching

The end result of cutting an incision through all fabric plies to a depth of 3/16 of an inch (.48 cm), or a seared "V" shaped notch on the perimeter of a pattern piece.

- To identify garment sections for assembling.
- To match corresponding seams for subsequent sewing operations.

Perimeter of Pattern / Cutting Line

The edge of a muslin or paper pattern piece or pattern outline as drawn on the marker.

- As a guide for cutting.

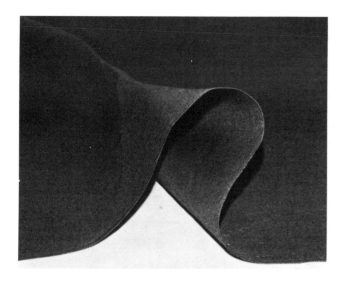

Ply

A single layer of fabric.

- In the sample room and couture house to cut out a sample garment or to cut a one-of-a-kind garment.

Plies / Multi-Plies

Two or more layers of fabric.

- To cut duplicate garments.
- To cut components for many garments.

Spread / Lay / Layup

The total number of fabric plies, one over the other, in a one-way or fold-back direction, for a particular cutting.

- When components for many garments must be cut simultaneously.

Spread with regard to structure or type of fabric as indicated on chart on page 101.

Spreading Fabric / Spreading of Goods

The process of superimposing a predetermined number of fabric plies on the cutting table either by hand or manually or by an electrically operated fabric spreading machine.

• When components for many garments must be cut simultaneously.

The end result of spreading is referred to as a *spread, lay* or *layup*.

14 ~ Hand Sewing Needles ————————————

Ball Point Needle
Beading Needle
Betweens Needle
Calyx-Eyed Needle
Chenilles Needle
Curved Needle
Darners Needle:
    Cotton Darners Needle

Yarn Darners Needle
Embroidery Needle / Crewel Needle
Glovers Needle
Milliners Needle / Straws Needle
Sharps Needle
Sailmakers Needle
Tapestry Needle
Tufting Needle

A hand sewing needle is a long, slender steel shaft, with an eye at one end. The shaft tapers to a fine point, ball tip or wedge end. Hand-sewing needles function to carry the thread through the fabric while hand sewing.

Needles are designed in a variety of sizes, types, and classifications, each developed for a specific use.

For each needle type, sizes range from a low number, indicating a coarse needle, to higher numbers, indicating a finer needle. Diameter of the needle shaft increases at the eye end proportionately to the length and size progression of the needle.

Needles are typed considering their use for various fabric structures and are identified by the eye size and/or point configuration.

Hand needles are selected with consideration for:
• Structure of fabric
• Weight and type of fabric
• Type of thread
• Size and weight of thread
• Intended use

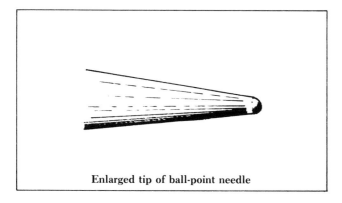

Enlarged tip of ball-point needle

Ball Point Needle

A needle designed with a rounded tip and a small rounded eye and designated as medium length; sizes range from 5 to 10.

- On knit and lingerie fabrics.

Ball point needle slides between, instead of piercing, the yarns as it penetrates the fabric. Reduces possibility of holes and runs in fabric such as jersey and tricot.

Beading Needle

An extremely fine, long needle designed with a small round eye; sizes range from 10 to 15.

- For beadwork.
- To string beads for fringe application.
- To sew sequins to fabric.
- To sew fine and lightweight silks.
- Where other needles would leave puncture holes or mar the fabric.

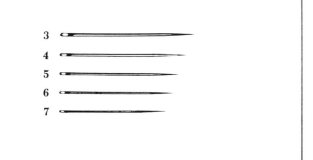

Betweens Needle

A needle designed with a small rounded eye and designated as short length; sizes range from 1 to 12.

- To produce short fine stitches as in tailoring, handwork, and openwork.

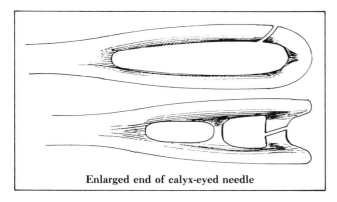

Enlarged end of calyx-eyed needle

Calyx-Eyed Needle

A needle designed with an oval eye and a slotted opening on the side, tapered to a fine point, ball tip or wedge end and designated as medium length; sizes range from 4 to 8.

- For ease in threading.
- By people who have difficulty threading other types of needles.

Thread is pulled into the eye through slot at needle edge.

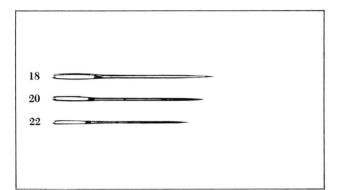

Chenilles Needle

A coarse needle designed with a long oval eye of extra proportion and designated as short length; sizes range from 13 to 26.

- To carry multiple strands of thread.
- To work with embroidery floss.
- For embroidery yarn.

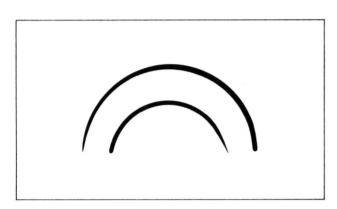

Curved Needle

A coarse, semicircular needle designed with a large oval eye and tapering to a sharply pointed end; ranging in measured length from 1 1/2 to 3 inches (3.8 to 7.6 cm).

- Where a straight needle would be impracticable.

Curved specialty needles labeled as upholstery, lampshade and mattress; intended for other uses; may be utilized to complete particular operation of garment construction.

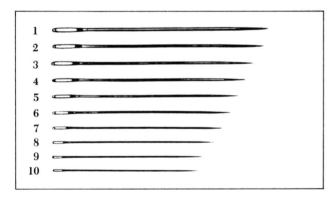

Cotton Darners Needle

A coarse needle designed with a long oval eye and designated as long length; sizes range from 1 to 10.

- To carry multiple strands of thread.
- When multiple stitches are woven on a needle as in darning, mending, and weaving.

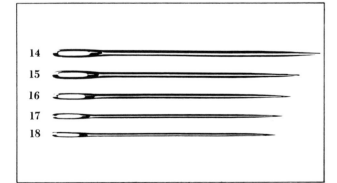

Yarn Darners Needle

A coarse needle designed with a large, long oval eye and designated as long length; sizes range from 14 to 18.

- To carry multiple strands of thread.
- For weaving.
- On loosely woven woolen and openweave knitted fabrics.

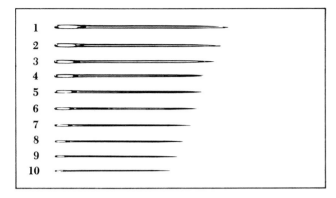

Embroidery Needle / Crewel Needle

A needle designed with a long oval eye and designated as medium length; sizes range from 1 to 12.

- To carry multiple strands of thread.
- For embroidery.

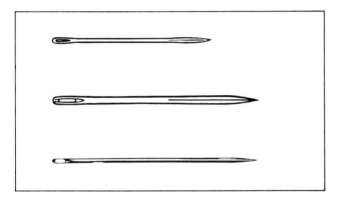

Glovers Needle

A needle, tapering to a three-faceted point, designed with a rounded eye and designated as medium length; sizes range from 3/0 (000) to 8.

Wedge-shaped point is designed to penetrate leather and plastic to avoid tearing or splitting.

Milliners Needle / Straws Needle

A needle designed with a small rounded eye and designated as long length; sizes range from 3/0 (000) to 12.

- Long stitches as in basting.
- Multiple stitches are woven onto the needle as in gathering and shirring.
- Multiple stitches are taken on the needle as in overcasting.

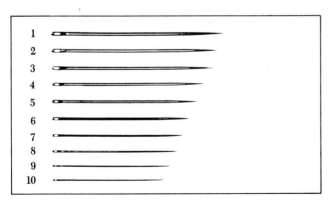

Sharps Needle

A needle designed with a small rounded eye and designated as medium length; sizes range from 1 to 12.

An all purpose needle:
- Size 1 to 5—For heavyweight fabrics.
- Size 6 to 8—For medium weight fabrics.
- Size 9 to 10—For fine and lightweight fabrics.
- Size 11 to 12—For sheer fabrics.

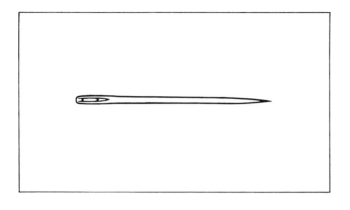

Sailmakers Needle

A coarse needle designed so that half its length is faceted, tapered to a fine point and designated as long length; sizes range from 14 to 17.

- To work with heavy leather; heavy coating and canvas punch work.

Wedge-shaped shank and sharply tapered point are designed to penetrate cloth to avoid tearing and splitting.
    Allows passage of multiple strand or heavy duty thread.

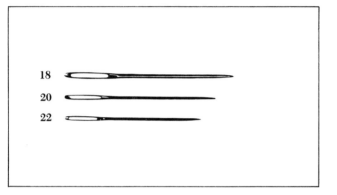

Tapestry Needle

A coarse, blunt-tipped needle designed with a long oval eye of extra proportion and designated as short length; sizes range from 13 to 26.

- To carry multiple strands of thread and embroidery floss.
- On openweave and loosely woven woolen and knit fabrics.
- To join sections of wool or knit garments.
- For needlepoint and tapestry work.

Tapestry needle may serve as a bodkin.
    Referred to as *wool needle*.

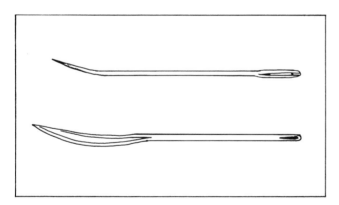

Tufting Needle

A coarse needle designed with a large oval eye and a slightly curved, flattened and faceted wide end tapering to a point; ranging in measured length from 1 1/2 to 3 inches (3.8 to 7.6 cm).

- Pointed end shaped to penetrate cloth to avoid tearing or splitting.
- To permit passage of multiple strands of yarn or thread through ply or plies of fabric.
- To permit passage of ribbon through fabric.

Specialty needles intended for other uses may be utilized to complete particular operation of garment construction.

15 ~ Sewing Machine Needles

Parts of the Needle
Point types:
   Ball Point Needle
   Leather Point Needle
   Round Point Needle / Set Point Needle

Twin Needles for Non-Industrial Machine
Machine Needle Size Chart
Machine Needle Blade Size Designations for
   Various Machines (Chart)

Sewing machine needles are made of steel. Their function is to carry the thread through the stitchmaking process of the machine.

Needles are manufactured in different sizes, types and classifications for industrial and home sewing machines, each developed for a specific purpose.

Size range from fine to coarse and are chosen with regard to interaction of yarn of the fabric and the type and size of thread. Higher numbers indicate thicker points and coarser needles with size of eye opening proportioned to diameter of the needle blade.

Type of needles identified by point configuration, are engineered with consideration for the various types of fabric structures.

Needles are standardized and classified with regard to the type and model number of machine on which they are used.

Different companies denote blade diameters or sizes differently as listed on table included.

Brand name home and industrial machines require needles of the same classification, type and make as the machine.

Needles for home machines and needles for industrial machines are not interchangeable.

Machine needle are selected for compatibility with:
- Structure of fabric
- Fiber content of fabric
- Weight of fabric
- Type and size of thread
- Length of stitch
- Formation of stitch
- Operation to be accomplished

The following charts have been compiled from data offered by manufacturers who supply the industrial and consumer markets with thread, needles, and fabrics.

Different needles, threads and fabrics interrelate with different machines and sewing procedures producing unpredictable results. As a rule, a test sample should be made before proceeding with the production of the garment.

The charts have been prepared as a guide, not as absolute standards.

Fine

Medium

Coarse

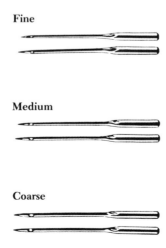

Parts of the Needle

Shank The upper end of the needle that fits into the needle bar and is held in place by a clamp or set screw.

Blade The long slender portion of the needle that extends from the base of the shank to the eye.

Point The portion of the needle at the lower end of the blade which tapers to a round or set point, ball point, or leather point.

Long Groove A depression in the blade of the needle that provides a protective channel for the thread as it moves from the take-up device to the eye.

Scarf or Spot A clearance cut extending above the needle eye, shaped to permit closer setting of shuttle, hook or looper to the needle for proper stitch formation and faster timing.

Short Groove A depression extending a short distance above and below the needle eye that provides protection for the needle thread as the needle passes through the fabric.

Eye The opening in the needle blade, through the long groove on one side and through the short groove on the other, which holds the thread in place during stitch formation.

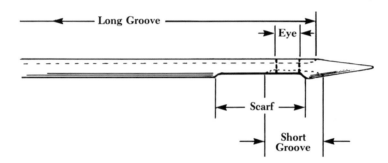

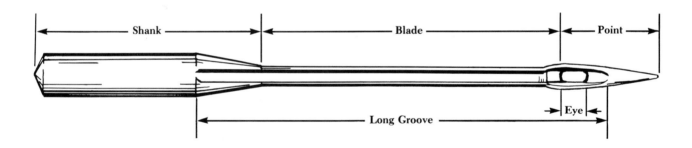

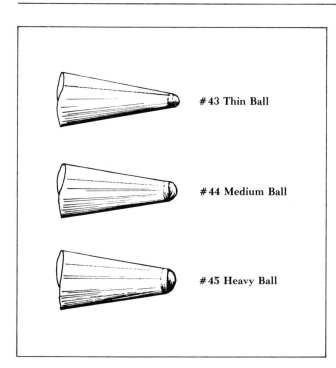

#43 Thin Ball

#44 Medium Ball

#45 Heavy Ball

Ball Point Needle

A slender steel shaft having a thickened shank and tapering below the eye to a tip forming a ball.

- To stitch:
    Knit and mesh fabrics;
    Hosiery and stretch materials;
    Web and rib-type elastic.
- On permanent press and synthetic blends to reduce puckering of seams.

Ball point needle slides between, instead of piercing, the yarns as it penetrates the fabric. It reduces the possibility of holes and runs, and eliminates picking or cutting of the fabric.

Referred to as a *cloth point needle.*

Machine Needle/Fabric Selection Guide
Ball Point

MACHINE NEEDLE SIZE	USED FOR FABRICS SUCH AS	TYPE AND SIZE OF THREAD	MACHINE STITCHES PER INCH
FINE 9	Lingerie fabrics Silk or nylon tricot, Ban-Lon®, silk jersey, Spandex Ribbed or nylon elastic Elastics	A Silk Synthetic, Nylon or Dacron Extra Fine Monocord Nylon (NYMO®) 100% Nylon Twist Extra Fine Cotton-Covered Polyester Core Extra Fine Cotton-Covered Dacron Core Extra Fine	14–25 10–12 12–15 12–15 12–14 12–25
11	Wool jersey, cotton knit, sweater knit, loosely constructed knit, stretchable knit Elastics	A Silk Polyester, Nylon or Dacron Fine Monocord Nylon (NYMO®) Cotton-Covered Polyester Core Cotton-Covered Dacron Core	12–15 10–16 10–16 12–14 12–14

Ball Point (continued)

MACHINE NEEDLE SIZE	USED FOR FABRICS SUCH AS	TYPE AND SIZE OF THREAD	MACHINE STITCHES PER INCH
11–14	Knit fabric of natural or synthetic fibers Closely constructed knit of nylon or polyester fibers Knit Qiana, lace Pile fabric with knit weave Woven or knit fabric with heat-set or fused surfaces Elastics	A Silk 100% Spun Polyester Textured Nylon Fine Polyester, Nylon or Dacron Fine Cotton-Covered Polyester Core Fine Cotton-Covered Dacron Core	12–16 16–22 10–14 10–12 10–15 10–15
14	Firm and medium firm knit constructed fabrics Double knit Bonded knit Jacquard knit Firm untextured warp knit Nubby knit that has stretch in both directions Rough textured novelty knit Power net Elastics Swimsuit fabric	A Silk 100% Spun Polyester Textured Nylon Regular Polyester, Nylon or Dacron Cotton-Covered Polyester Core Cotton-Covered Dacron Core	12–16 16–22 10–14 10–12 10–12 10–12
14 or WEDGE POINTED NEEDLE	Knit backed plastics such as vinyl, polyurethane, and crinkle patent Laminated fabrics Power net	Monocord Nylon (NYMO®) Textured Nylon Twisted Nylon Cotton-Covered Polyester Core Extra Heavy	8–10 8–10 8–10 8–10

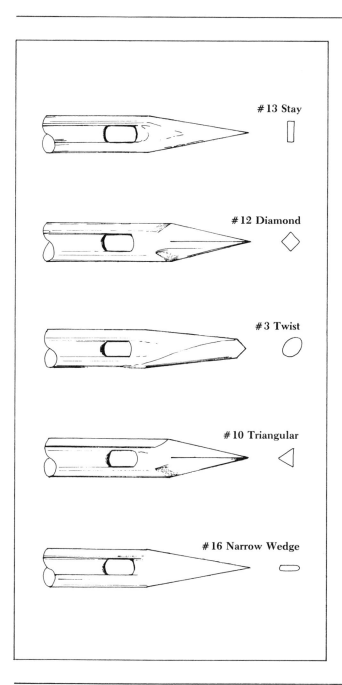

Leather Point Needle

A slender steel shaft having a thickened shank and tapering to any one of a variety of points, designed to puncture and cut openings for stitching.

- To sew leather, simulated leather, plastic, thermoplastic, rubberized, and laminated fabrics.

Cutting edge of leather point needle is designed to shape puncture and give stitching desired appearance.

Machine Needle/Fabric Selection Guide
Leather Point Needle

	USED FOR FABRICS SUCH AS	TYPE AND SIZE OF THREAD	MACHINE STITCHES PER INCH
	Leather such as tanned skin, suede split Animal skin Plastic Plastic laminated fabrics	Monocord Nylon Cotton-Covered Polyester Core Extra Heavy	6–8 6–8

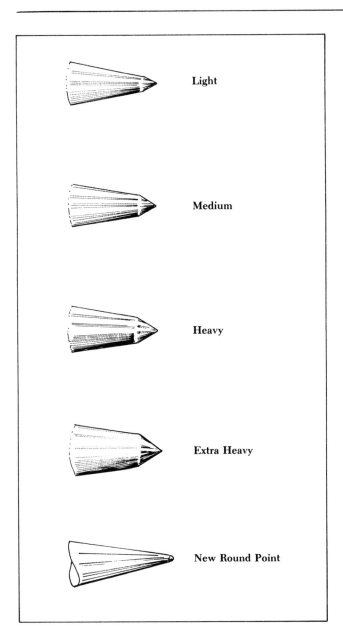

Light

Medium

Heavy

Extra Heavy

New Round Point

Round Point Needle / Set Point Needle

A slender steel shaft having a thickened shank and tapering below the eye to a fine pointed tip.

Set point varies from light to extra heavy. Size of eye opening proportioned to diameter of needle blade.

Needle is available for home machines in sizes 9, 11, 14, 16 and 18; for industrial machines in sizes ranging from 2 to 35.

Referred to as *cloth point needle.*

Machine Needle/Fabric Selection Guide
Round Point/Set Point

MACHINE NEEDLE SIZE	USED FOR FABRICS SUCH AS	TYPE AND SIZE OF THREAD	MACHINE STITCHES PER INCH
FINE 9	*Delicate, Sheer or Filmy Fabrics:* Lingerie fabrics Silk chiffon, georgette, organza Silk marquisite, net, tulle, illusion Silk or chiffon velvet Organdy, batiste, voile Ninon	A Silk Synthetic, Nylon or Dacron Extra Fine Monocord Nylon 150–100 Six-Cord Mercerized Cotton	14–25 10–25 10–12 14–22

MACHINE NEEDLE SIZE	USED FOR FABRICS SUCH AS	TYPE AND SIZE OF THREAD	MACHINE STITCHES PER INCH
MEDIUM FINE 10–11	*Fine Fabrics:* Voile, lawn, dimity, dotted Swiss, shirtings Synthetic sheers Paper taffeta, gossamer silk, crepe, satin Silk or synthetic velvet, panne, shantung Sheer woolens	A Silk Synthetic, Nylon or Dacron Fine Monocord Nylon Cotton-Covered Polyester Core Extra Fine 70 Waxed Cotton Extra Fine 80–100 Six Cord Mercerized Cotton	12–18 7–10 7–10 12–16 14–20 12–16
MEDIUM 11	*Lightweight Fabrics:* Percale, gingham, chambray, madras, poplin Cretonne, chintz, sateen, muslin, piqué, shirting Seersucker, handkerchief linen, challis Lace, surahs, silk or synthetic crepe, taffeta Faille, shantung, rayon, woven Qiana	A Silk Nylon Twist Monocord Nylon 60 Waxed Cotton 60–70–80 Six Cord Mercerized Cotton 50 Mercerized Cotton Quilting Cotton 100% Polyester Cotton-Covered Polyester Core Fine	12–16 7–10 7–10 12–16 12–18 12–16 6–12 8–10 12–14
MEDIUM 11–14	*Medium Weight Fabrics:* Bengaline, wool flannel, wool crepe, lightweight suiting Felt, fleece, pile imitation fur Cotton velvet, velveteen Linen	A Silk Nylon Twist Monocord Nylon (NYMO®) 100% Polyester Cotton-Covered Polyester Core Fine 60 Waxed Cotton 60–70–80 Six Cord Mercerized Cotton 50 Mercerized Cotton	12–16 7–10 7–10 8–10 12–16 12–16 12–18 12–16

MACHINE NEEDLE SIZE	USED FOR FABRICS SUCH AS	TYPE AND SIZE OF THREAD	MACHINE STITCHES PER INCH
MEDIUM COARSE 14–16	*Medium Heavyweight Fabrics:* Woolens, corduroy, crash, gabardine, cording Khaki, suiting, linen, broadcloth	A Silk Synthetic, Nylon or Dacron Cotton-Covered Polyester Core Regular 50 Waxed Cotton 30–40–60 Six Cord Mercerized Cotton 40 Mercerized Cotton Heavy Duty	10–14 7–10 10–14 10–14 10–12 10–14
COARSE 16–18	*Deep or Heavy Pile Fabrics:* Ticking Denim Sacking Coating	30–40 Six Cord Mercerized Cotton 40 Waxed Cotton Cotton-Covered Polyester Core Regular 100% Nylon 100% Polyester	 8–12 10–12 10–12 7–10 7–10
VERY COARSE 18	*Heavyweight Fabrics:* Duck, sailcloth, canvas, drill, tarpauline Tapestry Overcoating woolens, heavy weaves for coating Imitation fur	20–30 Six Cord Mercerized Cotton 40 Mercerized Cotton Heavy Duty 40 Waxed Cotton Cotton-Covered Polyester Core Extra Strong A Silk	 6–10 10–12 10–12 10–12 8–12

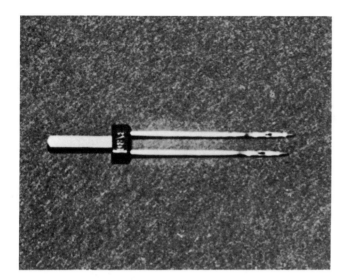

Twin Needle for Non-Industrial Machine

A unit formed by joining the thicker shank of two slender steel shafts both tapering to a fine or ball point.

- Simultaneously sewing two parallel rows of stitching a fixed distance apart.
- Topstitching.

Threads run side-by-side and do not cross during threading sequence.

Machine Needle Size Chart

SIZE NUMBER	DIAM. OF NEEDLE BLADE AT EYE (inch)
2	.017
3	.018
4	.019
5	.020
6	.0215
7	.023
8	.0245
9	.026
10	.028
11	.030
12	.032
13	.034
14	.036
15	.038
16	.040
17	.042
18	.044
19	.046
20	.048
21	.051
22	.057
23	.065
24	.072
25	.081
26	.091
27	.100
28	.110
29	.120
30	.130
31	.140
32	.150
33	.160
34	.170
35	.180

Common (Singer) Sizes	New Metric Sizes
5	50
6	55
7	60
9	65
10	70
11	75
12	80
13	85
14	90
16	100
18	110
19	120
20	125
21	130
22	140
23	160
24	180
25	200
26	230
27	250
28	280
29	300
30	330
31	350
32	380

Machine Needle Blade Size Designations for Various Machines

| BLADE DIAMETER | | UNION SPECIAL | SINGER | LEWIS BLIND-STITCH | AMERICAN COLUMBIA U.S. BLIND-STITCH | SCHMETZ | W & G OLD | W & G NEW | PFAFF | MERROW | REECE | MAUSER |
INCHES	METRIC											
.019	45	019	4			45	5/0					7/0
.020	50		5			50	4/0	20	5			6/0
.0215	55	022	6			55	3/0	22		3/0		5/0
.023	60		7 & 8	2		60	2/0	24	6	2/0		
.025	65	025	9			65		25				4/0
.028	70	027	10	2½		70	1	27	7	1	3/0	3/0
.030	75	029	11		1	75		30				
.032	80	032	12	3	1½	80	2	32	8	2	2/0	2/0
.034	85	034	13		2	85						
.036	90	036	14	3½	2½	90	3	36	9	3		
.038	95	038	15		3	95						
.040	100	040	16	4	3½	100	4	40	10	4	1	1
.042	105	042	17		4	105						
.044	110	044	18	4½	4½	110	5	44	11	5	2	2
.046	120	046	19	5		120	6	48	12	6	3	
.049	125	049	20			125		49				3
.052	130		21			130	7	52	13	7	4	
.054	140	054	22			140	8		14		5	4
.060	150	060				150	9		15	8		5
.063	160		23			160	10		16		6	
.067	170	067				170			17	9		6
.071	180		24			180			18		7	
.075	190					190			19			7
.080	200	080	25			200			20	10		8
.090	230	090	26			230			23			9
.100	250	100	27			250						10
.110	280		28			280						11
.120	300	120	29			300						12
.130	330		30			330						13
.140	350	140	31			350						14
.150	380		32			380						15
.156	400	156	33			400						16

Button & Carpet Thread
Cotton Thread:
    Cotton Thread/Cotton Basting Thread
    Mercerized Cotton Thread
    Mercerized Heavy Duty Cotton Thread
Darning Thread / Mending Thread
Embroidery Thread / Embroidery Floss
Industrial Thread
Metallic Thread
Monofilament Thread
Nylon Thread:
    Monocord Nylon Thread / Bonded Invisible
      Thread (Nymo®)
    Spun Nylon Thread / Twisted Invisible Thread
Polyester Thread:
    Polyester Core Thread / Cotton-Covered
      Polyester Core Thread
    100% Polyester Thread

Spun Polyester Thread
Quilting Thread
Silk Thread, Size A
Silk Thread, Size D
Six-Cord Thread
Thread Hank
Waxed Thread:
    Waxed Thread
    Heavy Duty Waxed Thread
Yarn

Thread-Fabric Selection Guide (Chart)
Thread Ticket Size (Chart)
Suggested Needle Sizes for Industrial Thread
Approximate Equivalent Ticket Numbers of
    Industrial Thread
Comparative Chart: Physical Properties for
    Industrial Thread

Thread is composed of flexible yarns made from fibers and/or filaments, bonded cords, or monofilaments.

Natural fibers such as cotton, linen and silk as well as a variety of synthetic fibers or filaments are used in making thread for home and industry.

Fibers are twisted or filaments bonded to form a unit or cord called a *strand*. Thread is formed by a combination of twisting and finishing two or more strands or by bonding multifilament synthetic yarns. Monofilament threads are made by an extrusion process with no twist imparted. The number of strands twisted or bonded identify the finished thread as two-, three-, four- or six-ply, or monocord.

Thread finishes include *soft finish, mercerization, glazing* and *waxing.*

Soft finished threads are made without special finishes or treatment but are lubricated for sewability.

Mercerization is a chemical bath of caustic soda (lye) applied to cotton or cotton-covered polyester core thread, producing qualities of greater strength, greater luster and smoother surface. Mercerization improves cotton's affinity for dye and color fastness. Mercerization reduces natural elasticity of thread.

Glazing is a process by which cotton or synthetic thread is starched and polished producing a stiffened thread with a smooth hard surface. Reduces possibility of thread untwisting during sewing process. It is applied to quilting, button and carpet, and poly-spun threads.

Waxing is the process of applying a lubricant of paraffin or silicone to thread. This process can be applied to any sewing thread. Waxed thread guides smoothly through hand needles, penetrates fabric smoothly and reduces thread friction during the sewing process.

The strength of thread is determined by the size, twist and finish of the yarn and the number of plies as well as the inherent characteristics of the yarn.

Cotton thread sizes range from low numbers, indicating coarse thread, to higher numbers indicating fine thread. This is based on the number of eight-hundred-forty-yard hanks of yarn needed to total one pound.

Synthetic thread is classified by a number system where the larger numbers indicate coarser thread. This is based on denier which is the weight in grams of nine thousand meters of yarn.

For silk, size range is designated by letters, starting with A, indicating fine thread, and progressing to D, indicating coarse thread.

Industrial thread for apparel manufacturing is selected for those qualities most compatible with fabric, type of stitch, procedure and method for sewing machine, and type of garment. Interrelationship of the thread and seam construction is planned whereby the thread breaks before the fabric tears.

Type of thread is selected with consideration for:
• Compatibility of thread and fabric fiber content

- Weight and type of fabric
- Method of construction employed
- Type of stitching
- Location of stitching
- Type of garment
- Use of garment
- Care of garment
- Life of garment

Different needles, threads, and fabrics interrelate with different machines and sewing procedures producing unpredictable results. As a rule, a test sample should be made before proceeding with garment production. The charts have been prepared as a guide, not as absolute standards.

The following charts have been compiled from data offered by manufacturers who supply the industrial and consumer markets with thread, needles, and fabrics.

Button & Carpet Thread

A heavy thread formed by twisting four strands of spun staple cotton fibers which have a glazed (glacé) finish.

Characteristic(s): Extra strong; heavily glazed; glaze stiffens thread restricting tangling; glazed surface allows smooth sewing procedure.

- To hand sew buttons and buttonholes.
- On heavy fabrics such as overcoating, canvas, duck, tapestry, upholstery, and leather.

Available in cotton, polyester, and polyester core; in a limited range of colors, and black and white.

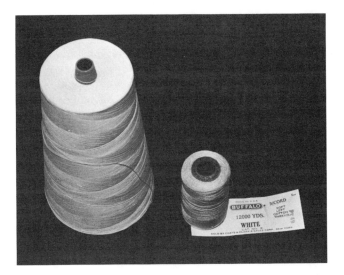

Cotton Thread / Cotton Basting Thread

A thread formed by loosely twisting two or more strands of spun staple cotton fibers.

Characteristics: Soft; lustrous; absorbent to dyes; breaks easily under tension; shrinks when laundered; lacks stretch or give.

- On cotton and linen fabrics.
- For hand basting.

No special finishes applied, considered an untreated thread.

Loose twist permits breaking, allowing for easy removal from garment. Thread breaks easily under tension and will not function well in a sewing machine.

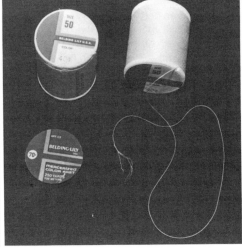

Mercerized Cotton Thread

A thread formed by twisting three strands of spun staple cotton fibers which have been mercerized.

Characteristic(s): Stronger than untreated cotton thread; lustrous; lacks stretch or give; mercerization gives cotton fibers affinity for dye allowing a wide range of colors; mercerization prevents color bleeding in laundering.

- For all natural fiber fabrics.
- On light to medium weight fabrics.

Available in retail stores in size 50; in a wide range of colors.

Black and white thread made in various sizes from fine to heavy.

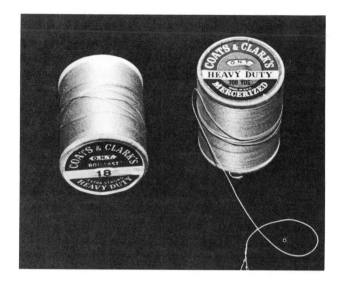

Mercerized Heavy Duty Cotton Thread

A size 40, heavyweight coarse thread formed by twisting three strands of spun staple cotton fibers which have been mercerized.

Characteristic(s): Stronger than untreated cotton thread; lustrous; lacks give or stretch; mercerization prevents bleeding in laundering.

- Where strength is required for hand or machine sewing.
- On seams which will be subject to strain.
- On heavyweight fabrics; heavy vinyl, coating, tapestry or upholstery fabrics.

Available in black and white only.

Darning Thread / Mending Thread

A cotton or silk thread formed by loosely twisting two strands of spun staple or filament fibers which may have a singed and/or mercerized finish.

Characteristic(s): Fine strands; soft and supple; strands may be separated for finer sewing; breaks easily under tension; cotton shrinks when laundered.

- In single or multiple plies for hand mending natural fiber fabrics.

Available in spools or hanks of two, four or six separable plies.

Not designed for use on sewing machines.

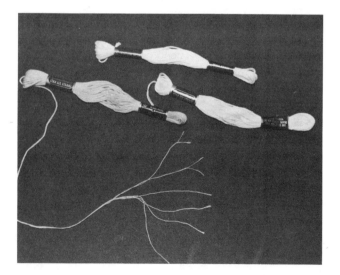

Embroidery Thread / Embroidery Floss

A mercerized cotton, silk or rayon thread consisting of two staple fiber strands loosely twisted which are again twisted to form a six-strand skein.

Characteristic(s): Strands may be separated for use singly or in groups. Strong; soft and supple; lustrous.

- Decorative hand stitches.
- Embroidery.
- Hand or machine smocking.
- French shirring stitches.

Industrial Thread

Natural, synthetic and blended fibers are designed and engineered in twisted and/or bonded types or monofilament to perform a full range of industrial sewing operations.

Different types and blends of natural and synthetic fiber threads have been developed to be compatible with the requirements necessary to the production of all categories of wearing apparel. Various finishes are applied to stabilize, strengthen and/or lubricate threads enabling them to function well at high speed.

Characteristics considered in the selection of thread for industry are:

UNIFORM EVENNESS—To permit even, rapid movement of the thread, through the fabric, under tension.
SMOOTHNESS—To withstand the function of high speed sewing.
ELASTICITY—To make supple stitches which will be less likely to break under seam strain.
STRENGTH—To hold seam secure through wear, laundering and use.

Industrial thread color is classified as:

FAST COLOR / BOILFAST COLOR—Colorfast to boiling water, soap and soda, bleaching, light, and perspiration.
WASHABLE DYE COLOR—Colorfast to 160° Fahrenheit (71° Celsius) laundering temperature.
ORDINARY DYE COLOR—Limited in colorfastness, requiring special cleaning procedure.

Industrial thread is wound in volume yardage on cones, parallel tubes, spools and king or base tubes (broad-based plastic tubes). Ready-wound bobbins containing the same thread as the upper needle are available for each type and make of industrial machine. Requirements for industrial thread change with the development of new fabric, machinery and methods of production. Thread is classified by cord and given a ticket number. Ticket numbers identify thread size within a given brand which may differ from the same ticket number of another brand. The charts list the most important thread ticket sizes.

Metallic Thread

A silver- or gold-toned synthetic thread constructed of loosely twisted strands of clear nylon filaments and laminated, flat or cylindrical metallic thread.

Characteristic(s): Coarse, stiff; glitters and/or shines; nylon provides strength and properties for sewing.

- Decorative hand and machine stitches.
- Embroidery.
- To weave openwork design.
- Hand or machine smocking.
- French shirring stitches.

Monofilament Thread

A continuous monofilament strand which is made by an extruding process producing a smooth uniform thread.

Characteristic(s): High elongation and elasticity; abrasion resistant; mildew and mold resistant; resists effect of sunlight and weathering; provides great seam strength.

- For permanent press apparel; quilted apparel.
- For men's suits and overcoats.
- For undergarments and foundation garments.

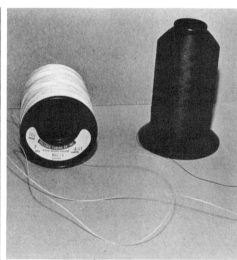

Monocord Nylon Thread / Bonded Invisible Thread (Nymo®)

A clear or dark, translucent one-cord thread comprising parallel continuous multifilaments of nylon and polyester bonded to form one strand.

Characteristic(s): Strength; elasticity and recoverability; abrasion and snarl resistant; non-shrinkable; longer seam life than other threads; least bulky for a given thread count; susceptible to fusion during high speed sewing.

- For hand and machine sewing medium weight fabrics.
- On synthetic fabrics; stretch and knit fabrics; woven or knit-backed bonded fabrics; laminated fabrics; fur or high pile fabrics; wash-and-wear fabrics.
- On double needle machines.
- Where flat seams are desired.
- For blind stitching to produce a less visible stitch.
- For topstitching tailored garments to produce flat seams.
- To reduce seam puckering.

Has twice the tensile strength of the same size cotton thread.

Translucence and lack of color blends with fabric eliminating need for an assorted stock of color thread.

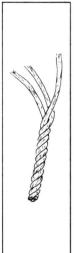

Spun Nylon Thread / Twisted Invisible Thread

A clear or dark, translucent thread produced by the twisting of three cords of monofilament synthetic yarns.

Characteristic(s): Strength; high elasticity and recoverability; abrasion and snarl resistant; non-shrinkable; longer seam life than other threads.

- For hand or machine sewing light and medium weight fabrics.
- On synthetic fabrics; stretch or knit fabrics; nylon tricot knits; woven or knit-backed plastics; laminated fabrics; fur or high pile fabrics; wash-and-wear fabrics.
- On double needle machines.
- Where a flat seam is desired.
- For blind stitching to produce a less visible stitch.
- For topstitching tailored garments to produce flat seams.
- To reduce seam puckering.

Has twice the tensile strength as the same size cotton thread.

Translucence and lack of color blends with fabric eliminating need for an assorted stock of color thread.

Polyester Core Thread / Cotton-Covered Polyester Core Thread

A thread formed by twisting two or more strands, each consisting of a continuous filament polyester core wrapped with mercerized cotton.

Characteristic(s): Core provides strength and elasticity; cotton wrapping provides heat resistance during sewing procedure; polyester core with diameter of size 60 cotton has the strength of size 40 cotton thread; lustrous.

- On knit, stretch and permanent press fabrics; woven and knit fabrics.
- For construction of jeans, overalls, and work clothes.
- Where a strong seam is desired.
- On fabrics made of synthetic, natural or blended fibers.

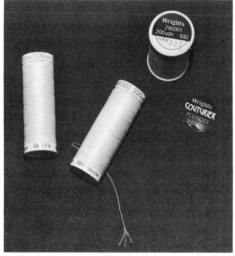

100% Polyester Thread

An electronically bonded thread made of three tightly twisted strands of long staple polyester filaments which may have a wax- or silicone-treated finish.

Characteristic(s): Stretchability and recoverability; non-shrinkable; smooth texture; extra strong. Resists sewing machine needle abrasion and heat; resists knotting and snarling during hand sewing. Wax finish allows thread to guide through fabric easily.

• On garments requiring strong durable seams.
• On synthetic and synthetic blend fabrics; polyester lightweight knit fabrics; stretch fabrics; permanent press fabrics.

Available in a wide range of colors.

Thread size comparable to size 50 mercerized cotton.

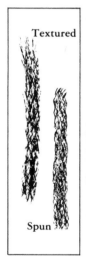

Spun Polyester Thread

A thread made by twisting two or more spun strands consisting of short staple 100% polyester filaments.

Characteristic(s): Stretchability and recoverability; strong; smooth texture; non-shrinkable. Resists sewing machine needle abrasion and heat; resists knotting and snarling during hand sewing.

• On double knit and stretch fabrics.
• *Fine*—On lingerie fabrics.
• *Heavy Duty*—On heavy fabrics and to sew on buttons.
• *Buttonhold Twist*—Topstitching, sewing on buttons and to make hand or machine buttonholes.

Quilting Thread

A strong, fine, glazed thread formed by twisting four strands of long staple cotton fibers which have been mercerized.

Characteristic(s): Strong for its diameter. Four-core construction prevents kinking and tangling. Glazed finish permits thread to glide through multiple fabric plies.

• Hand and machine quilting.

Wide range of non-bleeding fast colors.

Thread size comparable to size 40 mercerized cotton.

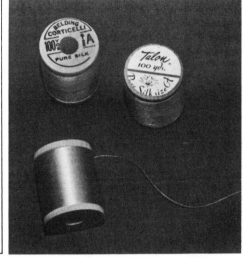

Silk Thread, Size A

A fine thread of natural fibers formed by tightly twisting two or more strands of continuous, gossamer multifilaments.

Characteristic(s): Lint or fuzz free; elasticity; durable; soft and supple; strong for its size; lustrous; leaves no imprint or indentation on fabric when pressed; can be molded with contour of garment parts; dye color faster than other threads; color will not fade after repeated cleaning; preshrunk; has highest strength and elasticity of all natural fiber threads.

- To sew silk, woolens and linens; nylon and polyester knits; high luster fabrics such as satin.
- To baste pile fabric where thread mars the surface.
- To baste fine and delicate fabrics.
- In tailoring to hold edge of collar, lapel, flap, pocket, and pleats in place for pressing.
- Thread tracing.

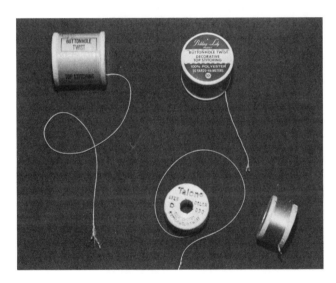

Silk Thread, Size D

A thick natural fiber thread formed by loosely twisting three strands which are composed of three separate, twisted plies of continuous gossamer filaments.

Characteristic(s): Lint and fuzz free; strong; heavy; soft and supple; smooth surface allows for smooth sewing procedure; dye color faster than other threads; color will not fade after repeated cleaning; pre-shrunk.

- Hand-worked buttonholes.
- Decorative topstitching by hand or machine.
- Hand-stitched decorative detail.
- To make arrowheads; bar tacks.
- Thread loops and belt carriers.
- To sew on buttons; hooks, eyes, loops and snap fasteners.
- Gathering thread for hand or machine sewing.

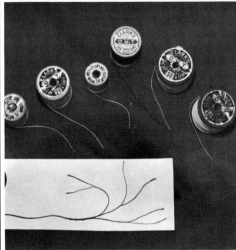

Six-Cord Thread

A firm, strong thread formed by tightly twisting six strands of spun staple cotton fibers.

Characteristic(s): Rounder; smoother; elasticity; most uniform of all threads; abrasion resistant to needle and fabric sewing operation.

- On cotton and linen fabrics.
- *Size 30*—Heavyweight fabrics.
- *Size 40*—Medium heavyweight fabrics.
- *Size 50*—Light and medium weight fabrics.
- *Size 60*—Fine or lightweight fabrics.
- *Size 80–100*—Fine fabrics.
- *Size 100–150*—Sheer fabrics.

Made in sixteen sizes from 8, the most coarse, to 155, the finest. Available in black and white only.

Thread Hank

Thread which has been pre-cut to specified lengths and bundled, tied or wrapped.

- In a simulated hand-stitch sewing machine (Federal Specification 801) to form saddle stitching on lapels, collars, cuffs, pockets and flaps, and coat fronts.
- In a button-attaching machine to simulate hand application.
- In hand tailoring for a variety of sewing procedures.

Waxed Thread

A mercerized cotton or poly-core thread to which a paraffin or silicone lubricant finishing process has been applied.

Characteristic(s): Finish makes thread stronger; eliminates tendency for tangling. Produces a smooth texture reducing shredding, fraying, and twisting of thread during sewing procedure.

- For sewing linen and 100% cotton fiber fabrics.
- On garments that require high temperatures during ironing.
- *Size 40 (Extra Strong)*—For heavy duty sewing in areas or seams receiving strain or heavy wear.
- *Size 50 (All Purpose)*—For medium weight cotton and linen fabrics, and underwear.
- *Size 60 (Fine)*—For sewing lightweight cotton and linen fabrics.
- *Size 70 (Extra Fine)*—For sewing and detail work on lightweight and sheer fabrics, and for sewing lingerie.

Heavy Duty Waxed Thread

A size 40, three-ply mercerized cotton or poly-core thread to which a paraffin or silicone lubricant finishing process has been applied.

Characteristic(s): Finish makes thread stronger; eliminates tendency for tangling; reduces shredding, fraying and twisting of thread during sewing process; produces a smooth texture.

- For hand and machine sewing on heavyweight fabrics.
- On seams subject to strain.
- To attach buttons.
- To apply zippers.

Available in black and white only.

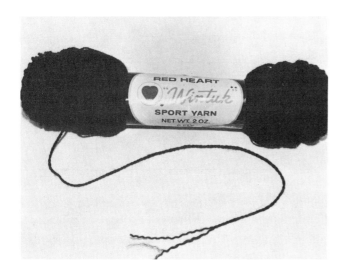

Yarn

A bulky strand comprised of two or more loosely twisted plies of spun wool, crimped synthetic or blended staple fibers.

Characteristic(s): Soft and supple; elasticity and bounce; springy and spongy.

- To make fringe, tassels, and pompoms.
- To embroider on loosely woven, open weave or knit fabrics.
- To sew novelty, sweater and loose knit fabrics.
- Cord substitute where soft fill is desired.
- Padding beneath buttonhole stitches.
- Filler beneath embroidery and couching stitches.

Thread/Fabric Selection Guide
Silk Thread

TYPE AND SIZE OF THREAD	USED ON FABRICS SUCH AS	TYPE OF HAND NEEDLE	SIZE OF HAND
INDUSTRIAL SIZE A	*Delicate, Sheer or Filmy Fabrics* Lingerie fabric Silk jersey Chiffon, georgette, organza, ninon Marquisite, net, tulle, illusion Silk or chiffon velvet Organdy, batiste, voile	Ball Point Beading Sharps Milliners	9–10 10
INDUSTRIAL SIZE A	*Fine Fabrics* Voile, lawn, dimity, dotted Swiss, shirting Synthetic sheer, synthetic or silk tricot Paper taffeta, pure silk, gossamer silk Crepe, crepe de chine, shantung Tissue faille Silk or synthetic velvet, panne Sheer woolens, wool and silk blends	Beading Sharps Milliners Betweens	8–10 8–10 8–10
INDUSTRIAL SIZE A-B	*Lightweight Fabrics* Silk sarah, crepe, taffeta, faille Shantung, satin, challis Rayon, Qiana, linen Wool flannel, jersey, crepe, suiting Bengaline	Beading Sharps Milliners Betweens	8–10 8–10 8–10
INDUSTRIAL SIZE A-B	*Medium Weight Fabrics* Ottoman, bengaline Wool worsted, flannel, jersey, crepe Suiting, fleece, mohair, cashmere Silk and wool blends Silk and linen blends Velvet, velveteen Felt	Sharps Milliners Betweens	6–8 6–8 6–8
INDUSTRIAL SIZE A-B-C	*Heavyweight Fabrics* Wool, wool suiting, wool coating Gabardine, melton, camel hair Textured linen	Sharps Milliners Betweens	1–5 4–8 4–8
SILK D BUTTONHOLE TWIST	Medium weight fabrics Medium heavyweight fabrics Heavyweight fabrics Hand and machine top stitching	Embroidery	1–6
SILK FLOSS	Embroidery	Embroidery	5–7
SILK DARNING	For darning or mending silk garments	Milliners	3–5

Thread/Fabric Selection Guide
Cotton Thread

TYPE AND SIZE OF THREAD	USED ON FABRICS SUCH AS	TYPE OF HAND NEEDLE	SIZE OF HAND
BASTING COTTON	100% cotton or lightweight linen fabrics	Sharps Betweens	6–10 6–10
COTTON	100% cotton or linen and lightweight linen fabric Organdy, batiste, voile, lawn, dimity Dotted Swiss, cotton shirting, handkerchief linen	Sharps Milliners Betweens	6–10 7–10 7–10
50 MERCERIZED COTTON	*Fine weight 100% Cotton or Linen Fabrics* 100% cotton or linen fabric Organdy, batiste, voile, lawn, dimity Dotted Swiss, cotton shirting, handkerchief linen *Lightweight 100% Cotton or Linen Fabrics* Percale, gingham, chambray, madras, poplin Chintz, sateen, muslin, piqué Seersucker, shirting, linen *Medium Weight 100% Cotton or Linen Fabrics* Lace, challis, flannel, velveteen, linen Corduroy, gabardine	Sharps Milliners Betweens Sharps Milliners Betweens Embroidery Darners Sharps Milliners Betweens Embroidery Darners	6–10 7–10 7–10 6–10 6–10 6–10 9–10 10 6–10 6–10 6–10 6–10 6–10
40 HEAVY-DUTY MERCERIZED COTTON	*Medium Heavy and Heavyweight Fabrics* Woolens, gabardine, heavy suiting Cording, corduroy, khaki, denim, sacking Ticking, linen	Sharps Milliners Betweens Embroidery Darners	2–6 3–6 3–6 1–10 5–10
QUILTING COTTON	Percale, gingham, chambray, madras, poplin Chintz, sateen, muslin, piqué Seersucker, handkerchief linen	Sharps Milliners Betweens	6–8 6–8 6–8
BUTTON AND CARPET GLAZED FINISH	Woolens, suiting, coating, overcoating Animal skin, fur Heavy leather Canvas, sailcloth	Cotton Darners Tapestry Chenille Glovers Sailmakers	1–10 18–22 18–22 3/0–8 7–14
DARNING COTTON	Cotton and linen fiber fabrics	Sharps Milliners Betweens Darners	8–10 8–10 8–10 10
EMBROIDERY FLOSS	Cotton and linen fiber fabrics	Embroidery	1–10

Thread/Fabric Selection Guide
Six Cord Cotton Thread

TYPE AND SIZE OF THREAD	USED ON FABRICS SUCH AS	TYPE OF HAND NEEDLE	SIZE OF HAND
150–100	Black or white *delicate* or *sheer* fabrics Lingerie fabric Organdy, batiste, voile	Ball Point Beading	8–10
80–100	Black or white *fine* fabrics Voile, lawn, dimity, dotted Swiss Shirting	Sharps Milliners Betweens	8–10 8–10 8–10
60–80	Black or white *lightweight* fabrics Percale, gingham, chambray, madras, poplin Chintz, sateen, muslin, piqué Seersucker, shirting, linen	Sharps Milliners Betweens Darners	6–10 6–10 7–10 10
50	Black or white *medium weight* fabrics Lace, challis, flannel, velveteen, linen Corduroy, gabardine	Sharps Milliners Betweens Darners	6–10 6–10 6–10 6–10
40	Black or white *medium heavy* or *heavyweight* fabrics Woolens, gabardine, heavy suiting Cording, corduroy, khaki, denim, sacking Ticking, linen	Sharps Milliners Betweens Embroidery Darners	2–6 3–6 3–6 1–10 5–10
30	Black or white *heavyweight* fabrics Duck, sailcloth, canvas, drill, tapestry Overcoating, imitation fur, heavy weaves	Darners Embroidery Tapestry Chenille Glovers Sailmakers	1–10 15–22 8–22 3/0–8 7–14

Thread/Fabric Selection Guide
Cotton or Poly-Core Waxed Thread

TYPE AND SIZE OF THREAD	USED ON FABRICS SUCH AS	TYPE OF HAND NEEDLE	SIZE OF HAND
70 WAXED COTTON EXTRA FINE	Delicate and sheer fabrics Organdy, batiste, voile	Sharps Milliners Betweens Beading	8–10 8–10 8–10
70 WAXED POLY-CORE EXTRA FINE	Lingerie fabrics Underwear fabrics Cotton knits	Ball Point	8–10
60 WAXED COTTON FINE	Fine fabrics Voile, lawn, dimity, dotted Swiss, shirting	Sharps Milliners Betweens	8–10 8–10 8–10
60 WAXED POLY-CORE FINE	Synthetic sheers Sheer woolens Wool and synthetic blends Cotton and synthetic blends Cotton or synthetic knit fabrics	Sharps Milliners Betweens Darners Ball Point	6–10 6–10 6–10 10 8–10
50 WAXED COTTON ALL PURPOSE REGULAR	*Lightweight fabric* of linen or all cotton fibers Percale, gingham, chambray, madras, poplin Chintz, sateen, muslin, piqué Seersucker, shirting, linen	Sharps Milliners Betweens Embroidery Darners	6–10 6–10 6–10 9–10 10
50 WAXED COTTON ALL PURPOSE REGULAR	*Medium weight fabric* of linen or all cotton fibers Lace, challis, flannel, velveteen, linen. Corduroy, gabardine	Sharps Milliners Betweens Embroidery Darners	6–10 6–10 6–10 6–10 6–10
50 WAXED POLY-CORE ALL PURPOSE REGULAR	Lightweight woolens Lightweight wool and synthetic blends Lightweight synthetic knits Cotton or synthetic knit fabrics	Sharps Milliners Betweens Embroidery Darners Ball Point	6–10 6–10 6–10 9–10 10
40 WAXED HEAVY DUTY	Medium heavy and heavyweight fabrics Woolens, gabardine, heavy suiting Cording, corduroy, khaki, denim, sacking Ticking, linen	Sharps Milliners Betweens Embroidery Darners	2–6 3–6 3–6 1–10 5–10

Thread/Fabric Selection Guide
Cotton and Polyester Blend Thread

TYPE AND SIZE OF THREAD	USED ON FABRICS SUCH AS	TYPE OF HAND NEEDLE	SIZE OF HAND
EXTRA FINE	*Lightweight* cotton and polyester blend fabrics Linings Lingerie, lightweight knits	Sharps Milliners Betweens Ball Point	8–10 8–10 8–10 8–10
ALL PURPOSE	*Medium weight* cotton, linen, woolen and polyester blend fabrics Acrylic and wash-and-wear fabrics Permanent Press fabrics Knit fabrics	Sharps Milliners Betweens Embroidery Darners	6–10 6–10 6–10 10 10
HEAVY DUTY	*Heavyweight* fabrics Coating, overcoating, suiting Making buttonholes Sewing on buttons	Sharps Milliners Betweens Embroidery Darners	1–5 3–6 3–5 1–7 1–7

Thread/Fabric Selection Guide
Cotton-Covered Polyester Core Thread

TYPE AND SIZE OF THREAD	USED ON FABRICS SUCH AS	TYPE OF HAND NEEDLE	SIZE OF HAND
EXTRA FINE	*Fine and lightweight fabrics* Synthetics and synthetic blends Chiffon, georgette, organza, marquisite, tulle, organdy Batiste, voile, crepe, crepe de chine, taffeta, rayon Synthetic knits, synthetic tricot and lingerie fabrics Lightweight knits	Sharps Milliners Betweens Ball Point	 8–10
REGULAR OR ALL PURPOSE	*Medium lightweight and medium weight fabrics* Synthetics and Synthetic blends Rayon challis, velvet, panne, shantung Ticking, denim, sacking, suiting, coating Knit fabrics	Sharps Milliners Betweens Embroidery Darners	6–10 6–10 6–10 10 10
EXTRA STRONG OR HEAVY DUTY	*Heavyweight fabrics* Duck, sailcloth, canvas, drill Tapestry, imitation fur, heavy weaves Overcoating, coating, suiting	Sharps Milliners Betweens Embroidery Darners Tapestry Chenille	1–3 3–6 3–6 1–6 1–6 18–22 18–22

Thread/Fabric Selection Guide
Polyester Thread

TYPE AND SIZE OF THREAD	USED ON FABRICS SUCH AS	TYPE OF HAND NEEDLE	SIZE OF HAND
100% POLYESTER (comparable to 50 Mercerized Cotton)	Polyester and synthetic blend fabrics Permanent Press fabrics Lightweight polyester knit fabrics Stretch fabrics	Sharps Milliners Betweens Ball Point	8–10 8–10 8–10 8–10
SPUN FINE	Fine, sheer and lightweight synthetic fabrics Lingerie fabrics Polyester jersey	Sharps Milliners Betweens Ball Point	8–10 8–10 8–10 8–10
SPUN REGULAR OR ALL PURPOSE	Medium, medium heavy polyester and synthetic blend fabrics Double knits, stretch fabrics Bonded fabrics Permanent press fabrics	Sharps Milliners Betweens Embroidery Darners Ball Point	6–10 6–10 6–10 10 10 6–10
SPUN HEAVY DUTY OR EXTRA STRONG	Heavyweight fabrics Polyester, synthetic blend woolens Coating, overcoating, suiting Imitation fur	Sharps Milliners Betweens Embroidery Darners Tapestry Chenille	1–3 3–5 3–5 1–7 1–7 18–22 18–22
SPUN BUTTONHOLE TWIST	For hand or machine details such as: Arrowheads, hand picking, detail work, tailoring details, fastening loops, worked buttonholes, gathering or shirring, thread loops, embroidery, hand finishing, zipper application, attaching fasteners, attaching buttons, decorative stitching, saddle stitch, and topstitching	Embroidery Darners Tapestry Chenille	1–7 1–7 18–22 18–22

Thread/Fabric Selection Guide
Nylon and Dacron Thread

TYPE AND SIZE OF THREAD	USED ON FABRICS SUCH AS	TYPE OF HAND NEEDLE	SIZE OF HAND
TWIST CONSTRUCTION SIZE A	100% Nylon, Dacron and synthetic blend fabrics Wash-and-wear fabrics Fur and high pile fabrics Laminated fabrics	Sharps Milliners Betweens	7–10 7–10 7–10
MONOCORD (BONDED CONSTRUCTION) SIZE A	Stretch fabrics Knit structure fabrics Nylon tricot Lingerie fabrics such as; Acetate, Acrylon, Arnel, Dacron, Dynel, Nylon, Orlon, Rayon	Ball Point Ball Point	6–10 8–10

Thread Ticket Size

SOFT AND GLACÉ FINISH COTTON THREADS

PLY	TICKET NUMBER
2	60–70–80–90 100–120–140–160
3	20–24–30–36 40–50–60–70 80–90–100–120
4	12–16–20–24 30–36–40–50
6	30–36–40 50–60

MERCERIZED THREADS—COTTON

PLY	TICKET NUMBER
2	00
3	B–A–0–00–000–0000

Soft and glacé finished cotton threads—The lower the number the coarser the thread.

Mercerized threads—The letter symbols indicate the size of the thread.

Ticket B is coarser than Ticket A. Ticket A is courser than Ticket 0.

Ticket 0 is coarser than Ticket 00, etc.

Suggested Needle Sizes for Industrial Thread

NYLON	4 CORD COTTON	DACRON	3 CORD COTTON	NEEDLE SIZES
13–15–22	—	13–15–23	90/3	9–10–11
22–23	—	23–30	80/3	10–11–12
23–33	—	30–46	70/3	11–12–13
33	60/4	46–46/2	60/3	12–13–14
33	60/4	46–46/2	50/3	14–15–16
46	50/4–40/4	46/2–69	40/3–36/3	16–17–18
46–46/2	40/4–36/4	69	36/3–30/3	17–18–19
46/2–69	30/4	69–92	24/3	18–19–20
69	24/4–20/4	92	20/3	19–20–21
92–99	16/4	138	16/3	20–21–22
99–138	12/4	—	12/3	21–22–23
138	12/4	207	10/3	22–23–24
207	10/4	207–346	—	24–25–26
277–346	—	346	8/3	26–27–28
415	8/4–(8/5)	—	—	30

Test sample should be made before proceeding with the production of the garment to determine the correct thread-needle size relationship.

Approximate Equivalent Ticket Numbers of Industrial Thread

REGULAR COTTON THREAD AND CORE SPUN THREAD	MERCERIZED	POLYESTER AND NYLON FILAMENT
16	F	105
20	E	90
24	D	69
30	C	61
36	B	53
40	A	42
50	0	38
60	00	32
70	000	30
90	0000	21
100	—	18
120	00000	14

Comparative Chart: Physical Properties for Industrial Thread*

	NYLON	DACRON	SILK	LINEN	COTTON
Tensile Strength	1	2	3	3	4
Loop Break	3	4	4	5	2
Elastic Recovery	1	2	5	5	5
Flex Life	2	3	3	4	5
Resistance to:					
Sunlight	3	3	4	5	5
Abrasion	1	2	4	4	5
Mildew	1	1	3	5	5
Heat	3	3	2	3	3
Acids	4	2	5	5	5
Alkali	3	4	5	5	5
Specific Gravity	1.14	1.38	1.31	1.50	1.50

*(1) Superior (2) Excellent (3) Good (4) Fair (5) Poor

17 ~ Aids & Tools for Garment Construction

Adhesive / Mucilage / Glue
Awl / Stiletto
Beeswax
Belting:
  Belting
  Non-Slip Belting / Rubberized Belting
Binding:
  Iron-On Seam Binding / Press-On Tape
  Lace Seam Binding
  Ribbon Seam Binding / Seam Binding
Bodkin
Bonding Strip / Fusible Adhesive
Bra Cup
Coat & Jacket Hanger
Cord / Cable Cord
Eyelet
Fitting Platform
Gauge:
  Cardboard Gauge
  Hemline Gauge / Hemline Marking Guide
  Scallop Gauge / Dressmaker's Gauge
  Sewing Gauge / Hem Gauge
  Sleeve Gauge / Sleeve Guide
Grosgrain Ribbon
Horsehair Braid
Magnet
Marking Pencil / Chalking Pencil
Needle Threader
Pins:
  Ball Point Pin
  Large Head Pin
  Straight Pin

Straight Pin Specifications Chart
T-Head Pin / "T" Pin
T-Head Pin Specifications Chart
Pin Cushion:
  Pin Cushion
  Emery Bag
Powdered Chalk
Punch:
  Eyelet Setter
  Hole Punch
  No-Sew Snap Setter
Seam Ripper
Shoulder Pads
Skirt Marker (Powder / Pin / Chalk)
Support:
  Boning / Feather Boning / Stay Strip
Tape:
  Double-Faced Tape
  Self-Stick Tape
  Tissue Tape
  Twill Tape
Thimble:
  Thimble
  Tailor's Thimble
Turner:
  Crease Turner
  Loop Turner
  Point & Tube Turner
Weights:
  Chain Weights
  Lead Disc Weights
  Lead Pellet Weights

Garment construction aids and tools include essential and/or accessory items, other than fabrics, patterns or equipment, required in the making of a garment.

Tools and aids for garment construction are used in a variety of ways during the development of the garment to facilitate sewing procedures.

Notions or findings are considered supplementary items used in manufacturing all types of garments. Essential are those needed for construction procedures performed on any garment; while accessories are items of specialized use.

Notions used by linear measure are available on spools or reels by the yard or are packaged in premeasured yardage.

Notions required in numerical quantity are packaged in limited amounts by the box, bag or card.

Aids and tools for garment construction are selected with consideration for:
- Utilization and efficiency
- Specific functional purpose
- Construction methods and procedures

Adhesive / Mucilage / Glue

A variety of cements, pastes, mucilages or glues which are selected for their compatibility with fabric.

- As a bonding agent for a glued seam.
- On a glued seam finish for leather or plastic.
- On a glued hem.
- To attach sequins, glitter or feathers.
- To attach appliqué motifs.

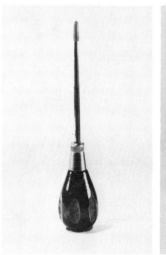

Awl / Stiletto

A pointed metal instrument, approximately 1/8 inch (3.2 mm) in diameter by 3 to 8 inches (8 to 20 cm) in length, with a wooden handle.

- To make holes for metal or thread eyelets; hammer-on-snaps.
- To make eye-end or keyhole buttonholes.
- To make punctures indicating grainlines, end of darts, and placement of trimming on sloper or pattern.
- To punch holes in leather, plastic or fabric.
- To spot points on pattern or sloper.
- To punch end of darts on sloper or pattern.
- To punch length- and crossgrain on pattern or sloper.
- To punch placement of pockets, trimmings or bands on patterns.

Beeswax

A block of a solid, natural or synthetic waxy substance.

- To strengthen thread for hand sewing.
- To coat thread surface to prevent knotting and tangling.
- To reduce friction of thread in sewing.
- To stiffen end of thread for ease in threading needle.
- To hold two or more strands of thread together.
- To eliminate static electricity in thread.

Available in large blocks or packaged with or without a slotted holder.

Belting

A stiff narrow band produced by the bonding of tightly woven fabric, buckram and compressed fiber.

- To make fabric-covered belts.
- To stiffen and reinforce a waistband of lightweight fabric.
- To prevent rolling and curling in waistbands.

Available in 1/2 to 3 inch (1.3 to 7.6 cm) widths; in premeasured lengths, shaped for contour belts, and waistbands; with adhesive backing for iron-on application.

Non-Slip Belting / Rubberized Belting

A grosgrain belting, 2 inches (5 cm) or less in width, woven with patterned rows of rubberized yarn which remain exposed on one surface.

- To complete the inside of a single-ply, self-fabric waistband.
- To produce a non-slip waistband.
- On waistbands to hold tuck-in blouses and shirts in place.

Iron-On Seam Binding / Press-On Tape

A narrow, lightweight ribbon of natural or synthetic yarns, approximately 1/2 inch (1.3 cm) in width, with two edges of bonding agent on the underside which may be activated by applying heat, steam or pressure.

- To eliminate the need for hand or machine hemming.
- To hem quickly a long edge or fold.
- To bind straight seam and edge.

Lace Seam Binding

A stretch or non-stretch lace ribbon produced in a variety of widths, weights, and patterns.

- On hems in place of seam tape or bias binding.
- On garments made of lace fabrics; knit and stretch fabrics.
- On edge of facing.
- As an edging.
- As an insert.

Available in 2-inch (5 cm) widths to be used as hem facing. Produced in a variety of natural and synthetic yarns for compatibility with fabric of the garment.

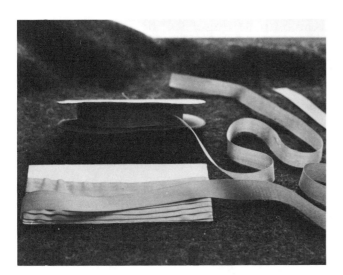

Ribbon Seam Binding / Seam Binding

A narrow, lightweight ribbon of natural or synthetic yarns; approximately 1/2 inch (1.3 cm) in width.

- To finish hem edges; straight-edge facings.
- As reinforcing strip for taped seam.
- To bind seams.
- To extend seams.

As stay:
- At seams;
- At waistlines;
- For gathering and shirring;
- At foldline of extended seam and facing.

Produced in a variety of synthetic yarns for compatibility with the fabrics of garments. Available in a diagonal cut to sew around curved edges.

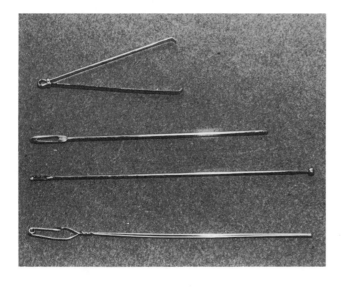

Bodkin

A blunt- or ball-end metal tool which may be designed as a large-eyed needle, tweezer or safety pin.

- To draw ribbon, cord, drawstring or elastic through a casing.
- To draw lacing through eyelet or grommet opening.
- To turn narrow belts and sashes.

Available in a variety of lengths, shapes and widths.

Bonding Strip / Fusible Adhesive

A bonding agent produced as a nonwoven fiber mesh strip, which is activated by applying heat, steam and/or pressure.

- To secure two plies of fabric.
- To hold facing and seam in place without stitching.
- To secure seam or fold-over allowance for vents and slashed openings.
- To hold interfacing to fabric.
- On lightweight fabrics when constructing buttonholes and pockets.
- Between plies to reinforce areas on lightweight and loosely woven fabrics for button placement.
- To adhere the hem of a garment by pressing.
- Where any hem stitch would detract from the smooth look of the garment.

Heat, steam, and pressure dissolve bonding agent into fabric plies. Available in 3/4, 1 1/2, 5 or 18 inch (1.9, 3.8, 12.7, 45.7cm) widths.

Bra Cup

A covered or uncovered foam rubber or synthetic batting, molded and/or stitched into a rounded conical shape.

- To shape swimsuit tops.
- To support shape of strapless garment.
- To support garment where a separate bra would detract from the appearance of the garment.
- In the construction of bra dresses and bra slips.

May be fashioned as separate cups or constructed as a unit; sized according to brassiere size.

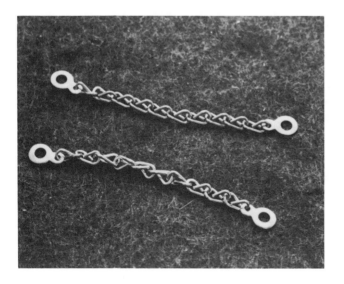

Coat & Jacket Hanger

A short length of metal chain or nylon braid designed with rings or loops.

- Attached at the back neckline of garments to provide a means for hanging garment on hook or peg.

Available in lengths from 1 1/2 to 4 inches (3.8 to 10 cm).

6			80
9			90
12			100
16			120
20			150
24			175
30			200
40			
50			300
60			
70			

Cord / Cable Cord

A soft cotton, cellulose or synthetic yarn rope, 1/8 to 1 inch (3.2 to 25.4 mm) in diameter, either twisted to form a cable or cylindrically shaped with a mesh of woven thread.

- As a filler for piping and cording; in tubing for belts and straps; trapunto.
- To make corded buttonholes and pockets.
- To make corded tucks.
- To delineate hem edge of bell sleeve and skirt.
- As a style feature to delineate and add body to hem edge of garment.

Eyelet

A round or square, metal tube, with an opening of approximately 1/4 inch (.6 cm). When applied to garment forms a flattened rimmed opening.

- To make a reinforced opening.
- For lacing and belt openings.
- To prevent openings from stretching out of shape.
- As a decorative design detail.

Available in nickel, gilt-finished anodized aluminum, and enameled brass; in kits or packaged units; in kits with buckle and belt.

Applied with hammer and attaching tool or eyelet setter.

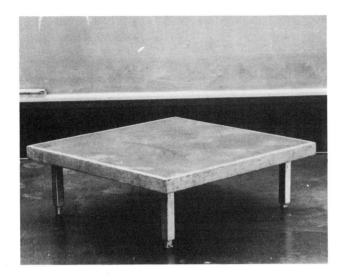

Fitting Platform

A low, table-like stand approximately 30 by 30 inches (76 by 76 cm) square and standing 6 to 8 inches (15 to 20 cm) high.

- To establish and mark hemlines of long garments.
- To establish and mark length of hem and train on bridal gowns.
- To establish and mark cuffs of trousers.

Cardboard Gauge

A hand-constructed tool, of Oak tag, cardboard, or plastic, notched at a desired measurement.

- To save time when measuring widths of the same size along a great distance.
- To measure:
    Specific design details such as tucks, hems, band, and trimmings;
    Position of buttonholes, buttons, and other fasteners;
    Seams and seam allowances.
- When larger measuring tools would be cumbersome.

Hemline Gauge / Hemline Marking Guide

A marking gauge, approximately 9 inches by 5 inches (23 by 12.7 cm) in which one long edge describes a shallow curve and the other a straight-edged rule.

- To measure and true curved lines of hems.
- To measure spacing for trimming or appliqué along a line parallel to the first.
- To measure widths of hems.
- To measure and mark tucks and pleating.

Printed lines indicate common curved hem depths. Slots mark straight hem depths.

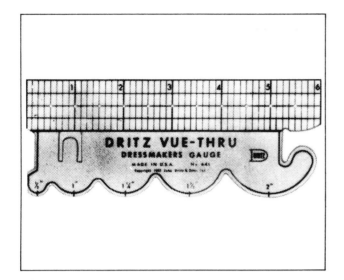

Scallop Gauge / Dressmaker's Gauge

A rule with a series of short, semicircular curves of different widths along one side and a straight edge on the other.

- To mark, measure, and space scallops.
- To measure size and placement of pleats and tucks.

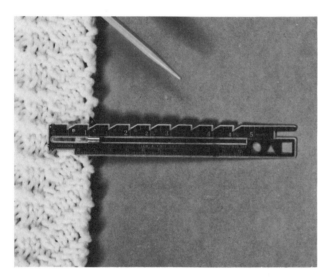

Sewing Gauge / Hem Gauge

A short rule provided with an indicator slide, which can be set at any point along the rule.

- Whenever a short, firm measure is needed.
- To save time in measuring hem widths.
- To measure and mark hem widths where a longer ruler would be cumbersome.
- To space distance between buttonholes, buttons, and other fasteners.
- To measure and mark tucks and pleating.
- To measure and space quilting lines.
- To measure and space hand or machine stitches for gathering or smocking.
- To measure spacing for trimming inserts or appliqués.

Gauge pivots on a pin to perform as a compass or for the circular measure of scallops.

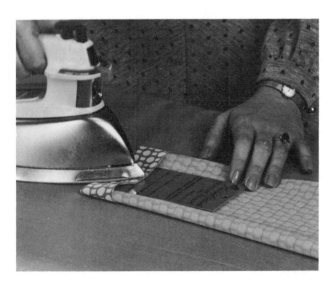

Sleeve Gauge / Sleeve Guide

A 3 by 5 1/2 inch (7.6 by 14 cm) rectangular guide with graduated hemline markings from 1/4 to 2 1/2 inches (6.4 mm to 6.3 cm), designated in inches and centimeters.

- To turn hems in small or limited areas.
- To hem sleeves and pants.
- To turn edge of pockets.
- To turn edge of appliqué design.

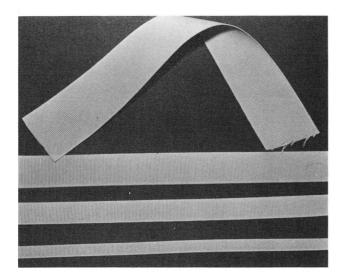

Grosgrain Ribbon

A narrow, firmly woven ribbed fabric produced with plain, satin or picot edge.

- Waistline stay.
- Ribbon waistband.
- Ribbon-faced waistband.
- Belting.
- Casing.
- Garment ties.
- Belt or sash.
- Banding.
- Decorative trim.
- Facing on straight edges.
- Facing on button closure in knit garments.
- Stay at zipper or placket closure in knit garments.
- To extend seam.

Available in a wide range of widths, colors, prints and geometrics.

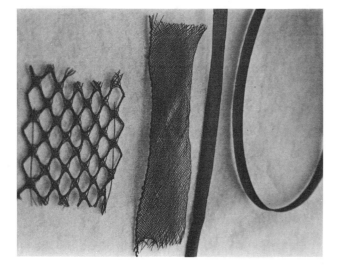

Horsehair Braid

A stiff, bias braid woven of transparent synthetic yarn which may include a heavy thread along one edge.

- To stiffen petticoats to create bouffant effect.
- To support dome silhouette.
- To finish and stabilize hem of garments made of heavy fabrics.
- On flared hem area of garments such as the lower edge of sleeves, wide collars, capes and dresses.
- On garments made of lightweight and sheer fabrics to produce soft curves.
- In late day or evening wear, formals, bridals and costumes.
- To stay zipper seams of pile fabrics.

Produced in a variety of widths and patterns. Heavy thread facilitates shaping for hem application. Width of horsehair selected according to the type of garment and edge or area on which it is applied.

Magnet

A bar, block or horseshoe form made in a grade of plain high carbon steel or high carbon alloy steel that has the property of attracting iron or steel.

- To pick up steel or stainless steel pins and needles.

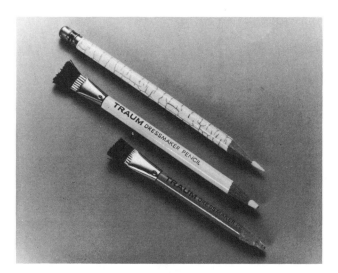

Marking Pencil / Chalking Pencil

An instrument with a clay chalk core, shaped and used like a pencil; sometimes equipped at one end with a small brush for erasure.

- To mark:
    A hem that is being measured;
    Fitting lines on the face or inside of the garment;
    Fabrics and garments where any wax substance would leave a stain.
- When draping in fabric.

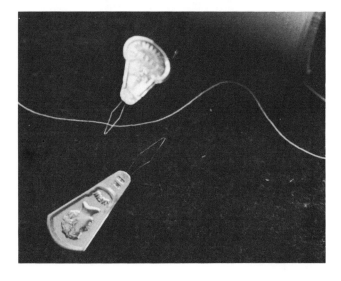

Needle Threader

A diamond-shaped loop of fine, flexible wire attached to a small flat metal or plastic plate.

- To ease threading of hand and machine needles.
- To ease threading of fine-eyed needles.
- To simplify needle threading when using multi-strand floss or yarn.

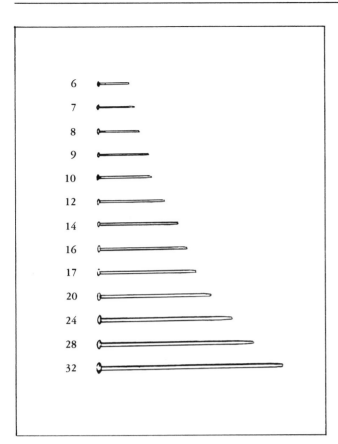

Ball Point Pin

A pin, from 1/2 to 1 5/8 inches (12.7 to 41.3 mm) in length, having a flattened or spherical head and a round ball tip.

- Instead of a pointed tip pin which would mar or damage the fabrics.
- On knit fabrics.
- On lingerie fabrics such as tricot, lace and spandex.

Ball point tip separates yarns and slips through weave instead of penetrating and cutting yarns.

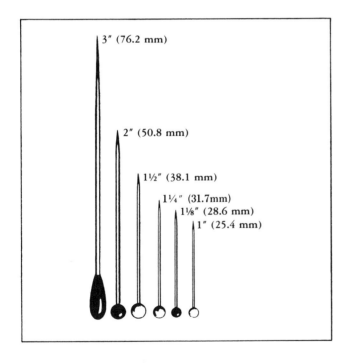

Large Head Pin

A pin, from 1 to 1 1/2 inches (25.4 to 38.1 mm) in length, having a sherical or ovoid head and a sharply pointed or ball tip end.

- On bulky, loosely woven or knit fabrics.
- To hold sequins or beads in place.
- To fasten loosely woven trimmings to garments.
- When high visibility is desired during pinning.
- Instead of push pins as a lightweight anchoring device.

Pin head may be made of glass or plastic. Large head allows ease of handling.

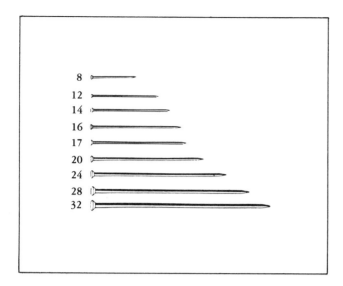

Straight Pin

A pin, from 1/2 to 1 5/8 inches (12.7 to 41.3 mm) in length, having a sharply pointed tip and a flat or round head.

- To anchor muslin to model form while draping.
- To assemble muslin patterns.
- To fasten fabric plies together in preparation for subsequent sewing operations.
- To fasten pattern pieces to fabric plies prior to cutting.
- To hold pattern draft in place while developing final pattern.
- For pin basting.

Extra long pins, 1 5/8 inches (41.3 mm), are used when working with heavy fabrics or pleating. Short pins, 1/2 inch (12.7 mm), are used when working with quarter scale patterns or muslin.

Available in steel, brass, and stainless steel.

Straight Pin Specifications

SIZE	LENGTH—INCHES (MM)	DIAMETER—INCHES (MM)
Dressmaker		
14	7/8 (22.2)	0.0285 (0.72)
16	1 (25.4)	0.0285 (0.72)
17	1 1/16 (27.0)	0.0285 (0.72)
20	1 1/4 (31.7)	0.030 (0.76)
24	1 1/2 (38.1)	0.036 (0.91)
Satin and Silk		
14	7/8 (22.2)	0.0255 (0.65)
16	1 (25.4)	0.0255 (0.65)
17	1 1/16 (27.0)	0.0255 (0.65)
Bank		
8	1/2 (12.7)	0.021 (0.53)
14	7/8 (22.2)	0.0285 (0.72)
17	1 (25.4)	0.0335 (0.85)
20	1 1/4 (31.7)	0.036 (0.91)
24	1 1/2 (38.1)	0.0455 (1.15)
28	1 3/4 (44.4)	0.0455 (1.15)
32	2 (50.8)	0.0455 (1.15)
44	2 3/4 (69.8)	0.046 (1.17)
Lills Ribbon Pleating		
6	3/8 (9.5)	0.021 (0.53)
7	7/16 (11.1)	0.021 (0.53)
8	1/2 (12.7)	0.021 (0.53)
9	9/16 (14.3)	0.021 (0.53)
10	5/8 (15.9)	0.021 (0.53)
12	3/4 (19.0)	0.021 (0.53)

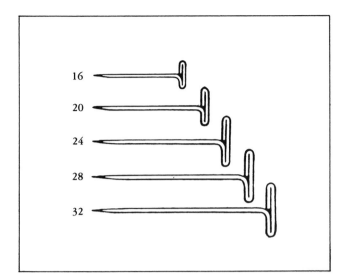

T-Head Pin / "T" Pin

A rigid metal wire, from 1 to 2 inches (25.4 to 50.8 mm) in length, with a sharply pointed tip and a T-bar shaped head formed from the wire.

- On bulky, loosely woven or knit fabrics.
- To anchor fabric to table during layout procedure.
- Instead of push pins as an anchoring device.
- To anchor fabric folds when forming pleats.

Size and shape of head allows for high visibility and easy removal.

T-Head Pin Specifications

SIZE	LENGTH—INCHES (MM)	DIAMETER—INCHES (MM)
16	1 (25.4)	0.030 (0.76)
20	1 1/4 (31.7)	0.0335 (0.85)
24	1 1/2 (38.1)	0.0455 (1.15)
28	1 3/4 (44.4)	0.0455 (1.15)
32	2 (50.8)	0.0455 (1.15)

Pin Cushion

A small, firmly stuffed pillow made in a variety of shapes and sizes.

- To hold pins and needles for easy accessibility.
- To store pins and needles safely.

May be attached to a clip or wristband; affixed to a weighted base or pin box. An emery bag may be attached.

Emery Bag

A small cushion stuffed with granulated corundum.

For machine and hand needles, and pins:
- To clean residual synthetic fabric resin;
- To sharpen;
- To remove rust spots.

May be attached to a pin cushion.

Powdered Chalk

A pulverized white or pink talc.

In container of the skirt marker tool:
- To mark hemline.

On powdered chalk board:
- As a tracing surface for lightweight or delicate fabrics;
- To transfer stencil or pounce patterns.

Eyelet Setter

A tool with a pair of prong and socket plates attached to opposing jaws; hinged, as a plier, at a spring-activated pivot point.

- To set metal eyelets or grommets into fabric.
- To puncture small holes prior to placement of grommets.

Designed to accommodate a variety of eyelet sizes; may be converted to an attachment for no-sew snaps.

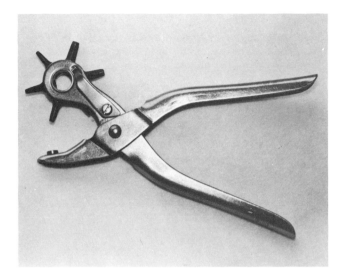

Hole Punch

A tool with a rachet-controlled size selector punch mounted on one jaw and a flat plate on the other; hinged, as a plier, at a spring-activated pivot point.

- To cut openings in belts to accommodate buckle prong.
- To cut eye openings of buttonholes.
- To cut eyelet or grommet openings for lacing.
- To cut openings in skins or vinyls for seam or edge finish lacing.

No-Sew Snap Setter

A tool with a pair of prong and socket plates attached to opposing jaws; hinged, as a plier, at a spring-activated pivot point.

- To install no-sew snaps into garment.
- To replace and repair no-sew snaps.

Snap setter may be equipped with rubber discs on prong and socket plates to protect decorative face of snap.
  Setter packaged for home and small shop use.

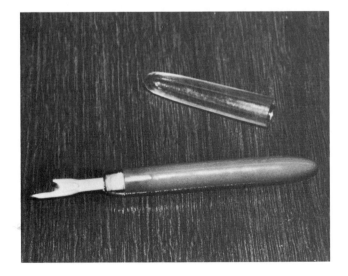

Seam Ripper

An instrument with a curved, hook-like blade tapering into two points of unequal length and attached to a handle.

- To cut seam stitches of garment for repair and correction.
- To remove stitches.
- To pick out basting threads.

Shoulder Pads

Padding, constructed or formed into a triangular configuration, which tapers to a diminishing thickness while maintaining maximum bulk along one edge.

- To add width to narrow shoulders.
- To camouflage rounded or sloping shoulders.
- To disguise uneven shoulder heights.
- To support shoulders of garment for correct drape.
- To maintain and support shoulder area of tailored garments.

Available in a variety of sizes, shapes, thicknesses, and weights and in materials such as cotton batting, felt, foam, or multiplies of canvas.

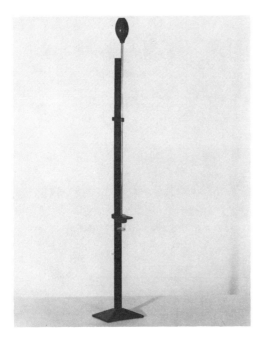

Skirt Marker (Powder / Pin / Chalk)

A ruler affixed to a weighted base; furnished either with an adjustable device which releases powdered chalk at a designated height by means of an attached pressure bulb and hose, or with an adjustable clamp for inserting pins or marking with chalk.

- To establish the hemline of garments while marking or pinning.
- To mark the hem lengths of garments from the floor level when garment is on the model form or live figure.

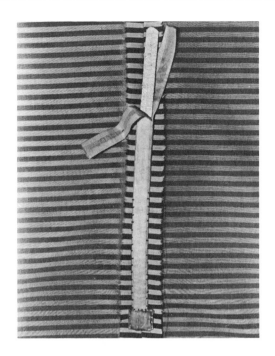

Boning / Feather Boning / Stay Strip

A firm flexible nylon strip, 1/8 to 3/4 inch (3.2 to 19 mm) wide, concealed in casing, or a flat, lightweight flexible strip of metal or plastic.

- To support:
    Built-up waistline;
    Strapless bodice;
    High-standing collar.
- To prevent:
    Crushing of cummerbund;
    Rolling and crushing of wide-shaped belts.
- To stiffen and maintain shape of corset.
- To maintain exaggerated silhouette of dome skirt.
- To produce hoop skirt in silhouette in outer garments and petticoats.

Applied to princess line, darts, center front, center back and/or seam.

Metal or plastic strip used for boning available in premeasured or finished lengths.

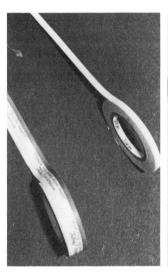

Double-Faced Tape

A roll of tape, 1 inch (2.5 cm) or less in width, with adhesive on both sides.

- As an aid when positioning zipper.
- To hold zippers in position for subsequent sewing operation.
- To hold fabric plies together before stitching.
- To hold a leather or plastic fabric together where pins would not penetrate or would mar fabric.

Available with an overlay of printed guide lines.

Tape may be rolled with removable protective overlay on one or both sides.

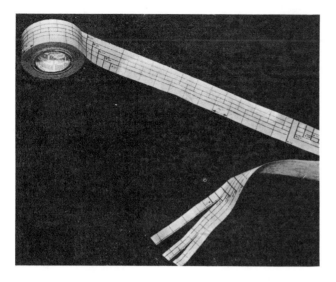

Self-Stick Tape

A roll of tape with an overlay of measured vertical and horizontal markings on one side and an adhesive on the other.

- As a guide for topstitching.
- As a seam allowance guide.
- On machine-needle plate as a sewing guide.
- To hold pleats in place during garment construction.
- To alter patterns.
- To position buttons and buttonholes.
- Along seam line to stabilize stretch or loosely woven fabrics.

Tape available scored for separation into narrow strips.

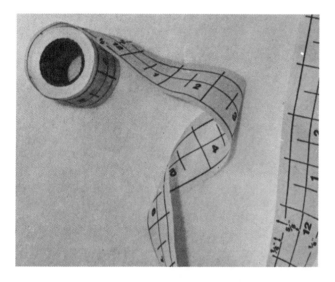

Tissue Tape

A roll of lightweight, non-adhesive tape, 1 1/4 inches (3.2 cm) wide, with measured horizontal and vertical markings on one side.

- To sew:
    Sheer fabrics such as chiffon, lace, and open-weave;
    Knit and pile fabrics;
    Leathers and plastics.
- As a seam stitching guide.
- To alter patterns.
- To position buttons, buttonholes, and pockets.
- As a guide for topstitching.

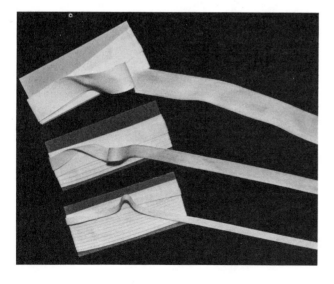

Twill Tape

A firmly woven ribbon, 1/4 to 1 inch (6.3 to 25.4 mm) in width, of natural or synthetic yarn.

- As a reinforcing strip.
- For stayed seams; taped seams.

At foldline of:
- One-piece extended facings;
- Extended pocket or slash seams;
- Straight edge closure or finish.

- As a waistline stay.

Thimble

A tapered metal, plastic or ceramic cap, with a patterned indented surface, which fits over the tip of the middle finger of the sewing hand.

- To protect finger while advancing or pushing the needle through fabric ply or plies during hand sewing.

Sizes range from 6 through 11. *Ceramic thimble* has smooth sides and indented cap.

Tailor's Thimble

A tapered metal band, with a patterned indented surface, which fits over the tip of the middle finger of the sewing hand.

- In tailoring.
- To protect finger while advancing or pushing the needle through fabric ply or plies during hand sewing.

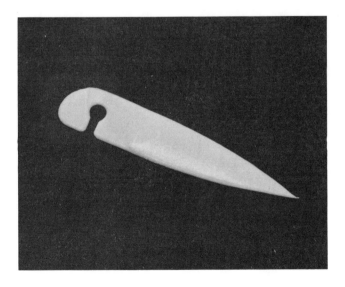

Crease Turner

A slender wooden or plastic tool, approximately 4 inches (10 cm) long by 1 inch (2.5 cm) wide, with one pointed and one rounded end.

- To push out corners of:
    Collars, pockets, and cuffs;
    Corners of faced garment areas;
    Corners of belts and sashes.
- As an aid in finger pressing.

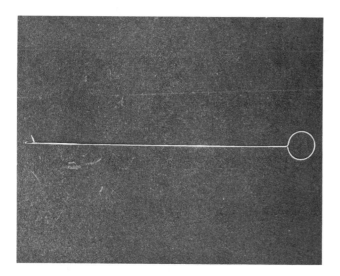

Loop Turner

A rigid wire, approximately 10 inches (25.4 cm) long, with a hook and latch at one end and a ring handle at the other.

- To turn:
    Narrow bias tubing when making frogs and corded buttons;
    Spaghetti and lingerie straps;
    Tie belts;
    Narrow bias or straight grain strip used for banding;
    Bias strip when making passementerie trimming.
- To pull cord through bias tubing.
- In place of a bodkin.

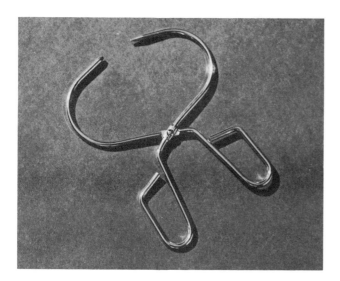

Point & Tube Turner

Metal tongs designed with curved arms, 1/4 inch (6.4 mm) in diameter, one of which is tapered to a point and the other shaped to a blunt end.

- To turn:
    Points of collars, cuffs, pockets and flaps;
    Tubing for loops, spaghetti straps, and strapping;
    Belts and sashes.

Chain Weights

A chain in any one of a variety of metals, weights and lengths.

- To obtain a uniformly weighted hem.
- To control and improve drape of garment.
- On coat and jacket hems.
- On Chanel-type jackets.
- To prevent a hem area from shifting.
- To prevent garment from riding up on body.

Chain is attached along hem allowance, a measured distance from finished edge and is exposed on a finished hem.

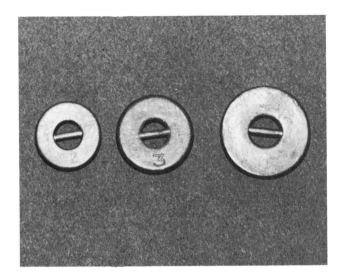

Lead Disc Weights

A square or round lead disk in any one of a variety of weights and sizes.

- To establish and hold drape of cowls.
- To control drape of hem.
- To prevent a hem area from shifting.
- To hold hem detail in place.
- At the front corners of facing on hem of jackets.
- At lower edge of pleats and slashed openings.
- To control and improve drape of garment.

Weights may be purchased with fabric covering or may be covered with a self or lighter weight fabric.

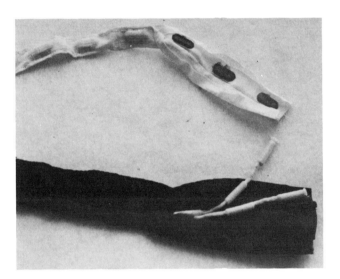

Lead Pellet Weights

A lead-pellet string encased in a fabric or uncovered, made in a variety of weights and sizes.

- To obtain a uniformly weighted hem.
- To add weight and body to hem of lightweight garments.
- At edge of exaggerated bell or kabuki sleeves.
- To prevent:
  - A garment hem from shifting;
  - A garment from riding up on body.
- To control and improve drape of garment.

18 ~ Basting

Diagonal Basting / Tailor Basting
Even Basting
Machine Basting
Pin Basting
Press Basting
Slip Basting
Uneven Basting

Basting is a means of temporarily holding together two or more plies of fabric or trimming during various phases of garment construction.

It is used as a guide for sewing and to hold a garment together for fitting before the final hand or machine stitching.

Methods of basting and basting stitches are used to transfer construction symbols from the back to the face side of the fabric and to indicate guidelines.

The type of basting stitches and processes selected depends on:
- Placement of construction techniques
- Purpose of temporary stitch
- Placement of final stitch
- Type and weight of fabric
- Method of production and manufacturing

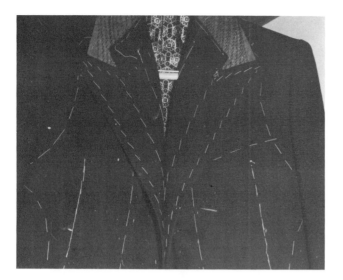

Diagonal Basting / Tailor Basting

An even or uneven stitch taken at an angle to the direction of the grain or seam, producing a pattern of parallel slanting lines.

- To hold several layers of fabric together.
- During any construction procedure where facings and interfacings are part of the tailoring process.
- Where seams are turned to the underside of garment section.
- On collars, lapels, cuffs, pockets, facings, interfacings, and linings.
- To hold turned edges flat and in place before pressing.
- To hold buttonhole strips together during construction process.
- While machine stitching to prevent slippage of garment section or seams on satin, napped, or pile fabrics.
- To hold underlining or backing to garment fabric.
- To hold edges of faced openings together.

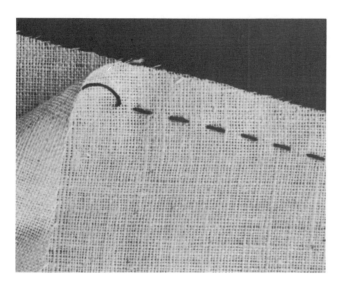

Even Basting

A series of hand stitches where the length and spacing of the stitch are each 1/4 inch (6.4 mm).

- To join and fit parts of the garment.
- On seams where there will be some strain in fitting.
- To hold seams, darts, collars, necklines, or sleeves together before final stitching.
- On curved seams and seams with ease.
- To hold interfacing and facing in place before stitching.
- To hold lining in position before hand or machine stitching.
- As a guide when machine stitching.

Worked so that the stitches are easily removed after permanent stitching.

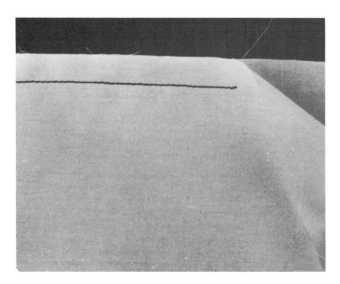

Machine Basting

The joining of garment sections using an easily removable chainstitch or a row of single needle lockstitches sewn with decreased thread tension and increased stitch length.

- On some fabrics as an alternative to hand basting.
- Only on firm and hard fabrics that will not be marred by the machine stitching.
- As a means of marking.

Not recommended for pile, silk or satin fabrics as needle marks remain on the fabric.

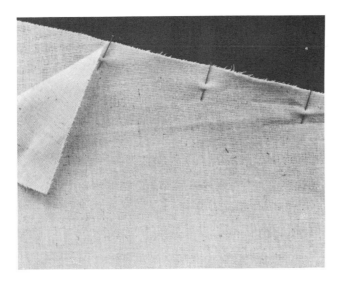

Pin Basting

A process of joining seams or garment sections by pinning. Pins are placed perpendicular to the seam line at regular intervals.

- As a preliminary method of holding two or more fabrics together before thread basting.
- To position trimming.
- To keep layers of fabric from shifting while being basted or machine stitched.
- When pinned section is to be immediately machine stitched.
- When the fit of the garment is assured.

Press Basting

The process of creasing a seam edge by ironing or finger pressing.

- To turn under edges of hems or seams before thread basting or stitching.
- To turn under seam edges before top stitching.
- In conjunction with a hem or sleeve guide.
- On straight edges as a guide for subsequent sewing operations.

Used only on lengthgrain straight edges as crossgrain, bias, or curved edges will stretch.

Slip Basting

A series of hand stitches alternating between the folded seam edge of one ply and the folded seam edge or seam line of another ply.

- To match seams, stripes, plaids, checks, or border print fabrics on the face of the garment.
- To baste fittings and alterations on the right side of the garment.
- To attach sleeves to armholes when garments are fitted on the body or model form.
- To join intricately curved seams or difficult construction details from the right side of the garment.
- To position lining in place.

When joining process is complete, the seam resembles even basting and the stitching produces a flat seam on the inside.

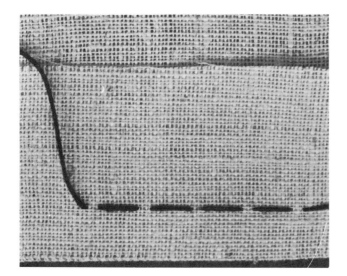

Uneven Basting

A series of hand stitches about 1/2 inch (12.7 mm) in length and at 1/8 inch (3.2 mm) intervals.

- Where there is little or no strain of the garment parts.
- As a guide line for inserts or placement of trimmings.
- To hold hemline in place before final stitching.
- In place of thread tracing to indicate grain and style lines.
- To attach underlining or backing to fabric.
- To hold interfacing, lining; pleats and folds in place.

May be used as a marking stitch.

Bias Hemming / Bias Facing
Bias Binding:
   Single-Fold Bias Binding
   Double-Fold Bias Binding
Cording / Corded Piping
French Piping / French Binding
Tubing:
   Cord-Filled Bias Tubing
   Self-Filled Bias Tubing

Welt Piping / Piping
Bias Preparation Methods:
   Bias Prepared for Apparel Manufacturing
   Commercially Prepared Bias
   Self-Prepared Bias
Bias Application Methods:
   Bias Application with Binder Attachment Set
   Bias Application with Binder Foot Attachment
   Bias Application without Attachment

Bias is prepared as a strip of matching or contrasting fabric. In construction it is used to conceal, finish, and strengthen seams and raw edges or as a substitute for facings. Bias may be used as decorative binding, piping, or tubing.

Bias for binding, piping, and tubing is a *true bias* and is defined as the diagonal line established by a 45° angle, intersecting length- and crossgrain of a square. The bias of the fabric offers the greatest stretch, flexibility, and elasticity needed to conform to a curved edge.

Bias may be self-prepared, specially manufactured for industry, or commercially prepared and purchased in retail stores.

Commercially prepared, precut, and folded bias bindings are also known as *bias tape* or *bias fold*. They are available in a variety of widths and in fabrics of cotton, silk, synthetics and blends.

The type, width, and placement of bias selected depends on:
• Style and design of garment
• Type of garment
• Use of garment
• Care of garment
• Choice of fabric
• Method of construction
• Availability of machines and attachments
• Procedure for production

Bias Hemming / Bias Facing

A commercially or self-prepared bias strip of fabric, approximately 2 inches (5 cm) in finished width. A prefolded 1/4 inch (6.4 mm) seam allowance on both sides included.

- As a stay for French shirring or gathering.
- To eliminate the bulk in hem of garments made of heavy fabrics.
- To replace hem fold when altering the length of garments.
- On hems where stretch and flexibility of hem area is necessary.
- As a decorative band on face of garments.
- To make a casing.

May be folded in half and used as binding. Commercially prepared bias available in natural or synthetic fiber fabrics.

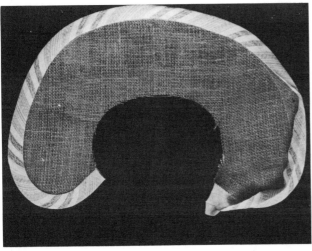

Single-Fold Bias Binding

A commercially prepared fabric strip which includes a prefolded 1/4 inch (6.4 mm) seam allowance on each side, or a self-prepared strip measured to include the desired finished width plus two seam allowances.

- Instead of facing on children's and infants' wear; garments made of sheer fabrics, where the size and shape of facing would detract from appearance of the garment.
- Instead of facing to reduce bulk.
- To conceal collar and neckline edges.
- As a carrier for boning or stays in strapless garments.
- As a casing for elastic and drawstrings.
- As a stay to tape and strengthen curved seam line.
- As a stay at waistline or on waistline seam.
- To strap and reinforce curved seams of crotch and sleeve underarm.
- On curved hems to conceal raw edge.
- To finish neckline and sleeveless garment edges.
- To finish hem edge of sleeves.
- To enclose hem edge.

May be pre-shaped by steaming and/or stretching to conform to curved edge. Commercially prepared bias is available in natural and synthetic fiber fabrics.

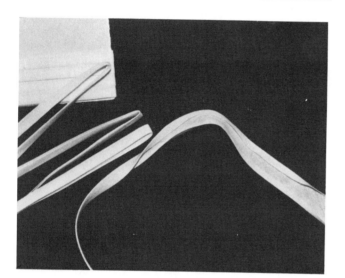

Double-Fold Bias Binding

1. A commercially prepared fabric strip, 2 inches (5 cm) or less in finished width with two pre-folded 1/4 inch (6.4 mm) seam allowances, includes a slightly off center fold line.
2. A self-prepared strip measured and folded to include the desired finish width and seam allowances.

- As a finish on seam edges to prevent raveling.
- To enclose raw seam edges on fabrics that irritate the body.
- To enclose raw hem edges for bound hem finishes.
- To enclose hem edges as decorative finishes.
- To enclose collar, cuff and pocket edges for decorative finishes.
- To finish pocket openings.
- To finish neckline and slash openings.
- To conceal unfinished edges of lace, trimmings, and ruffles.
- To bind waistline seams.

Pre-shaped by steaming and/or stretching to conform to curved edges. Commercially prepared bias available in natural or synthetic fiber structures.

Cording / Corded Piping

A commercially or self-prepared bias strip stitched to enclose a cord filler, and produced with a seam allowance.

- As a design detail to show on face of garment.
- To produce a dimensional effect to piping.
- At waistline seam instead of belt or sash.
- As a decorative effect for seams of collars, cuffs and pockets.
- To emphasize princess line seam.
- To add body and stiffness for a standout effect at hem edge.
- To outline and emphasize bands applied to garment part or section.

Commercially prepared cording. Available in a variety of fabrics, weaves and filler sizes.

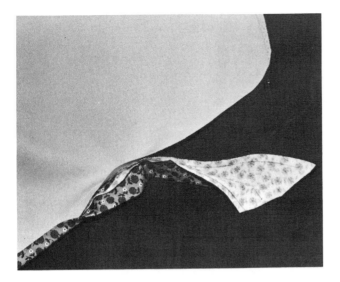

French Piping / French Binding

A folded bias strip stitched through both seam allowances to the garment edge and when doubled back conceals the raw edges to produce a welt.

- As a finish on sheer or transparent fabrics.
- As a trimming or decorative finish for necklines, armholes, sleeve edges, pockets, and hemlines.
- To finish edge of scallop design.
- To provide a firm and dimensional edge to garments.
- To finish edges which show on both sides.
- As a decorative finish on lingerie and children's wear.
- To finish top edge of strapless garments.
- To bind and finish edge of lace.
- To conceal the gathered edge of ruffles.

May be referred to as *book edge finish* in some production rooms.

Cord-Filled Bias Tubing

A commercially or self-prepared bias strip enclosing a cord which when stitched and turned produces a stuffed, clean-finished tubing.

- To add body and firmness to tubing.
- As spaghetti straps; ties, belts and bows; belt carriers; lacings; drawstrings.
- For continuous or individual loop closures.
- To make corded ball buttons and frog closures.
- To form and outline appliqué design.

Commercially prepared tubing is available in a variety of fabrics, weaves, and diameters.

Self-Filled Bias Tubing

A commercially or self-prepared bias strip which when stitched and turned produces a self-stuffed, clean-finished tubing.

- For finished straps made of sheer and transparent fabrics.
- As button loops; belt carriers; ties, belts and bows; spaghetti straps; lacings; drawstrings.
- To make corded ball buttons and frog closures.

Commercially prepared tubing is available in a variety of fabrics, weaves and diameters.

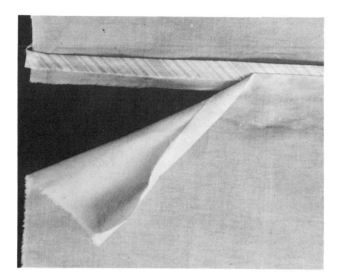

Welt Piping / Piping

A folded bias strip, available in a variety of widths of the same or contrasting fabric, inserted between the plies of the seam, to show on the face of the garment.

- For decorative effect of seam edge.
- At waistline seam instead of belt or sash.
- To trim a convex or concave scalloped edge.
- As an insert for emphasis in tier-seamed garments.
- To accentuate and add decorative detail to hemline of garment.
- To add design detail and point of interest to garments made of striped, checkered or plaid fabrics.
- To outline and emphasize bands applied to garment parts.

Prepared in advance and then stitched into seam.

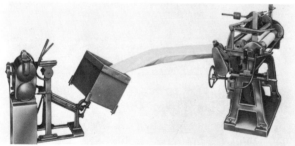

Cloth sewn into tubular form

Bias Prepared for Apparel Manufacturer

Bias produced by a series of machines in a multi-step operation. The cloth is automatically sewn into tubular form, made into bias-cut tubular cloth, wound into rolls, and slit into specific widths.

- By apparel manufacturers coordinating bias trim to garment fabric and design.
- On reels in conjunction with binder attachment set for application to garment.

Cut in widths from 1/2 to 3 inches (1.3 to 7.6 cm) and prepared with or without a center fold.

Bias-cut tubular cloth wound into rolls

Manual single knife slitter

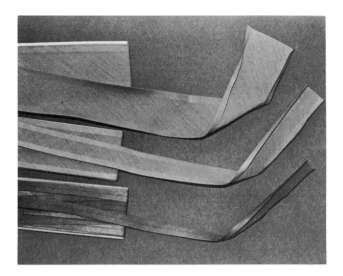

Commercially Prepared Bias

Bias produced by a series of machines in a multi-step operation. The cloth is automatically sewn into tubular form, made into bias-cut tubular cloth, wound into rolls, slit into specific widths, and prepared with 1/4 inch (6.4 mm) prefolded edges or with prefolded edges and an off-center fold.

- Where garment and bias fabric characteristic need not correspond.
- On a single or sample garment or for mass production.

Prepared in packaged form as a notion. Available for industrial use in volume yardage on reels; in finished widths from 1/4 to 3 inches (0.6 to 7.6 cm); as single-fold binding, wide single-fold binding, or hem facing.

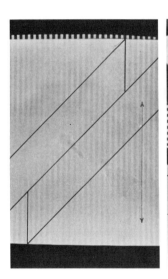

Self-Prepared Bias

1. A bias strip cut from a lay of cloth following lines established directly on true bias of fabric.
2. A bias strip using commercial pattern pieces or paper draft with 45° lines on a planned layout.

- When cutting a single or sample garment where bias trim is made of the same or contrasting fabric.

Width of bias planned with regard to placement, design and/or effect desired.

Bias Application with Binder Attachment Set

A binder set consisting of: feed dog, regular or compensating binding foot, and funnel-shaped feeder attached to throat plate or machine bed. Set is designed to roll and fold both sides of the reel-fed bias forming a piping-enclosed garment edge as plies are guided beneath needle in one operation.

- To apply bias to edge or top work on mass-produced garments where piecework methods are employed.

Funnel feeder is designed for a specific bias width. Funnel feeder is designed to apply bias in single- or double-fold application.

Bias may be applied as a round or flat finish.

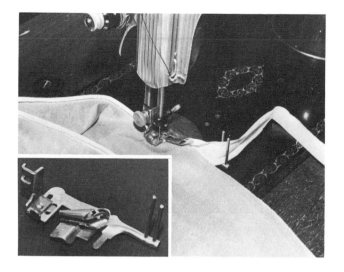

Bias Application with Binder Foot Attachment

A plate with a funnel-shaped feeder fixed to a shank to be attached to presser bar. Plate is designed to fold reel-fed or self-prepared bias over and enclose garment edge as plies are guided beneath needle.

- To apply bias for edge or top work on mass-produced garments where piecework methods are employed.
- On single or sample garments where many yards of fabric will be bound.

Foot is designed for specific use with regard to the class and type of home or industrial machine.

Plate is designed with or without guides for directing bias.

Prefolded commercially prepared bias may be used with attachment foot.

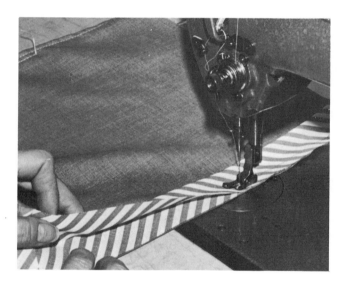

Bias Application without Attachment

A method of applying commercially or self-prepared bias strips to a garment edge or area in one or more steps by machine and/or hand stitching.

- On single or sample garments where choice of application depends upon garment, fabric, design and/or effect desired.

20 ~ Casing

Casing with Drawstring
Casing with Elastic
Casing with Heading
Inside Applied Casing
Outside Applied Casing
Self Casing

A casing is a fold-over edge or applied strip which is an intregal part of the garment.

Casings are established at the edge of garments or span seam or style lines and may be constructed on unfitted and/or one-piece garments.

A casing encloses a drawstring or an elastic to draw in the garment circumference to fit corresponding body areas. They are utilized on garments designed to accommodate more than one size. A casing is planned 1/4 inch (6.4 mm) wider than the elastic or drawstring.

Drawstring may be made of cord, braid, ribbon, leather strip or fabric tubing.

Elastic may be ribbon or rib-type, or webbing.

The type or method of application for casings selected depends on:

• Style and design of garment
• Use of garment
• Care of garment
• Type and weight of fabric
• Type and width of drawstring or elastic

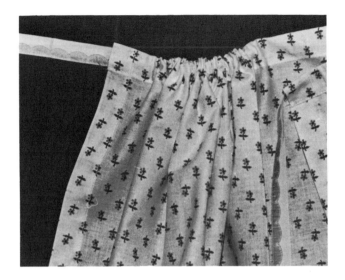

Casing with Drawstring

A self or applied casing enclosing a drawstring.

- To allow wearer to control garment circumference for body comfort.
- On waistlines of skirts, pants, shorts, blouses, and jackets.
- To draw in predetermined fullness.
- To change style effect by allowing drawstring manipulation at necklines, sleeves, waistline area of one-piece garments, and waistline of upper-torso garments.

Drawstring may be cord, braid, ribbon, leather strip or fabric tubing. It may be planned to emerge on inside or outside of garment; from openings such as eye slits, buttonholes, machine-worked or metal eyelets, grommets, or seam openings.

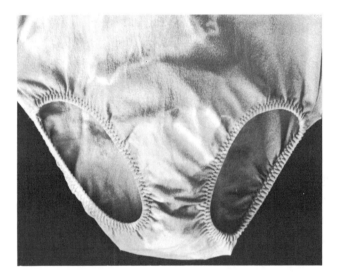

Casing with Elastic

A self or applied casing enclosing an elastic.

- On children's wear to facilitate ease in dressing.
- To support a garment on a figure with no waistline indentation.
- On waistline of garments made of knit or stretch fabrics eliminating need for placket and band.
- On waistlines of skirts, pants or shorts; garments covering the upper torso; blouson bodice.
- On upper edge of strapless garments.
- On necklines allowing adjustable style effects.
- At lower edge of sleeve and pants legs; camisoles.

Elastic may be ribbon or rib type or webbing; available in various widths.

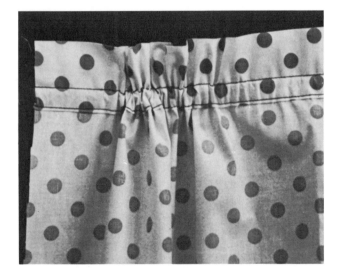

Casing with Heading

A self or applied casing established a measured distance from the finished edge. Forms an edging when elastic or drawstring is enclosed.

- To create a ruffled edge.
- On waistlines of skirts, pants, and shorts.
- On waistlines of blouses and jackets.
- On edges of sleeves, pant legs, and hoods.
- On neckline of garments.
- On sheer, light and medium weight fabrics.

Width of heading and casing determined by design of garment and effect desired.

Inside Applied Casing

A separate strip of fabric applied to the inside of the garment either at an edge or the span of a seam or style line.

- On curved edges.
- Instead of self-casing on garments made of thick or bulky fabrics.
- A measured distance from the edge of the garment to create a ruffle, flounce, or peplum.
- To encase boning.

Strip may be ribbon, bias tape; or of the same or lighter weight contrasting fabric.

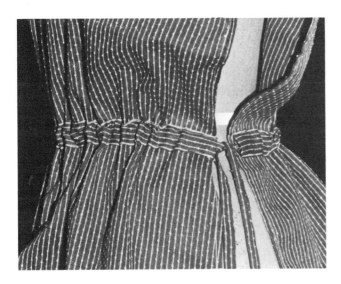

Outside Applied Casing

A separate strip of fabric applied to the face of the garment either at an edge or the span of a seam or style line.

- To emphasize a design element.
- A measured distance from the edge of the garment to create a ruffle, flounce, or peplum.

Strip may be ribbon, bias tape, or of the same or contrasting fabric.

Self Casing

A fold-over, machine-stitched finish at the edge of a garment section.

- On straight edges and shallow curves.
- On waistlines of skirts, pants, and shorts.
- On waistlines of blouses and jackets.
- On edge of sleeves, pants legs, and hoods.
- On shallow neckline curve of peasant blouse or garment.
- On sheer, light or medium weight fabrics.

Width of self casing is determined by design of garment and effect desired.

Decorative Elastic Band
Elastic Braid / Ribbon Braid / Rib-Type Braid
Elastic Ribbon / Non-Roll Ribbed Elastic
Elastic Cord
Elastic Edging
Elastic Thread

Elastic Webbing
Elastic in a Casing
Elastic Sewn to Garment
Elastic for Lingerie
Elastic for Swimwear

Elastic is a product processed from rubber or a synthetic substance which is cut, extruded or rolled into cores, wrapped, and braided or woven; or may be produced in flat, thin uncovered bands or strips.

Elastic is thread, cord, braided or woven ribbon or fabric which has resilience and flexibility. The stretchable core substance is covered with cotton, silk, synthetic or yarn blends.

Amount of stretchability in elastic is determined by fiber content, size of core, method of weaving or braiding, and finished width.

Elastic is identified by the core and/or yarn from which it is produced, its methods of construction, and/or its intended use.

Webbing or woven elastic of firm or soft construction retains original width when stretched; braided elastic becomes narrower when stretched.

Both types of elastic may be applied to garments in any of a variety of methods. Elastic may be applied directly to garment by a lockstitch, zig-zag or overedge machine or may be enclosed in a casing.

Pajamas, lingerie, intimate apparel, and swimwear require special purpose elastics.

Elasticized shirring is made with multiple rows of elastic thread.

The type of elastic selected depends on:
• Construction of garment
• Width of elastic
• Fiber content of fabric
• Gripping power of elastic
• Weight compatibility to fabric
• Type and style of garment
• Use of garment
• Care of garment
• Figure type and size range

Face of Garment

Inside of Garment

Decorative Elastic Band

Woven or braided strip 1 to 2 1/2 inches (2.5 to 6.4 cm) in finished width, cut to a predetermined length and applied to draw in a garment edge.

- On knit or woven fabrics.
- At waistline, end of sleeve and bottom of pants leg.
- As an inset waistband.
- On an unfitted edge to draw in fullness.
- On garments spanning more than one size range.
- On a figure with no waistline indentation to support a garment.

Available in solid colors, prints or geometric designs. Degree of stretchability varies with the fiber, weave, and manufacturing method.

Elastic Braid / Ribbon Braid / Rib-Type Braid

A premeasured length of elastic, ribbon or rib-type braid applied to draw up a predetermined fullness to fit body measurements.

- Applied directly to garment.
- In a self or applied casing.
- Concealed in waistband for garments made of knit fabrics.
- As inside ply of waistband.
- On unfitted garments.
- On skirts and pants designed without darts.
- On garments designed without plackets.
- On garments spanning more than one size range.
- Instead of stable waistband to eliminate constriction.
- At garment edge or spanning garment section.

Elastic varies from 1/4 to 3 inches (0.6 to 7.65 cm) in width. Type and size of elastic chosen depends upon the style and fabric of garment. The degree of elasticity, type of yarn and hand produced in braid construction determine the intended use of braid such as for swimwear, lingerie, intimate apparel, and infants' clothing. Elastic is available in soft and hard stretch.

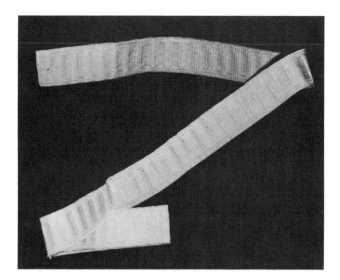

Elastic Ribbon / Non-Roll Ribbed Elastic

A rib patterned, non-curl resilient band, of rubber or synthetic core and natural or synthetic yarn woven and/or braided, 3/4 to 2 inches (1.9 to 5.1 cm) in width.

- In concealed waistbands for garments made of knit fabrics.
- As inside ply of waistbands.
- In a self or applied casing.
- Applied directly to garment.

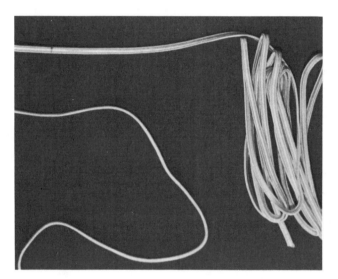

Elastic Cord

A round or oval gimp-covered core of elastic sewn directly to the garment or enclosed in the bite of patterned hand or machine stitches.

- A measured distance from garment edge of sleeve, pant leg or waist.
- To produce a ruffle or flounce effect.
- Singly where a delicate line of gathering is desired.
- On waistline of one-piece garments.
- On shift or tent garment to change style.
- On children's and infants' wear.
- Enclosed in patterned bite as base stitching for machine smocking.
- To produce elasticized shirring.

Available in a range of diameters and expandability.

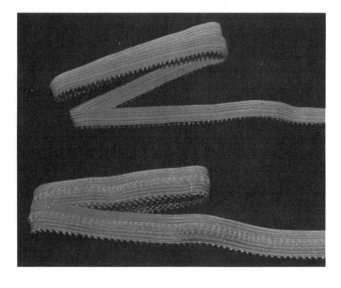

Elastic Edging

Yarn- or thread-covered elastic core woven, knitted or braided into a soft ribbon strip or band with a scalloped, picot or other decorative edge along one or both lengths.

- Where other elastic may interfere with comfort of garment.
- Where a casing is inapplicable.
- To finish garments made of knit or stretch fabrics.
- At edge of waist, neck, sleeve or leg openings.

May be applied on outside or inside of garment; to extend beyond garment edge. Made in widths up to 5/8 of an inch (1.6 cm).

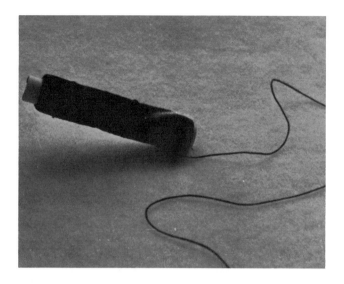

Elastic Thread

A stretchable thread consisting of a rubber core, wound and covered with cotton, synthetic, blended or metallic yarn.

- To produce elasticized shirring; waffle shirring; an elasticized waistline; shirred ribbon decorative waistband.
- Individually or in multiple rows.
- On garments designed to accommodate more than one size range.
- For tube tops and halters.

Amount of control for elasticized shirring or gathering is determined by length of stitch; type and expandability of elastic; number and spacing of parallel rows of stitching; and their interrelationship with the fabric.

Thread is used only in the bobbin of a lockstitch and zigzag machine. Thread is firm and pliable and the maximum stretch and recovery.

May be used to produce an expandable chain stitch.

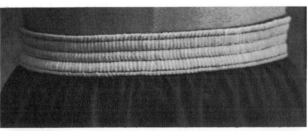

Elastic Webbing

A soft, resilient woven band, 3/4 to 1 1/4 inch (19 to 32 mm) in finished width, cut to a predetermined length.

- Applied directly to garment.
- On inside waistline of boxer shorts and pajamas.
- On garments spanning more than one size.
- To support a garment on a figure with no waistline indentation.
- To draw in complete or partial circumference of garment as design dictates.
- On children's and infants' wear.

Woven construction allows webbing to maintain original width when stretched.

May be referred to as *pajama webbing*.

Elastic in a Casing

A self or applied casing enclosing a premeasured elastic, which draws in a predetermined fullness of a garment section or design detail to correspond to a specified body measurement.

- On waistline of skirts, pants or shorts; garments covering the upper torso; blouson bodice; garments made of knit or stretch fabric eliminating need for placket and band.
- On upper edge of strapless garment.
- On upper and lower edges of camisoles.
- At neckline to allow for different style effects.
- On lower edge of sleeve or pants leg.
- A measured distance from sleeve or pants leg edge to create a ruffled end.
- On children's wear to facilitate ease in dressing.
- To support a garment on a figure with no waistline indentation.

Elastic may be braid, rib type or webbing. Casing may be applied to face or inside of garment.

Elastic Sewn to Garment

Premeasured elastic applied to garment.

- To draw up a predetermined fullness to fit a smaller corresponding body measurement.
- On waistline area of shift or tent silhouette to change the style.
- At waistline of one-piece garments.
- On jumpsuits and rompers.
- At waistline edge of skirts, pants or shorts; blouse or jacket.
- As finished edging on intimate wear and lingerie.
- A measured distance from sleeve or pant leg edge, to create ruffled end.

Elastic may be applied by zigzag or overedge machine. Elastic cord may be encased within zigzag machine stitches. Film of elastic or webbing may be attached by multiple rows of parallel stitching.

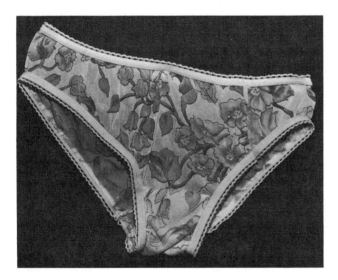

Elastic for Lingerie

Thread-covered elastic core woven, knitted or braided into a soft strip or band in a variety of widths and patterns.

- At waistline of petticoats and intimate apparel.
- At leg opening of intimate wear.
- As edging on brassieres and girdles; on body suits.
- On infants' and children's wear.
- At a measured distance from garment edge.

May be woven with picot finish along one or both lengths. Made in stretchable lace patterns. Elastic is softer resulting in a less constrictive garment.

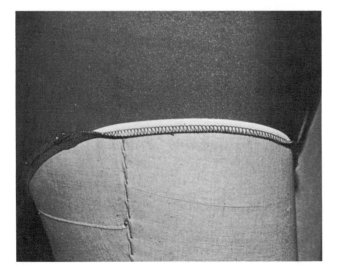

Elastic for Swimwear

Nylon- or polyester-covered synthetic rubber core braided or woven into band or ribbon with or without a decorative edge.

- On swimwear to retain resilience when wet.
- Applied directly to garment.
- Enclosed in a casing.
- As an edging at top, waist or leg of swimwear.

Elastic manufactured in widths and sizes for waist, leg, bra, and neckline of garment. Width of elastic chosen by location of application to garment.

Rayon unsuitable for swimwear as it "wets out."

Bias Facing
Combination Shaped Facing / All-In-One
    Shaped Facing
Outside Facing
Self Facing / Extended Facing / One-Piece Facing
Shaped Facing

Facing is a means by which the raw edges of a garment are finished with the same, contrasting or lighter weight fabric.

Facings are composed of one or more sections joined to span seamed or darted parts of the garment and are cut to fit or conform to the edge they will finish. They are identified as shaped, extended or bias facings.

They are usually applied to lie flat on the *inside* of the garment, but may be applied to lie on the *face* of the garment producing a decorative finish.

Facings are found on necklines with or without collars, front and back openings, sleeveless armholes, waistlines, and lower edges of garments.

The type and application of facing selected depends on:
• Style and design of garment
• Purpose and use of garment
• Care of garment
• Type and weight of fabric
• Methods of construction techniques

Bias Facing

A true bias strip of fabric, commercially or self-prepared, approximately 3 inches (7.6 cm) or less in width, which is folded and molded to conform to a curved edge.

- As a substitute for shaped and fitted facings of garments.
- As a waistline facing where a visible waistline band is not desired.
- To face a curved slot seam.
- Instead of facing on a collared neckline.
- To finish edges of slashed openings.
- On garments made of sheer fabrics where other facings would detract from the appearance of the garment.
- Instead of other facings on heavy fabrics to eliminate bulk.
- At waistline of pants, skirts or jackets.

May be used as a form of decorative trim on the face of the garment.

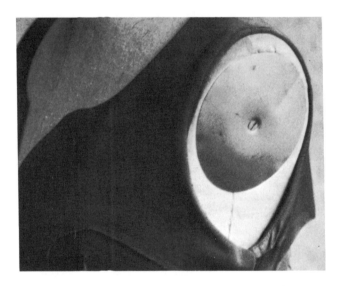

Combination Shaped Facing / All-In-One Shaped Facing

A facing unit cut and shaped to conform to a garment area which has more than one edge to be clean-finished.

- To reduce bulk.
- When separate facings would overlap.
- When facing for garment would be too narrow.
- At neckline and armhole combinations for halters, vests and boleros.

Outside Facing

A shaped, one-piece, bias or bias tape facing planned to be visible on the face of the garment.

- As a decorative functional finish.
- To conceal raw edges.

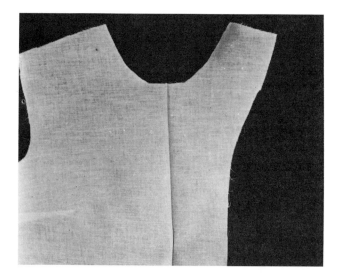

Self Facing / Extended Facing / One-Piece Facing

A facing unit cut as an integral part of a garment section which folds back to fit and conform to the remaining area and edges.

- On straight-edged closures or finishes.
- To avoid seam line produced by joining separate facings.
- To reduce bulk due to seam line when making garments of heavy fabrics.
- To eliminate distortion of edge on garments made of knit fabrics.
- On garments made of sheer fabrics, where the seam would detract from the appearance of the garment.

Shaped Facing

Fabric cut in the same shape and grain as the garment area and edge to be finished.

- To maintain shape and avoid distortion of garment areas and edges.
- To prevent stretching of edges.
- On waistlines of skirts, pants or trousers.
- On contoured waistbands.
- On curved or irregularly shaped edges.

Facing width is determined by type of opening or edge.

Buckle:
  Buckle
  Concealed Hook Buckle
  Covered Buckle
  Clasp / Interlocking Buckle
  Hook & Eye Buckle / Anchor Buckle
  Overall Buckle
  Spring-and-Hook Type Buckle / Ratchet Buckle
Dog Leash Fastener
Drawstring
Eyelet:
  Hand-Worked Eyelet
  Metal Eyelet
Frog
Fur Tack
Grommet
Hook:
  Hook
  Bra & Swimsuit Hook
  Hook & Bar (Prong)
  Hook & Bar (Sew-On)

Hook & Eye:
  Hook & Eye
  Covered Hook & Eye
  Gimp-Covered Hook & Eye / Fur Hook & Eye
  Hook & Eye Tape
Hook & Loop:
  Hook & Loop Fastener / Velcro® Fastener
  Hook & Loop Tape / Velcro® Tape
Lacing
Paired Rings
Snap:
  Snap
  Covered Snap
  Hammer-On Snap / No-Sew Snap
  Hammer-On Snap Tape / No-Sew Snap Tape
  Snap Tape
Suspender Clip
Tab
Thread Eye
Ties
Toggle

Fasteners are used to hold garment sections closed, in place, or together. They are designed for a variety of specific or special holding purposes. Functional closures may be designed with concealed or surface-type fasteners.

Fasteners are used for decorative as well as functional purposes. They may be used at the discretion of the designer as a focal point in designing, to add originality, and to enhance the look of the garment.

The type of fastener selected depends on:
• Style and design of garment
• Type of garment
• Type of garment closure
• Use of garment
• Care of garment
• Placement and position of fastener
• Method of application
• Weight, type and texture of fabric.

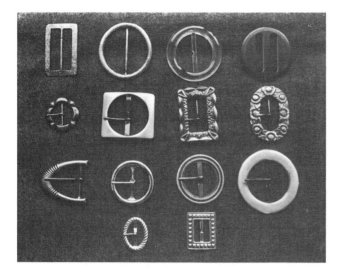

Buckle

A device, in a variety of sizes and shapes, consisting of an open rim having a single or center bar, with or without a prong.

- To close an attached or unattached belt.
- To anchor free ends of tab on sleeves, shoulders, and pockets.
- As a design detail for garment closure.

Available in a variety of materials with or without fabric covering.

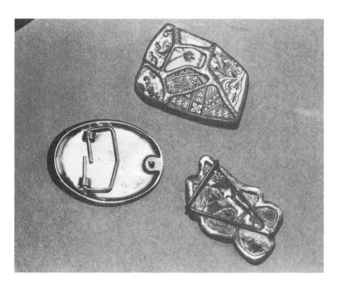

Concealed Hook Buckle

A plate, in a variety of sizes and shapes, designed with a concealed hook or clip at one end, and a bar through which the belt is attached at the other end.

- To close an attached or unattached belt.
- To anchor free ends of tab on sleeves, shoulders, and pockets.
- As a design detail for garment closure.

Face of buckle may be designed or adorned in a variety of details and materials.

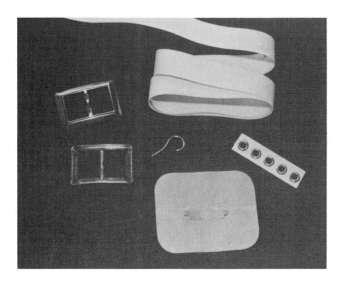

Covered Buckle

A two-piece buckle form or mold; the top section is covered with a ply or plies of fabric or other material and clamped into a corresponding base section.

- To match or complement garment fabric.
- To accentuate or contrast garment fabric.
- To correspond buckle with matching trim.
- As a design feature.

Available in a kit. Kit contains adhesive sheets for stabilizing and strengthening fabric for covering. Kit is available with belting strips and eyelets.

Buckles are available with or without a prong; in a variety of sizes, shapes and widths.

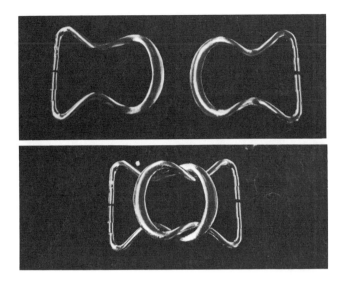

Clasp / Interlocking Buckle

A pair of circular, square or oblong shapes, made of metal, plastic or wood. Shapes allow interlocking when one is slipped through the other.

- On coats and jackets.
- On belts and tabs.

Available in a variety of sizes.

Hook & Eye Buckle / Anchor Buckle

A two-piece metal fastener consisting of a hook and opposing opening, both designed with aperture for attaching.

- On end of belts or tabs.
- On outerwear and sportswear for garment closure.

Available in a variety of shapes, sizes, and weights.

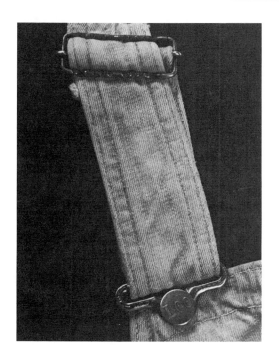

Overall Buckle

A two-piece fastener composed of a metal rim, with one side designed for attaching to the garment and the other shaped to engage the shank of an opposing pivot button.

- To fasten suspender or strap of overall to bib section.
- On shoulder straps of sportswear similar to overalls.
- On aprons, children's wear.

Fastening rim made in a variety of widths to accommodate straps of different widths.

A strap-adjusting bar buckle is used in conjunction with overall buckle.

Spring-and-Hook Type Buckle / Ratchet Buckle

A two-piece metal fastener consisting of a hinged spring clip and a hinged opposing plate. The hinged plate has one or more openings, any one of which allows the clip to pass through and snap back to secure the closure. Both pieces of the fastener are designed with a prong for attachment to garment.

- On rain gear and slickers for civilian, military and professional use.
- On active sportswear and outerwear as a functional and/or decorative fastener.

Plate may be designed with up to five openings for adjustability.

Grommet opening may be used instead of the hinged opposing plate.

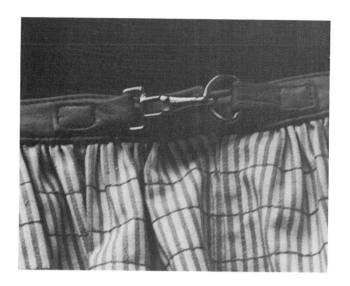

Dog Leash Fastener

A two-piece metal fastener consisting of a metal bar with a hooked end, closed by a spring clip to form a complete loop, and an opposing opening. Both designed with aperture for attachment to garment.

- To close a belt.
- In place of toggles on sportswear and rain gear.
- To hold belt to belt loop or carrier.
- In conjunction with a half-belt attached to waistline of the garment.

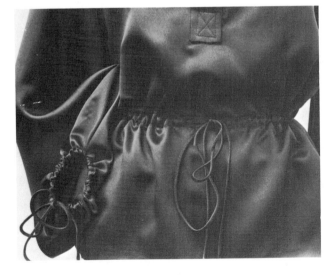

Drawstring

A long narrow strip, which when pulled through a casing on the garment, gathers or draws in garment circumference.

- On hoods.
- On lower end of sleeves or pants.
- At lower and upper edges of camisoles.
- At waistline of upper and/or lower torso garments.
- At empire, waistline or hipline of one-piece garments.
- To create blouson.
- To change style effect by allowing drawstring manipulation of garment at neckline, sleeve, and bodice waistlines.
- On sportswear such as windbreakers and sweatshirts.
- On ski wear and swimwear.

Drawstring is designed longer than flattened casing or garment section. It may be made of cord, braid, ribbon, leather strip, or fabric tubing. Drawstring is planned to emerge on inside or outside of garment; from openings such as eye slits, buttonholes, machine-worked or metal eyelets, grommets, or seam openings.

Drawstring allows for flexibility and individual control of circumference adjustment.

Hand-Worked Eyelet

A circular opening made with an awl, stiletto or mechanical punch, and worked with buttonhole twist in a series of closely worked buttonhole or blanket stitches.

- As an opening to accommodate lacing; cuff links or studs.
- To accommodate loop shank of button attached by a separate clip.
- On belts with a pronged buckle.
- On fine or delicate fabrics.

Metal Eyelet

A round or square metal tube, with an opening of approximately 1/4 inch (6.4 mm), which when applied to garment forms a flattened rimmed opening.

- To make a reinforced opening.
- To prevent openings from stretching out of shape.
- As decorative design detail.
- To accommodate lacing.
- On belts with pronged buckle.
- Instead of metal eye for hook closure.

Metal may be nickel, gilt-finished anodized aluminum, and enameled brass. Available in kits (with or without buckle and belt) or packaged units. Applied with hammer and attaching tool or eyelet setter.

Frog

A two-piece closure consisting of a loop and a Chinese ball button. Closure is formed by the twisting, plaiting, interlocking or looping of cord, soutache or bias fabric tubing.

- As a decorative closure.
- To accentuate closure details.
- To accentuate ethnic-styled garments.

May be purchased ready-made or may be self-prepared. Available in a variety of shapes and sizes.

Fur Tack

A two-piece fastener consisting of snaps, clasp or clip which has been concealed within a decorative shell.

- To hold separate collar or fur piece to coat or jacket.
- To fasten opposing ends of a fur piece.

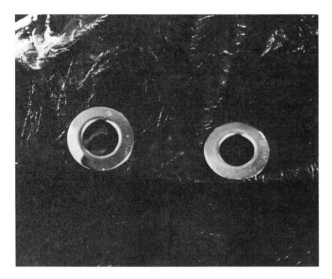

Grommet

A metal tube, in any of a variety of shapes and sizes, which when applied to garment forms a flattened rimmed opening.

- To finish and strengthen punched openings.
- To make reinforced openings for lacing, thick tubing, and cord.
- On non-overlapping closures such as opposing ends of belts, midriffs, waist-cinchers, and corselettes.
- As opening to accommodate scarf, ribbon or belt.
- In conjunction with rachet buckle.
- On belts for wide or square prong of buckle.
- As decorative design detail.

Applied with hammer and attaching tool or grommet setter.

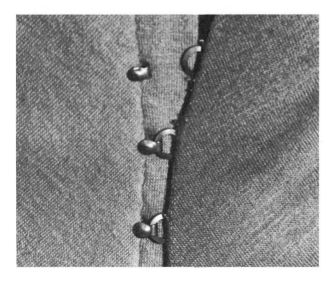

Hook

A metal fastener shaped into an engaging hook consisting of a bill and a base and designed with openings for attaching to garment.

- Paired with metal eyelets openings, metal loops or metal eye.
- In conjunction with lacing.
- As a lap or buttoned closure.
- As a decorative closure.
- On fitted garments where there may be a strain on the clothing.
- In a series to fasten an entire garment opening.
- As a closure for camisoles, corselettes, torsolettes, midriffs and foundation garments.

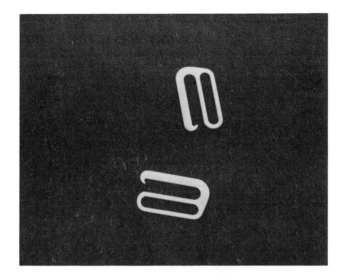

Bra & Swimsuit Hook

A flat metal or plastic plate, similar to an oblong rim buckle, designed with one open section, shaped so as to engage and hold an elastic or fabric loop.

- As a bra closure.
- For removable shoulder straps on lingerie and intimate apparel.
- On swimwear straps and closures.

Fastening rims are made in a variety of widths to accommodate straps of different sizes.

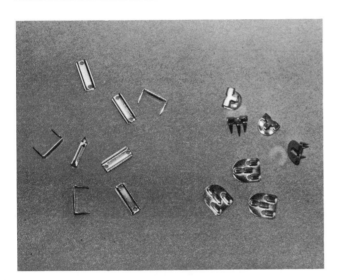

Hook & Bar (Prong)

A set of shaped metal plates, one of which is curved to form a broad hook or bill, the other a raised bar receptacle; both designed with prongs for attachment to garment.

- On heavyweight fabrics.
- On garments where there will be a maximum of strain.
- On waistbands of dungarees, trousers, and slacks.
- On lapped closures.
- On garments where easy snap-in retention is desired.
- On garments subject to harsh and excessive laundering.

Available in a variety of sizes, shapes, and weights.

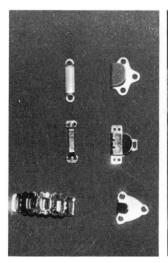 

Hook & Bar (Sew-On)

A set of shaped metal plates, one of which is curved to form a broad hook or bill, the other a raised bar receptacle; both designed with openings for attachment to garment.

- On lapped closures.
- On waistbands of skirts, shorts, pants, and trousers.
- On loosely woven fabrics.

Available in a variety of sizes, shapes and weights. Bar available with adjustable eye combinations.

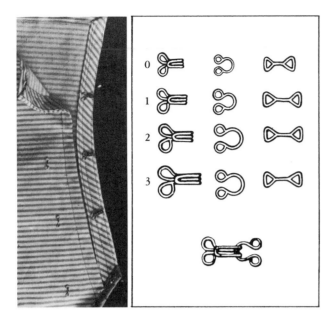

Hook & Eye

A set of wire fasteners, one of which is shaped into an engaging hook consisting of a bill and base and the other a receptacle eye formed into a bar or loop and base.

- Where there may be strain on the closure.
- At the top of zipper plackets.
- At a single point of garment opening such as neckline or waistline.
- In a series to fasten an entire garment opening.
- To close waistband of skirts or pants.
- On waistline stay.
- As a supplement to other fasteners.
- At waistline of dress; seam zipper closure.
- As a closure for foundation garments.

Finishes are brass, nickel or black-enameled coated metal.
    Straight eye intended for use on lap closures. Round eye intended for use on abutted edge.
    Sizes 00 to 3 for lightweight fabrics; sizes 3 to 5 for heavier or coarser fabrics.

Covered Hook & Eye

A set of wire fasteners, one of which is shaped into an engaging hook consisting of a bill and base and the other a receptacle eye formed into a bar or loop and base. The set is covered with a series of blanket or buttonhole stitches concealing the metal.

- Where metal of fastener would detract from the appearance of the garment.
- For an inconspicuous application on garments made of pile or napped fabrics.
- Where there may be strain on the closure.
- At top of zipper plackets.
- In a series to fasten entire garment opening.
- At a single point of garment opening such as neckline or waistline.
- As a supplement to other fasteners.
- On fine and lightweight fabrics.
- As a surface fastener for decorative purposes.

Various size hooks and eyes are selected for specific uses.

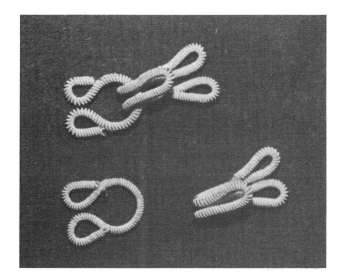

Gimp-Covered Hook & Eye /
Fur Hook & Eye

A set of wire fasteners, one of which is shaped into an engaging hook consisting of a bill and base, and the other a receptacle eye formed into a bar or loop and base. The set is covered with reinforced cord.

- Where metal of fastener would detract from appearance of the garment.
- On garments made of pile or napped fabric.
- On fur or fur-like fabrics.
- As a surface fastener for decorative purposes.

Size of hook is four times larger than the largest metal eye available.

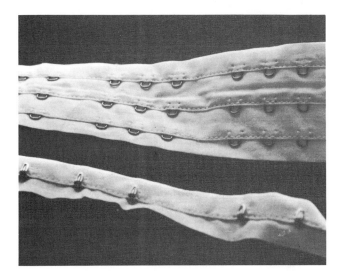

Hook & Eye Tape

A pair of tapes with opposing hook and eye attached at regular intervals.

- In areas where there is much strain.
- In the same manner as a zipper.
- In place of zipper closure.
- On foundation garments.
- In conjunction with zippers in swimwear, girdles, corselettes and other foundation garments.
- When multiple hook and eye application is desired.

Hook and eye tape relieves strain on zipper when garment is first closed and prevents zipper from becoming disengaged or broken because of excessive strain.

Tapes are available in a variety of widths; hooks and eyes in a variety of space intervals. Sold by the yard or cut to specific length to conform to a section of a garment.

Designed for lap or centered application. Base fastening of hook and eye may be concealed by additional fabric.

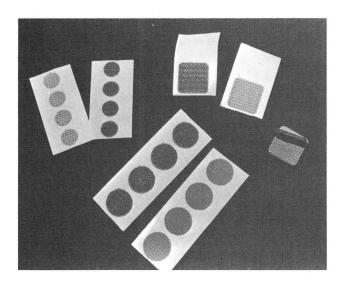

Hook & Loop Fastener / Velcro® Fastener

A woven nylon hook and loop fastener consisting of two mating units, in a variety of sizes and shapes; one unit is designed with minute flexible hooks and the other with many small soft loops.

- Instead of buttons, snaps, or hooks and eyes.
- On garment details such as detachable collars, cuffs, and trimmings.
- On lab coats and uniforms.
- On belts.
- On wrap-around garments.
- On garments to facilitate ease in dressing.
- When rapid removal of garment is desired.
- On closures in garments made for the handicapped.

When opposing units are pressed together, hooks engage loops forming a strong closure which opens when units are peeled apart.

Available in sew-on, iron-on or stick-on form.

Hook & Loop Tape / Velcro® Tape

A woven nylon hook and loop fastener consisting of two mating tapes; one tape is designed with minute flexible hooks and the other with many small soft loops.

- To form an adjustable closure.
- When a secure closure is desired.
- On civilian, military and professional clothing; protective clothing.
- On leg and neck wraps; belts.
- On garments to facilitate ease in dressing.
- When rapid removal of garment is desired.
- On closures in garments made for the handicapped.
- On garment details such as detachable collars, cuffs, and trimmings.
- As a substitute for other types of closures.

When opposing tapes are pressed together, hooks engage loops forming a strong closure which opens when tapes are peeled apart. Tapes are available by the yard or in strips in a variety of widths; as sew-on, iron-on, or stick-on.

Attached to end product by sewing, adhesive, dielectric, heat-activated ultrasonic and mechanical methods.

Lacing

Ribbon, cord, braid or tubing in which two free ends are pulled alternately through opposing eyelets, grommets or buttonholes, or under hooks.

- On belts, corselettes, midriffs, vests and tabards.
- On leggings and pants.
- As a decorative design detail.

Paired Rings

A pair of metal, plastic or wooden rings held together by a looped- and stitched-end of a belt. The rings function as a buckle when the free belt end is slipped through both and doubled back over the first and through the second.

- On raincoats, trench coats, and sportswear.
- On sleeves of outerwear.
- To tighten sleeve width.
- As a design feature.

Rings are available in a variety of sizes and shapes

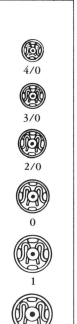

4/0

3/0

2/0

0

1

2

3

4

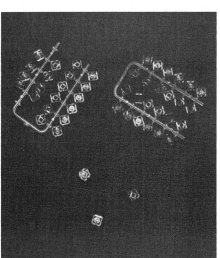

Snap

A pair of opposing circular or square plates, molded with mating ball and socket; both designed with openings for attachment to garment.

- On garments where there is little or no strain at the opening.
- Where a smooth flat closure is desired.
- In conjunction with buttons to hold lap of garment in place.
- In between buttons to prevent garment opening from gapping.
- Behind decorative buttons when there is no buttonhole.
- To fasten the topmost corner of an opening.
- In a fly-front concealed closure.
- In place of buttons and buttonholes on loosely fitted garments.
- As part of a lingerie strap holder.
- On removable dress shields and crotch linings.

Sizes 4/0 (0000) to 1/0 (0) are used on sheer and medium weight fabrics. Sizes 1 to 4 are used on heavier fabrics.

Snaps are available in nickel, brass, black-enameled coated metal; plastic or clear nylon. Clear or transparent plastic snap is used where a metal snap would detract from appearance of garment.

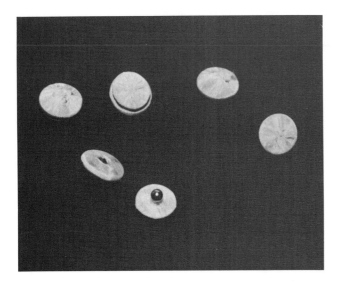

Covered Snap

A pair of opposing circular or square metal plates molded with mating ball and socket; both designed with openings for attachment to garment. Pair is covered with lightweight fabric that is color-matched to garment fabric; may be self-covered or ready-made.

- On fur and outerwear such as coats and jackets.
- On garment sections individually or in a series.
- On garments where the shine of the metal would detract from the appearance of the garment.

PARTS OF THE NO-SEW SNAP FASTENER

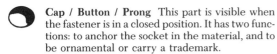 **Cap / Button / Prong** This part is visible when the fastener is in a closed position. It has two functions: to anchor the socket in the material, and to be ornamental or carry a trademark.

Socket The resilient member of the fastener. The stud snaps into it and thus performs the actual fastening operation.

Stud The portion of the fastener which engages the socket, and with it comprises the actual closure.

Post / Eyelet This is the very bottom part of the fastener when it is in a closed position, and serves only to anchor the stud in the material.

Screw Stud Stud equipped with screw—wood, machine, drive, or self-tapping thread—for use in metals, plastic or wood.

Reversible Stud / Gypsy Manufactured with an eyelet attached to make possible an assembly back-to-back with a socket or another stud, to make a double or reversible closure.

Nail Stud Assembled with a brad or nail for driving into soft material.

Rivet A specially designed single-pointed rivet for anchoring certain types of closures to the material. Used primarily on work clothing.

Staple A special double-pointed rivet for anchoring some types of closures to material. Used primarily on work clothing.

Rivet & Burr A metal reinforcement often used in place of a thread bar tack, or sometimes in addition to it.

Capped Post Cap shell and eyelet assembled. Ordinary post but designed to look like a cap. It is used on applications where the post will be visible, or where a reversible feature is desired.

Hammer-On Snap / No-Sew Snap

A pair of metal plates molded with mating ball and socket and designed with a pronged backing plate which cleats through all garment plies attaching snap section to garment.

- In place of buttons.
- On playclothes, children's wear and sleepwear.
- On sport clothes and work clothes.
- On jeans, overalls and trousers.
- On belts.
- As a fastener for outerwear and leather goods.
- On industrial or professional garments where other fasteners are not applicable.
- On garments to facilitate ease of dressing.

Face surface of snap may be decorative in size, shape or color.

May be purchased in packaged form with an applying tool or attaching plier; or in industrial quantities.

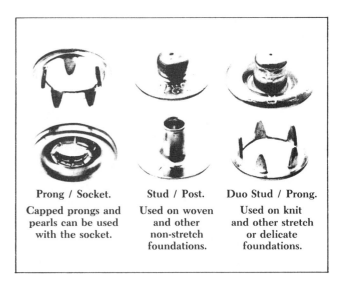

Prong / Socket.
Capped prongs and pearls can be used with the socket.

Stud / Post.
Used on woven and other non-stretch foundations.

Duo Stud / Prong.
Used on knit and other stretch or delicate foundations.

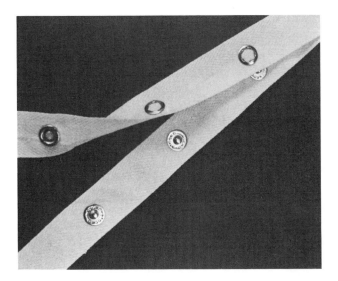

Hammer-On Snap Tape / No-Sew Snap Tape

A pair of woven tapes with opposing no-sew snaps attached at regular intervals.

- On children's wear and playwear.
- On inseam of pants.
- On garment sections that are to be detached for laundering.
- To eliminate need for individual snap application when multiple snaps are needed.
- On garments to facilitate ease of dressing.

Tapes are available in a variety of widths; snaps in a range of space intervals. Designed for lap applications.

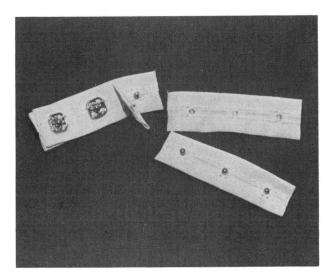

Snap Tape

A pair of woven tapes with opposing snaps attached at regular intervals.

- To eliminate need for individual snap application when multiple snaps are needed.
- On garments to facilitate ease in dressing.
- On placket openings.
- On lingerie and intimate apparel.
- On crotch of bodysuits.

Tapes are available in a variety of widths; snaps in a range of space intervals.

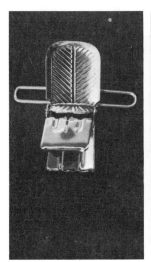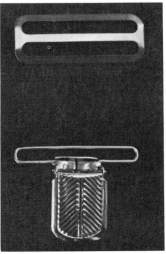

Suspender Clip

Two opposing, lightweight metal or plastic plates activated by a spring at hinged end to which a rim, designed to accommodate strap at band, is also fastened.

- To grip waistbands and waistlines.
- On straps and bands that support garment.

Fastening rim made in a variety of widths to accommodate straps of different widths.

A strap-adjusting bar buckle is used in conjunction with suspender clip.

Tab

A decorative strip, of a desired shape and size, made of self-fabric, folded tape, grosgrain ribbon, or strapping.

- To secure or fasten a button, buckle, no-sew snap or lacing.

A variety of designs may be made by twisting, plaiting or looping cord, from cut and sewn pieces of fabric, or combinations.

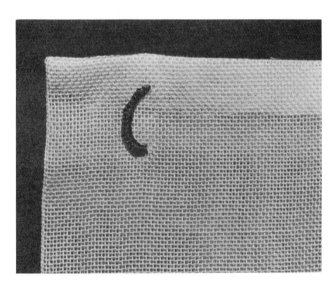

Thread Eye

A chain or thread loop of 1/4 inch (6.4 mm) or less, placed to accommodate a wire hook.

- In a place of a metal eye.
- When a softer closure is desired.
- Where there will be little strain in the area of the closure.
- On fine, sheer and soft fabrics.

Also may be used to form buttonhole loops and belt carriers.

Chain is made of sewing thread or buttonhole twist thread. Blanket stitch or thread chain may be used.

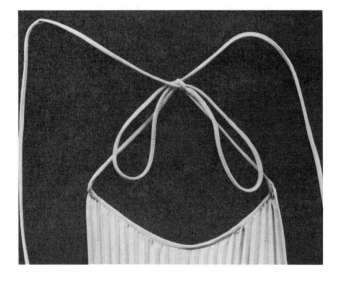

Ties

Opposing pairs of ribbon or clean-finished self or contrasting fabric strips attached to a garment.

- On center front, center back or side seams of blouses, jackets, dresses or pants.
- To hold garment fullness in place.
- To fasten aprons, pinafores, or tabards.
- On lower edges of sleeves or pants.
- On halter necks and backs.
- To fasten garments at shoulder.
- As a single pair, grouped, or in a series.

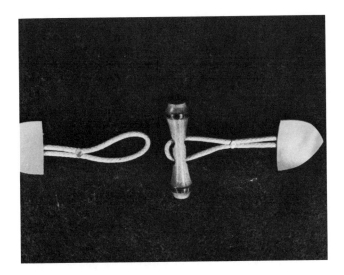

Toggle

A paired closure formed by two loops, one of which has a bar-shaped button affixed. Both designed with prefinished ends for attachment to the *face* of the garment.

- On sportswear; coats, jackets and sweaters.
- On garments made of heavy fabric or fur.
- Where buttonholes would be difficult to construct.
- As a design detail.

Made in a variety of sizes, shapes, materials, and finishes.

Side View Button Dimension Chart
Button Size Chart
Corded Button
Covered Button

Sew-Through Button
Shank Button
Button Attaching Clip / Jet Clip
Reinforced Button

A button is a three-dimensional form attached to a garment. A button is slipped through an opening for fastening the garment.

Buttons may be used for decorative as well as functional purposes. Novelty buttons of irregular shapes, sizes and designs are used as trimming.

There are two types of buttons.

1. The sew-through button has two or four holes for attaching the button to the garment.

2. A button with a metal, fabric, plastic, or thread shank which provides concealed attachment to the garment. The shank also provides the space needed to accommodate the thickness of the garment ply.

Buttons are available in a wide range of sizes and designated by line (ligne) inches or centimeters, indicating the diameter of the button.

Buttons are made in many shapes and contours. Dimensional variations of a button are flat, half-ball, and full-ball. Button surfaces may be smooth, raised, patterned, or adorned.

A wide variety of natural or man-made materials are used to make buttons. Button materials include pearl, wood, bone, fiber, fabric, glass, jewels, plastic, steel and other metals. Button forms or molds may be covered with fabric or other material to complement the garment. Cord, braid and other fibers may be formed into buttons.

The type of button selected depends upon:
• Style and design of garment
• Type of closure
• Purpose of closure
• Type, weight, and texture of fabric
• Care of the garment
• Size and shape of button
• Design and type of button
• Number of buttons used
• Placement of buttons
• Method of application

Side View Button Dimension Chart

Flat Button   Half Round Button   Full Round Button

Button Size Chart (actual size)

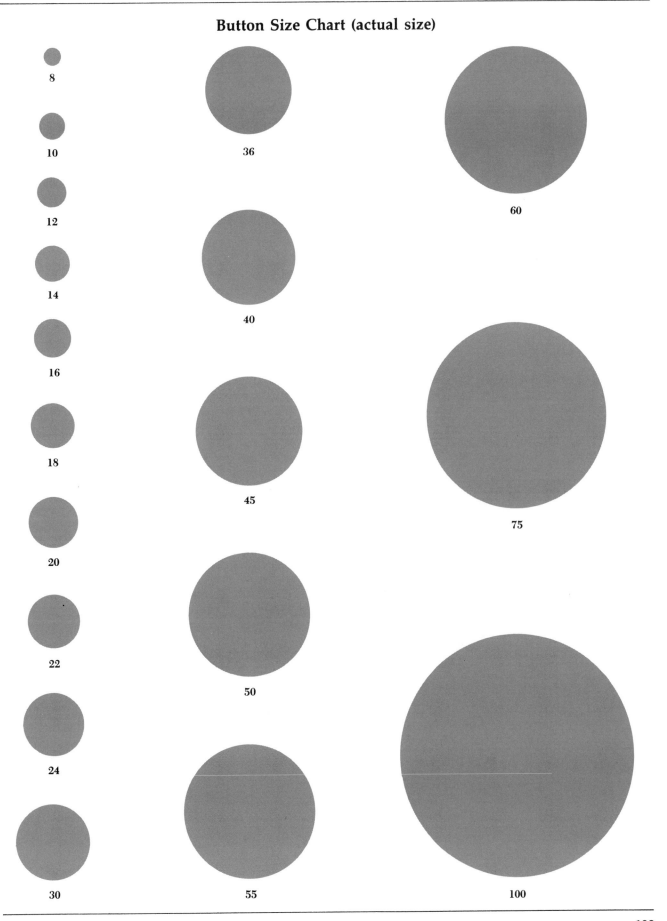

8

10

12

14

16

18

20

22

24

30

36

40

45

50

55

60

75

100

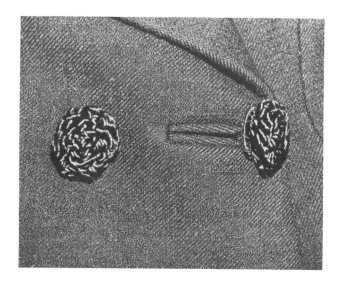

Corded Button

A button produced by twisting, looping, twirling, plaiting or knotting cord, soutache, dyed-string, fabric thread or fabric tubing.

- With loop buttonholes.
- With frog closures.
- As a design feature.

Button is available ready-made or may be self-prepared. When button is made spherically, it produces a *Chinese ball button*. Thickness of cord and manner of looping determines size of button.

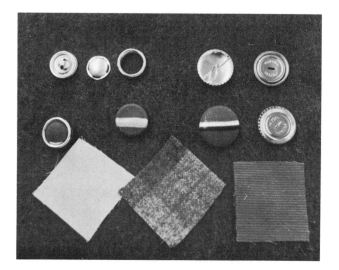

Covered Button

A two-piece button form or mold; the top section is covered with a ply or plies of fabric or other material and clamped to the bottom shank base section.

- When button is:
    To match or complement the garment fabric;
    To accentuate or contrast the garment fabric;
    To correspond with matching trim.
- As a design feature.

Button may be fully covered, outlined by metal rim, or decoratively stitched on the surface. It is available with a metal or fabric shank.

Buttons are available in kits for self-fabric covering or commercially prepared.

Sew-Through Button

A disk designed in a variety of shapes, thicknesses and surface patterns with two or four holes punched equidistant from the center to facilitate attachment to the garment.

- On sleepwear, tuck-in garments and at waistlines beneath belted closures where a flat, thin button is most comfortable.
- On back closures.
- On men's shirts, buttondown collars, and collar bands.
- On band closures.
- On inside of waistbands in conjunction with other closures.
- To hold suspenders.
- As a reinforcing button.
- On children's and infants' wear.
- On garments made of thin and sheer fabrics where shank of button would detract from appearance and wear of garment.

Button may be sewn flat or with a worked-thread shank. Thread design for attaching four-hole button may be formed into a cross, parallel line, square, or leaf pattern. Large-holed buttons may be attached with fabric tubing, ribbon, cord, lacing, or wires.

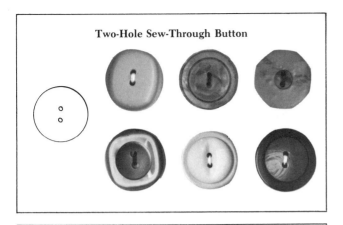

Two-Hole Sew-Through Button

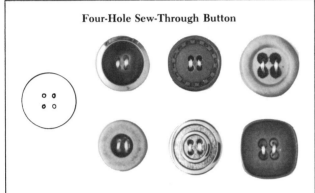

Four-Hole Sew-Through Button

Shank Button

A three-dimensional form, designed in various shapes, sizes and surface patterns, in which the protruding part of the underside is made of metal, fabric or plastic and through which the means of attachment to the garment passes.

- Where a visible means of attaching button would detract from the appearance of the garment.
- For closures on garments made of heavy and bulky fabrics.
- On garments where a sew-through button would not complement the style or use of the garment.

Shank provides the space needed to accommodate the thickness of the garment overlap and allows button to rest on top of the buttonhole. It eliminates distortion and crowding of buttonhole. Shank permits the closure to fasten smoothly. Unobstructed face surface of shank button allows freedom of design. Stem and size of shank varies with type and use of button. Shank and attaching thread do not show on the face of the garment.

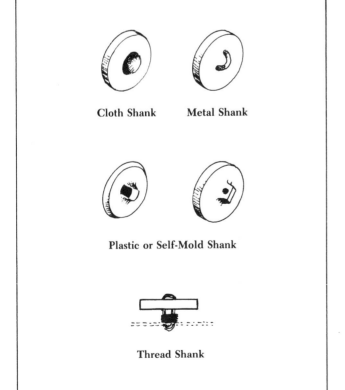

Cloth Shank   **Metal Shank**

Plastic or Self-Mold Shank

Thread Shank

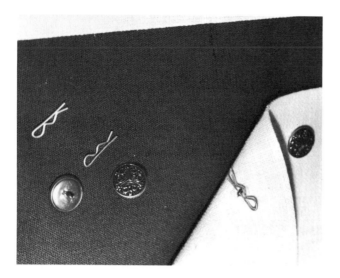

Button Attaching Clip / Jet Clip

Molded plastic or heavy gauge bent wire with a centered arch or arches on one prong forming a split pin.

- To attach wire loop shank button.
- As a substitute for sewing buttons to garment.
- When buttons must be removed for garment care.

Button shank is passed to back of garment through eyelet for clip attachment. Arched section prevents clip slippage.

Reinforced Button

A flat, two- or four-hole button attached on the underside of the garment, behind, and to the top button and all garment plies.

- At points of great strain on garments of heavy materials.
- On soft and loosely woven fabrics to prevent pull-through of fabrics or pull-off of buttons.
- To prevent top buttons from tearing fabric.
- On jackets and coats.
- On waistbands.

Double square of fabric, ribbon or binding may be substituted for the small button to eliminate bulk, for softer reinforcing or to prevent irritation of body.

25 ~ Buttonholes & Openings

Bound Buttonholes:
 Corded Bound Buttonhole
 Welt Bound Buttonhole
Bound Buttonhole Facing Finish:
 Eye Slit
 Patch Slit
Hand-Worked Buttonhole
Hand-Worked with Cord Buttonhole
Loop:
 Fabric Loop / Rouleau
 Soutache Braid Loop / Cord Loop

Crochet Loop / Chain-Thread Loop
 Thread Loop / Worked-Thread Loop
Machine-Fused Buttonhole
Machine-Worked Buttonhole
Machine-Worked with Cord Buttonhole
Opening in Skins
Open Slit Buttonhole
Slot Buttonhole / In Seam Buttonhole
Tailored Buttonhole / Keyhole Buttonhole
Buttonhole Machine
Buttonhole Machine Attachment (Non-Industrial)

A buttonhole is an opening in a garment large enough to accommodate a button. There are three types of buttonholes, each has its variations.

1. *Worked buttonholes* are made by hand, by a home machine attachment, or by a commercial buttonhole machine. Hand- or machine-worked buttonholes are made on the outside or face of the garment after the garment is completed.
2. *Bound buttonholes* are made of separate strips of fabric. They are planned and constructed before the facing is applied.
3. *Loops* are made of bias tubing, thread or cord. They are placed in the seam or fold edge.

Buttonholes are made on the overlap of the garment. Women's garments button right over left and men's garments button left over right. Garments may be planned for vertical or horizontal buttonhole placement. On designs with a tab-front closure lengthwise placement is preferred.

The type and size of buttonhole or opening selected depends on:

• Type of garment
• Design and style of garment
• Compatibility with garment
• Type and weight of fabric
• Purpose of opening
• Method of application
• Placement of button
• Size and shape of the button
• Number of buttons required

Corded Bound Buttonhole

A buttonhole in which the opening is formed by a variety of construction methods using corded piping in matching or contrasting fabrics.

- Where a rounded effect is desired.
- To add strength and body to buttonhole strips.
- To prevent stretching of buttonhole strips.
- On garments made of spongy or textured fabrics that will not hold a crease.

Corded bound buttonhole is made on garment section before facing is applied.

Welt Bound Buttonhole

A buttonhole in which the opening is formed by a variety of construction methods using strips or piping in matching or contrasting fabrics.

- On tailored garments.
- Where a crisp look is desired.
- On firmly woven opaque fabrics with body such as wool, cotton, linen and synthetics.

Welt bound buttonhole is made on garment section before facing is applied.

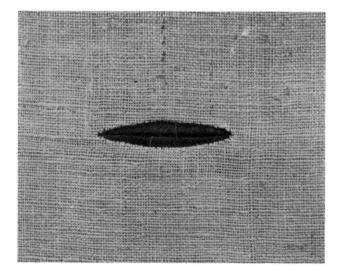

Eye Slit

The finished shape of the facing opening in which the hand-felled edges form an ellipse.

- To complete the opening made on the facing or underside of the bound buttonhole.

Patch Slit

A clean-finished opening on the facing, shaped to match the buttonhole by the application of a stitched, slashed, and turned strip.

- To complete the opening made on the facing or underside of a bound buttonhole.
- On fabrics that ravel easily.
- To reinforce loosely woven fabrics.
- On fabrics where hand felling would not hold.
- On garments that may be worn open.

When finished, opening is shaped like the buttonhole. Applied to the facing side of the garment after facing is attached.

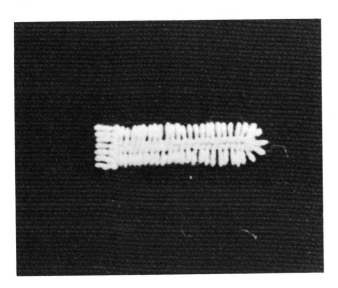

Hand-Worked Buttonhole

A buttonhole made with buttonhole twist, silk or other sewing thread, in a series of closely spaced purl stitches worked around the opening.

- In place of bound buttonholes where the underlay of the patch would add bulk or show on the face of the garment.
- On fabrics that will not ravel.
- On thin, firm fabrics such as organdy, lawn, batiste, dotted swiss and other sheers.
- On fragile fabrics where machine buttonholes would fray or damage the garment.

Worked on the face of the garment after interfacing and facing are applied. Used in horizontal or vertical placement. Buttonhole may be finished with a bar tack.

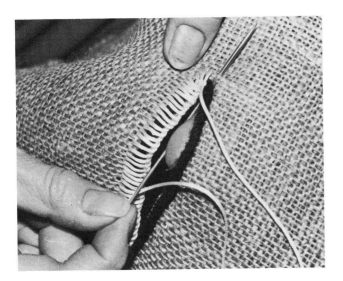

Hand-Worked with Cord Buttonhole

A buttonhole with a filler cord or gimp placed along the cut edge between the layer of fabric and the hand-worked buttonhole stitch.

- On firm fabrics that will not ravel.
- On fragile fabrics where machine buttonholes would fray or damage the garment.
- To add strength and body to hand-worked buttonholes.
- To produce a raised effect.

Worked on the face of the garment after interfacing and facing are applied. Buttonhole may be finished with a bar tack.

Fabric Loop / Rouleau

A loop made of self or cord-filled tubing in matching or contrasting fabrics.

- Individually or in a continuous row.
- In place of a buttonhole as a decorative finish or closure.
- As a single top closure at the neckline of the garment.
- Under collars to hold shirt or blouse closed.
- Where other types of buttonholes would mar the fabric.
- On garments made of silk, crepe or jersey.
- Where other types of buttonholes would detract from the appearance of the garment.
- On a closure for narrow fitted sleeves.
- On cuffs of sleeve.
- In conjunction with other closure fasteners.

Loops are placed to extend beyond edge of garment. Buttons for loop closure may be positioned as a center or lap application.

Soutache Braid Loop / Cord Loop

A loop made from a commercial braid or cord.

- On garments where fabric loops would be too heavy.
- As a decorative detail.
- To coordinate with other soutache trim on the garment.
- Individually, grouped or in a continuous row.
- At neckline closures of blouses, dresses, coats and jackets.

Purchased as a braid to be self-prepared into loops or as commercial braid pre-formed into loops and sold by the yard.

Crochet Loop / Chain-Thread Loop

A loop characterized by a series of hand-worked interlocking loops or by a prepared chain-stitched cord.

- Where a fabric loop construction would show on the face of the garment.
- Where fabric is too heavy for fabric or cord loops.
- As an alternative to:
    Worked-thread loops;
    Metal eyes.
- In place of other types of loops.
- As a single top closure at neckline of garment.
- Under collars to hold shirt or blouse closed.
- At waistline to hold belt in position.
- As lingerie strap holder in a garment.

Chain is formed by hand looping of stitches or may be purchased ready-made. May be made in buttonhole twist or garment sewing thread.

FASHION PRODUCTION TERMS

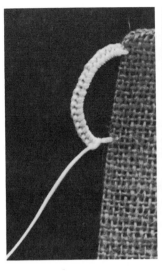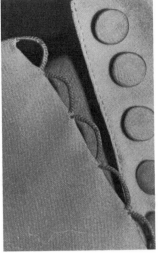

Thread Loop / Worked-Thread Loop

A loop formed by a series of buttonhole stitches worked over a core or base of preliminary stitches, which spans the garment ply accommodating the size of the button.

- When fabric is too thick or too heavy for fabric or cord loops.
- As an alternative to metal eyes for hook and eye closures.
- On garments made of lace where buttonholes are not desired.
- On garments made of sheer and fine fabrics where fabric loop construction would show on the face of the fabric.
- Where other types of buttonholes would mar the fabric.
- On women's, children's and infants' wear.

Loops made in buttonhole twist, fine silk, or machine sewing threads. May be made individually or in a series.

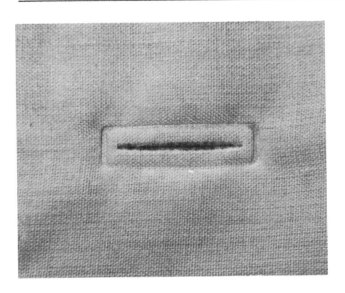

Machine Fused Buttonhole

A buttonhole opening formed in the fabric, without the use of thread, by a machine designed with a patterned horn tip which vibrates at a high speed generating heat to melt, reform and fuse the opening.

- On one-hundred percent thermoplastic fabric.
- On wool and blended fabrics in conjunction with adhesive lining.
- To produce eyelets.

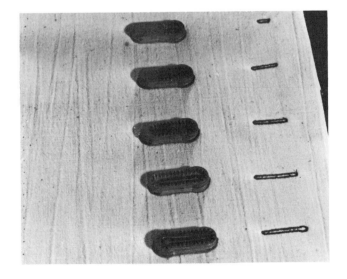

Machine-Worked Buttonhole

A buttonhole made by a commercial machine, a special attachment on a home machine, or a planned zigzag machine stitch simulating hand-worked buttonholes.

- On garments made of lightweight and sheer fabrics where bound buttonholes would be too heavy or too bulky and would show on the face of the garment.
- In place of bound buttonholes in less expensive garments.

Worked on the face of the garment after interfacing and facing are applied. Buttonhole may be finished with a bar tack.

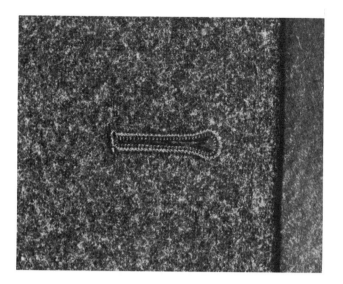

Machine-Worked With Cord Buttonhole

A machine-made buttonhole stitch worked over a filler cord or gimp placed along the finished edge.

- To add strength and body to machine-worked buttonholes.
- To produce a firm raised effect.
- To reduce stretching of buttonholes.

Buttonhole is made after interfacing and facing are applied. May be finished with a bar tack.

Opening in Skins

A buttonhole formed by a rectangular cut opening with abutted strips held in place by glue or stitching.

- On heavy skins and vinyl to eliminate bulk.
- On fabric that will not fray.
- With contrasting strips to produce a decorative effect.

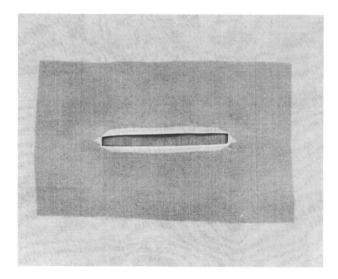

Open Slit Buttonhole

A clean-finished opening produced by stitching, slashing, and turning a patch of fabric which is applied to the face of the garment.

- On fur, fur-like fabrics, leather and vinyl.
- On bulky fabrics.
- When self-fabric cannot be used for buttonhole strips.
- As an opening on the garment ply when a casing and drawstring are used.

Author's Note: Sheer fabric is used merely to show construction.

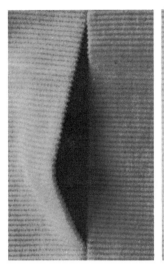
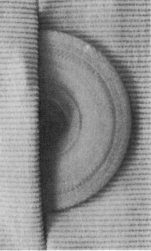

Slot Buttonhole / In Seam Buttonhole

A finished opening in a stitched seam.

- Where a necessary button-placement corresponds with a seam line such as at waistlines, tabs, yokes, or midriffs.
- When other types of buttonholes would interfere with design such as where bands or inserts are planned.
- As a planned decorative closing.

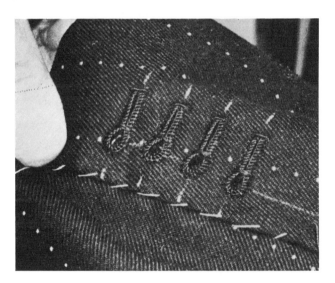

Tailored Buttonhole / Keyhole Buttonhole

A machine- or hand-worked buttonhole in which the end nearest the extension edge is rounded into an eye.

- On men's and women's tailored suits and coats.
- On heavy, thick or firm fabrics.
- To provide more room for the button shank.

Buttonhole will not be distorted when the garment is buttoned. It may be constructed with filler cord or gimp and finished with a bar tack.

Buttonhole Machine

A machine designed so that a cam-controlled sewing motion guides a vibrating needle bar to produce a thread-worked buttonhole on the finished garment.

- To produce:
    Open-end buttonholes;
    Fly-bar end buttonholes;
    Eye or no-eye lapel buttonholes;
    Eyelets.

Various machines can be adjusted to produce a wide range of buttonholes of different lengths, stitch density and bite, with or without eyes. Models made for cutting before or after stitching; made to produce rounded ends and purl stitching for knit garments.

Buttonhole Machine Attachment (Non-Industrial)

A buttonhole foot attachment to work in conjunction with cams inserted into stitch pattern control units or push-button operated stitch pattern controls.

- To produce:
  Open-end buttonholes;
  Fly-bar end buttonholes;
  Eye or no-eye lapel buttonholes.

Non-industrial attachments can be adjusted to produce a wide range of buttonholes of different lengths, stitch density, and bite. Buttonholes made by attachments and stitch pattern controls are cut after stitching.

Parts of the Zipper
Closed End Zipper / Dress Zipper
Conventional Zipper / Regulation Zipper /
   Skirt or Neckline Zipper
Decorative Zipper / Industrial Zipper
Invisible Zipper
Reversible Zipper
Separating Zipper
Trouser Zipper
Two-Way Zipper / Dual Opening Zipper
Zipper Application:
   Hand-Stitched Zipper Application
   Machine-Stitched Zipper Application
Zipper Insertion:
   Dress Placket Zipper Insertion /
      Side Seam Zipper Insertion

Exposed Decorative Zipper Insertion /
   Exposed Industrial Zipper Insertion
Exposed Zipper in a Slash Insertion
Fly-Front Concealed Zipper Insertion
Lap Zipper Insertion
Slot Zipper Insertion /
   Centered Zipper Insertion
Trouser Fly Zipper Insertion
Zipper with Underlay
Zipper Foot Attachment:
   Left or Right Adjustable Zipper Foot
   Grooved Zipper Foot for Invisible Zippers
   Roller Zipper Foot for Invisible Zippers
   Single-Toed Zipper Foot / One-Sided
      Zipper Foot / Cording Zipper Foot
   Two-Toed Zipper Foot / Slit Zipper Foot

A zipper is a fastening device which makes a complete closure by means of interlocking teeth or coils.

The three types of zippers are:

1. Conventional or regulation
2. Separating
3. Invisible

Conventional or *regulation* zippers are closed at one or both ends. They are inserted either beneath the garment seam folds which completely conceal the zipper, or in a slashed opening as an exposed zipper.

The *separating* zipper is open at both ends allowing the zipper to disconnect completely. It can be concealed beneath the seam folds or inserted as a decorative zipper where tape and teeth will show on the face of the garment.

The *invisible* zipper is a self-concealing zipper, closed at one end, applied to the seam line with no visible means of stitching.

Zippers are used at front, back, side and princess line seams or sleeve openings.

Zippers may be inserted horizontally for pocket, design detail, or fashion accent.

Each zipper is applied either by a special foot attached to the machine or by hand stitching in a lapped, centered or exposed application.

All zippers are available in various weights, sizes, and colors.

The weight of zippers is determined by the type of tape and structure.

A *coil-constructed* zipper is a continuous strand of nylon or polyester twisted into a spiral and attached to a synthetic tape. It is flexible and lightweight.

A *chain-constructed* zipper consists of individual metal or plastic teeth attached to a cotton or cotton blend tape. It is heavier and more rigid than the coil-constructed zipper.

The type, length and application method for zippers selected depend on:

• Style and design of garment
• Type and use of garment
• Construction of garment
• Care of garment
• Type and weight of fabric
• Compatibility with fabric and garment
• Type of opening

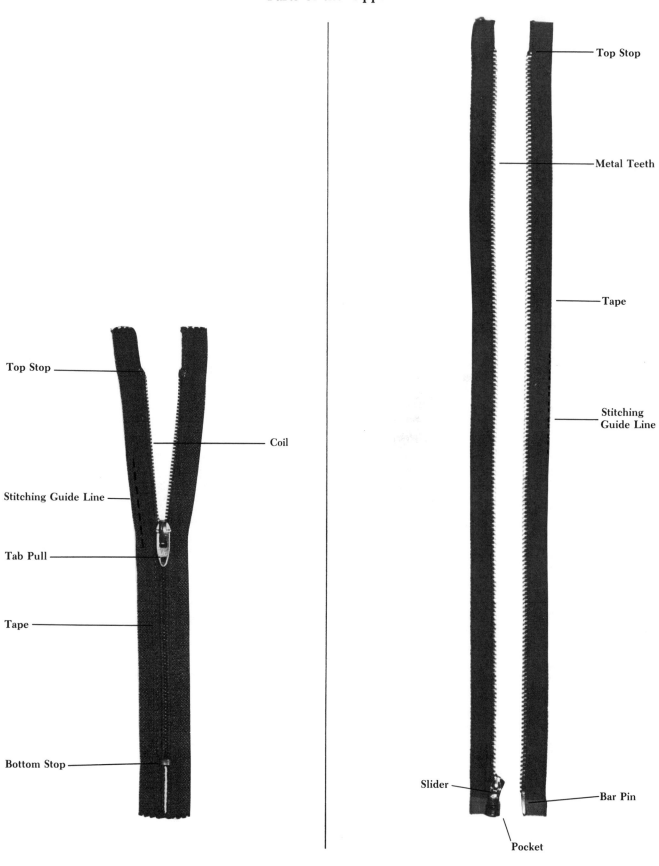

Top Stop

Coil

Stitching Guide Line

Tab Pull

Tape

Bottom Stop

Top Stop

Metal Teeth

Tape

Stitching Guide Line

Slider

Pocket

Bar Pin

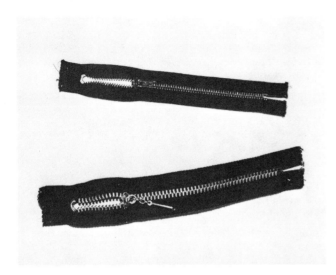

Closed End Zipper / Dress Zipper

A conventional or regulation, metal or synthetic zipper, 2 to 14 inches (5.1 to 35 cm) in length, closed at both ends by a metal or plastic bar spanning both tracks of teeth or coils.

- In a garment seam which is closed at both ends of placket opening.
- On garments fitted at the waistline.
- At the underarm or center back seam of dresses.
- Where an opening extending into the neckline would detract from the appearance of the garment.
- In pocket openings for functional or decorative design.

Centered or lapped zipper application construction method may be used.

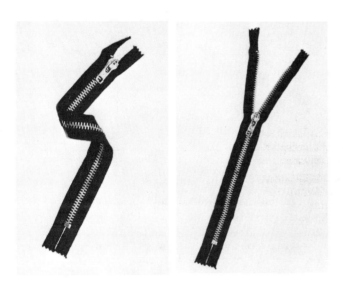

Conventional Zipper / Regulation Zipper / Skirt or Neckline Zipper

A regulation or conventional chain- or coil-constructed zipper, 4 to 36 inches (10 to 90 cm) in length, closed at one end by a bar spanning both tracks of teeth or coils.

- On skirt and neckline openings; trousers, slacks and pants.
- On bodices that open from the waistline upward.
- On the finished edge of fitted sleeves.
- On center seam of hood to convert hood to collar.
- For underarm dress opening; long-sleeve opening.

Zippers for skirt or short-neck openings available in lengths from 4 to 10 inches (10 to 25 cm); for blouse, dress, house coat, and robe openings in lengths of 16, 18, 20, 22, 24, 30 and 36 inches (40.6, 45.7, 50.8, 55.9, 61, 76.2 and 91.4 cm).

Centered or lapped application method may be used. Applied with hand or machine stitches.

Decorative Zipper / Industrial Zipper

A zipper with a large metal or plastic tooth size and a pull tab.

- As a design detail.
- As an exaggerated functional closure.
- As a novelty touch to garments.
- In contrasting color to emphasize design feeling.
- To enhance look of a garment.

Zippers available in regulation or separation types. Pull tab may be designed as a large ring or pendant.

Invisible Zipper

A zipper constructed so that the chain is concealed beneath the tape when the zipper is closed, leaving only the pull tab visible.

- Where any other zipper application would detract from appearance of the garment.
- To produce a smooth, continuous seam line.
- Where break in continuity of fabric design would detract from style of the garment.
- On matte jersey, lace, and velvet and other napped fabrics.
- On lower edge opening of fitted sleeves.
- On fitted bodice openings from the waist to the neckline.
- On necklines of garments, skirts and slacks.

Zipper is applied before seam is stitched, which differs from usual construction method. It is applied with a specially designed zipper foot and no stitching shows on the face of the garment.

Zipper is available in featherweight nylon coil for lightweight fabrics and in metal tooth chain for firmer or heavier weight fabrics. Available in lengths from 7 to 22 inches (18 to 56 cm).

Reversible Zipper

A zipper constructed with a pull tab on both sides of the slide.

- On reversible coats, jackets, and vests.
- On skirts, tops and other garments that are designed to be worn with either side face out.

Available in conventional and separating types.

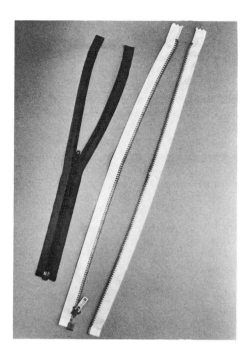

Separating Zipper

A zipper constructed with individual, vertical pin or bar stops which lock together through the slide and pocket enabling the slide to join the parallel teeth or coils.

- On any garment with a completely opened front.
- On parkas, coats, jackets or vests.
- On detachable hoods.
- To separate linings from dual season coats and jackets.
- To separate fleece or fur lining in hunting or sport clothes.
- On snowsuits and leggings.
- On cardigan sweaters.
- Horizontally, to add or delete portion of a garment to increase or decrease lengths.

Separating zipper may be inserted by centered or lapped applications. Hand or machine stitches may be used.

Zipper is available with lightweight or heavyweight teeth and tape.

Length for lightweight fabrics is 10 to 22 inches (25 to 56 cm); for heavyweight fabrics, 14 to 24 inches (35 to 61 cm).

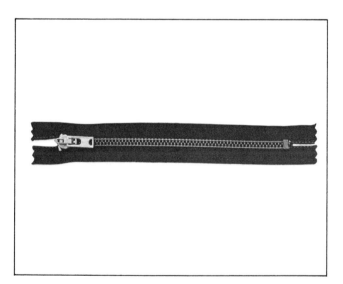

Trouser Zipper

A regulation or conventional metal zipper, of 6, 9, or 11 inches (15.2, 22.9 or 28 cm) in length, closed at one end with metal bar spanning both tracks of teeth.

- On dungarees, jeans and overalls.
- On men's trousers and slacks.
- Where a heavyweight zipper with strong teeth is necessary.

Slider has special bar support to withstand frequent laundering. Zipper is designed with wide tapes allowing for double stitching.

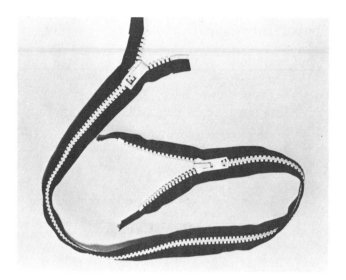

Two-Way Zipper / Dual Opening Zipper

A separating zipper constructed with two identical vertical bar strips, slides and pockets at the top and bottom of the zipper teeth or coil; insertion of the bars into their slides and pockets, locks and enables the zipper to be closed from either or both ends.

- On snowsuits, jackets and pants; ski wear and sportswear.
- On children's clothing to facilitate dressing.
- On closures in garments made for the handicapped.

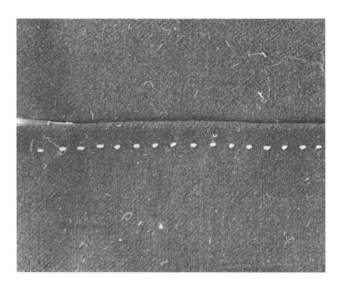

Hand-Stitched Zipper Application

A centered, lapped or concealed fly-front zipper application which utilizes a modified back or prick stitch to produce evenly spaced stitches, spanning a few threads, visible on the face of the garment.

- On garments not subject to hard wear or laundering.
- On sheer or lightweight fabrics.
- On loosely woven, stretch or knit fabrics.
- On sample room garments.
- On couture garments.
- On garments where machine stitching would detract from the appearance of the garment.

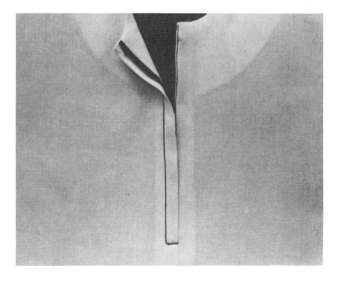

Machine-Stitched Zipper Application

A centered, lapped or fly-front zipper application utilizing a regular or standard lockstitch or chainstitch machine to produce stitches visible on the face of the garment.

- On garments subject to hard wear.
- On trousers, jeans and overalls.
- On active sports clothes.
- On sportswear garments.

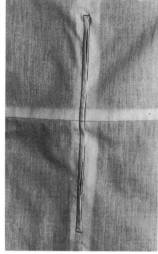

Dress Placket Zipper Insertion / Side Seam Zipper Insertion

A zipper applied in a garment seam which is closed at both ends of the placket or opening.

- On garments fitted at the waistline.
- At the underarm or center back seam of dresses.
- Where an opening extending into the neckline would detract from the design concept.

Centered, lapped or invisible zipper insertion construction methods may be used.

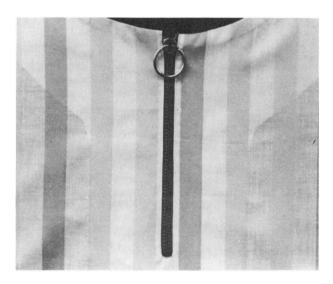

Exposed Decorative Zipper Insertion / Exposed Industrial Zipper Insertion

A zipper insertion utilizing a metal or plastic decorative zipper in which the enlarged teeth and wide tape show on the face of the garment.

- Where the conspicuous exposure of the zipper is desired as a decorative feature.
- On the center front of garments for functional and decorative purposes.
- As pocket closures.
- On active sportswear and industrial garments.
- For easy accessibility and removal of garment.

Pull tab may be designed as a large ring or pendant. Tape and teeth may contrast. May be a regulation or separating zipper.

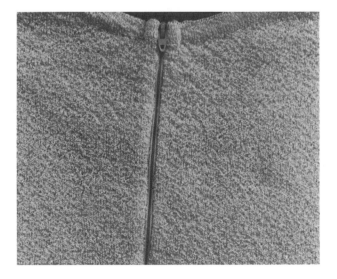

Exposed Zipper in a Slash Insertion

A zipper inserted into a slashed opening so that the chain is left exposed.

- Where the garment section or part has no placket opening.
- On garments where there is no seam and an opening is necessary.
- On pockets of garments.
- On pocket sleeves of sport jackets and outerwear.
- On sweater knit and jersey fabrics.

May be applied so that top stitching shows on the seam fold of each side; stitch is not visible on the face of the garment.

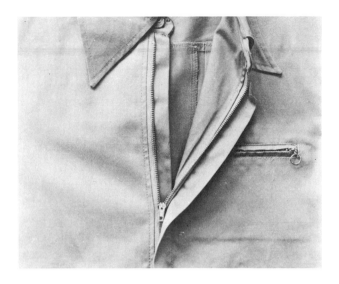

Fly-Front Concealed Zipper Insertion

A zipper insertion having one side of the zipper tape stitched to a facing which is then turned back and stitched a measured distance from the folded edge to form an extension beyond the garment closure line. This conceals the other half of the zipper which is aligned and stitched to close at center of the lap.

- On jackets and coats.
- On rain or snow weather gear.
- On sportswear garments.
- On center or asymmetrical garment closures.
- In conjunction with other fasteners for winter garments.
- On garments where other fasteners and other zipper applications would detract from the appearance of the garment.
- On garments where the extended lap is part of wearing and design allowance.

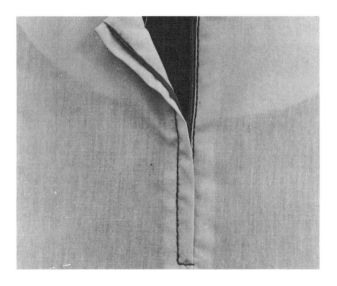

Lap Zipper Insertion

A zipper insertion in which the folded seam edge of a garment section is stitched along the stitching guideline on the zipper tape. The folded edge of the second garment section, when stitched 1/4 to 1/2 inch (6.4 to 12.7 mm) from the folded edge, forms a tuck concealing the entire unit.

- On the left side seam opening of dresses, skirts, and pants.
- On skirt and dress plackets.
- On the center front and center back opening of garments.
- As a concealed primary closure on outerwear and sportswear fastened with buttons, toggles, and snaps.
- On the lower end of fitted sleeve openings.
- For regulation or separating zippers.

Inserted by hand or machine application. When completed, only one line of stitching is visible.

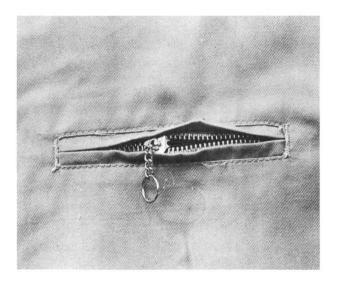

Slot Zipper Insertion / Centered Zipper Insertion

A zipper insertion in which the two seam edges of the garment are folded, abutted or faced over the center of the zipper chain and stitched approximately 1/4 to 1/2 inch (6.4 to 12.7 mm) parallel to the finished seam line.

- On the center back placket in skirts, slacks and shorts.
- In the princess seams of gored skirts.
- On the center front and center back opening of dresses and blouses.
- On the lower end of fitted sleeve openings.
- On parkas, snowsuits, boating jackets and other sportswear.
- On hoods of coats and jackets.
- On leather, suede and vinyl.

Used for conventional or separating zippers. Inserted by hand or machine stitching. A row of stitching is visible on each side of the closure.

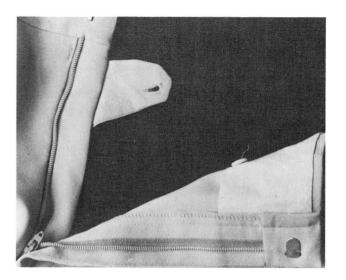

Trouser Fly Zipper Insertion

A zipper insertion in which one side of the zipper tape is double stitched to a facing which is then turned back and stitched 1 1/2 inch (3.8 cm) from the folded edge; thereby producing a lap concealing the other half of the zipper which is stitched to an underlay extending beyond the center front line.

- On men's and boys' trousers.
- On dungarees.
- On women's trousers to imitate men's wear design.

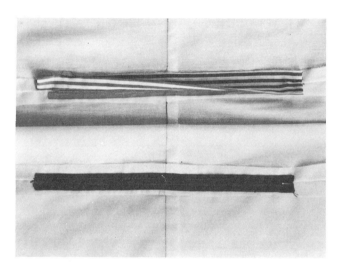

Zipper with Underlay

A strip of self-fabric or ribbon applied behind the zipper chain on the ply closest to the body.

- To protect the undergarment and body from the zipper teeth.
- To support the belt which overlaps the closing.
- As a guard for the zipper.

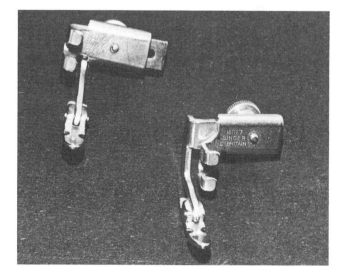

Left or Right Adjustable Zipper Foot

A single-toed, rigid presser foot notched on both sides to accommodate the needle for left or right construction operation; designed with a shank fixed to an adjustable, horizontal slide bar.

- To permit sewing close to the raised edge of zipper teeth or coil.
- To permit sewing both sides of a zipper construction in the same direction.
- For centered, lapped or fly-front zipper insertion.

Designed for a specific type and class of home sewing machine.

Grooved Zipper Foot for Invisible Zippers

A plastic or metal presser foot having a wide base with tunnel openings to the right and left of the needle hole; designed with a shank for attachment to presser bar.

• To apply an invisible zipper to garment seam.

Grooved zipper foot is available in one-piece metal construction for industrial machine; in plastic and packaged with a choice of base for coil or metal chain zippers and an assortment of shanks for various types and classes of home machines.

Grooves or tunnels on foot are designed to hold coil or teeth upright, positioning zipper, permitting close stitching.

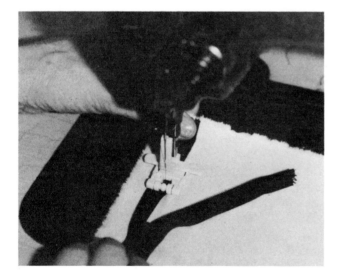

Roller Zipper Foot for Invisible Zippers

A zipper foot having a wide base set with a grooved roller at the front to feed zipper coil to the right or left of the needle opening; designed with a shank for attachment to machine.

• To apply a synthetic or metal invisible zipper to garment.

Roller zipper foot is available in one-piece metal construction for industrial machine; in plastic and packaged with a choice of base for coil or metal chain zippers and an assortment of shanks for various types and classes of home machines.

Grooves or tunnels on zipper foot designed to hold coil or teeth upright, positioning zipper, permitting close stitching.

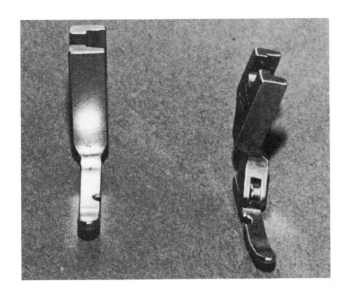

Single-Toed Zipper Foot /
One-Sided Zipper Foot / Cording Foot

A metal presser foot with a hinged or rigid, single- right- or left-toed base notched to accommodate needle; designed with a shank for attachment to presser bar.

- To permit sewing close to the raised edge of zipper teeth or coil.
- To stitch close to a raised edge.
- For centered, lapped and fly-front zipper insertion.

Designed to fit a specific class and type of machine; with needle slot for either left or right edge sewing.

Two-Toed Zipper Foot / Slit Zipper Foot

A metal presser foot with a hinged or rigid, narrow two-toed base with a circular opening at top of split to accommodate needle; designed with a shank for attachment to presser bar.

- To permit sewing close to the raised edge of zipper teeth or coil.
- To apply zippers in garments made of heavyweight fabrics.
- When zipper application is followed by subsequent sewing operation performed by the same operator in mass produced or sample garments.
- For centered, lapped or fly-front zipper insertion.

Designed to fit a specific class and type of machine.

Band Hem
Blind-Stitched Hem
Book Hem
Bonded Hem
Bound Hem:
   Double-Fold Bias Binding /
     Bias Tape / Bias Fold
   Single-Fold Bias Binding /
     Bias Tape / Bias Fold
   Bound Hem / Hong Kong Finish
   Net Binding
Double Fold Hem
Double-Stitched Hem
Ease in a Hem
Edge-Stitched Hem
Faced Hem
Flat Hem:
   Flat Hem / Plain Hem / Turned Flat Hem
   Pinked Flat Hem
   Stitched & Pinked Flat Hem

Glued Hem
Horsehair Hem
Interfaced Hem
Machine-Stitched Hem
Mitered Hem
Overedged Hem
Padded Hem
Rolled Hem:
   Hand-Rolled Hem
   Machine-Rolled Hem
Taped Edge:
   Iron-On Seam Binding / Press-On Tape
   Lace Seam Binding
   Ribbon Seam Tape / Seam Binding
Weighted Hem:
   Weighted Hem with Lead Disk
   Weighted Hem with Lead Pellets
   Weighted Hem with Metal Chain
Wired Hem

Hems are the finished lower edges of a garment and are designed to prevent raw edges of material from fraying or tearing. Hems may be turned to the back or inside of the garment, made on the face of the garment as a decorative finish, or left unturned and finished with a decorative stitch pattern.

A hemline is the designated line along which the hem is to be folded, faced or finished.

Hems may be hand or machine stitched or may be held in place or finished with bonding agents. Bonding agents are procedures used to expedite garment construction replacing the need for hand or machine stitching. Different stitches are designed to duplicate the stitch pattern and appearance of handwork. Blind stitching may be done in a variety of stitch configurations not visible on the face of the garment. Machine-stitched hems may be made to show on the face of the garment for functional or decorative purposes.

The type of hem or hem finish selected depends on:
• Type of fabric
• Finish of fabric
• Weight and hand of fabric
• Style and design of garment
• Type and use of garment
• Care of garment
• Current methods of production and manufacturing

Band Hem

A hem which results when a shaped, bias or straight grain, double-ply strip, which may be folded or seamed, is applied to garment edge.

- At the hem edge of a skirt or sleeve.
- To introduce color or texture contrast to a garment edge.
- To increase length of a garment.

Band may be applied to enclose garment ply to produce a clean finish. Applied with regard to type of fabric and use of garment to permit selection of seam finish.

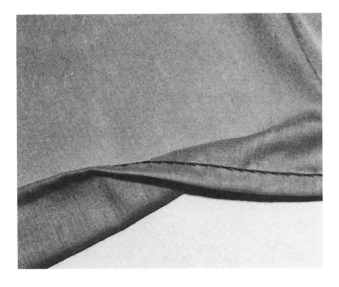

Blind-Stitched Hem

A folded hem secured by a series of interlocking loop stitches not visible on the face of the garment.

- Between hem and garment ply.
- At hem edge of a garment.
- On hems with or without tape or binding applications.

The type of blind stitch machine used is determined by type of fabric, placement of hem, use of garment, type of thread used, and count of loop stitch required. Zigzag and lockstitch may be used as blind stitch.

Book Hem

A hem with the raw edge folded under and secured to the garment ply by concealed blind stitches.

- To finish hems of an unlined jacket and coat.
- On garments where exposed stitches would detract from the appearance of garment.
- On garments where exposed stitches and raw edges would be subject to abrasion.
- On men's tailored garments.

Stitches may be made with thermoplastic thread which bonds hem to garment when activated by heat, steam, or pressure.

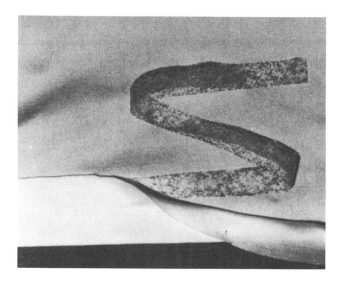

Bonded Hem

A hem which results when a strip of bonding agent is placed between fold of hem and garment and fused by the application of heat.

- To adhere the hem of a garment by pressing.
- Where any hem stitch would detract from the smooth look of the garment.
- On a fabric in an area where a hem stitch would show.
- For washable and dry cleanable garments.

Bonded hem is suitable for woven and knit fabrics.
   Bonding strip is available in a variety of widths: 3/4, 1 1/2, 5, 18 inches (1.9, 3.8, 12.7, 45.7 cm).

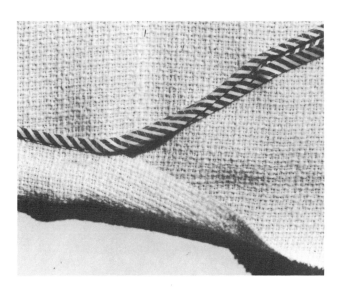

Double-Fold Bias Binding / Bias Tape / Bias Fold

A bias strip of various widths, commercially or self-prepared with two pre-folded 1/4 inch (6.4 mm) seam allowances and a slightly off-center fold; applied to encase the raw edge of the hem prior to hand or machine hemming of garment.

- To finish and bind raw edge of hems on unlined coats and suits for a clean finish.
- As a decorative binding to finish the hem area of a garment.

Bias strip is available commercially in cotton, silk or synthetic fabrics with pre-folded edges and center fold; in finished widths from 3/8 to 1 inch (9.5 to 25.4 mm).

Single-Fold Bias Binding / Bias Tape / Bias Fold

A bias strip of various widths, commercially or self-prepared with two pre-folded 1/4 inch (6.4 mm) edges; in which one edge is applied to hem edge prior to hand or machine hemming of garment.

- In place of seam or lace binding to conceal raw edges of fabrics that ravel easily.
- On hems where stretch and flexibility of the hem area is necessary.
- On garments made of heavy fabrics where a self hem fold would create bulk.
- To face hems.
- To replace the hem fold when altering the length of a garment.

Bias strip is available commercially in cotton, silk or synthetic fabrics with prefolded edges; in finished widths from 3/8 to 3 inches (9.5 to 38.1 mm).

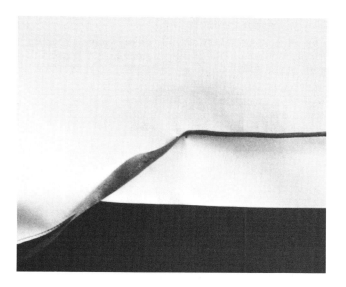

Bound Hem / Hong Kong Finish

A hem finish obtained by a bias strip applied to conceal and bind the raw hem edge. The unfinished edge of the bias strip is hidden between the hem and garment ply.

- When a flat finish is desired.
- On thick material which may fray.
- On hems of unlined vest, jacket or coat.
- On hems of tailored garments.
- On hems of garments made of heavy fabrics.

Raw edge of hem may be encased in a binding of self or contrasting fabric, or lace.
  May be referred to as a *welt-finished edge*.

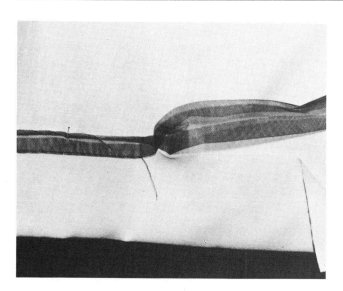

Net Binding

A lightweight strip of synthetic, meshlike, transparent binding applied to conceal and bind the raw hem edge.

- When a transparent hem finish is needed to complement the fabric.
- As a hem finish for such fabrics as lace, velvet, and chiffon velvet.
- To add body to the hem edge of scallops.

Self-prepared and commercially available in a variety of widths and weights.

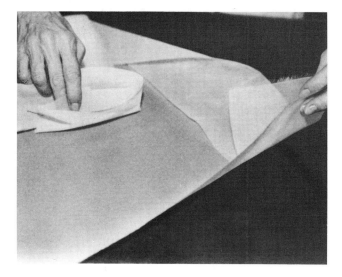

Double Fold Hem

A deep width, straight-grain hem characterized by two full depth folds.

- For transparent fabrics where garment needs a deeper and heavier hem.
- On a straight hemline.
- On lightweight and sheer fabrics such as organdy and chiffon.
- On rugged wearing apparel and where garments are laundered frequently.

This type of hem adds weight and body to lower edge of garment.

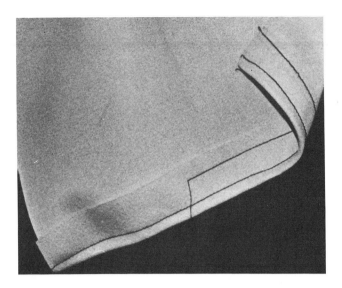

Double-Stitched Hem

A hem secured by two rows of hand or machine hemming stitches; one row applied midway along hem depth and the other along upper edge.

- On bulky or heavy knit fabrics.
- To hold a weighted hem in place.
- To prevent a hem from pulling down.

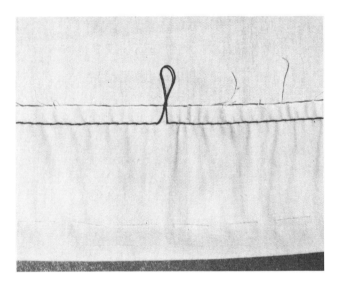

Ease in a Hem

The excess circumference, of a folded hem, which is drawn flat against the garment ply by pulling a heavy thread which has been machine stitched 1/4 inch (6.4 mm) from the cut edge of the ply.

- On garments where the hem area is greater than the corresponding garment area.
- To pull into place, the extra fullness of the hem area.
- To adjust excess fullness in flared and circular skirts, tops and capes; in tent dresses; and in bell sleeves.

Edge-Stitched Hem

A straight-grain hem in which the initial raw edge is turned under, 1/4 inch (6.4 mm), and machine stitched before final hemming.

- To prevent straight grain edge from raveling.
- To give body to a limp hem.
- On lightweight and medium weight fabrics; sheer fabrics.
- To produce a strong edged-finish for machine washable garments.

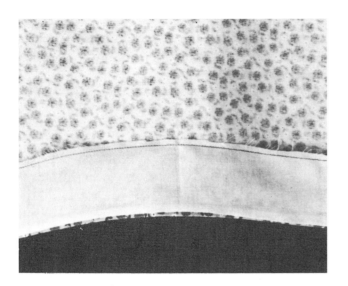

Faced Hem

A clean-finished hem produced on a shaped edge by stitching a similarly formed section of fabric on the face of the garment, followed by reversing the piece to the inside.

- On hems that are shaped.
- Where it is not possible to make a folded hem.
- On garments of heavy fabrics to reduce bulk.
- On garments made of lace to maintain the illusion of the fabric.
- On scalloped edges.
- To lengthen a hemline

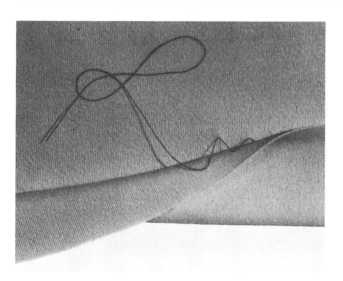

Flat Hem / Plain Hem / Turned Flat Hem

A hem produced by a turned-up fold with an unfinished edge void of preliminary machine stitching, tape, or binding application.

- On garments where a flat unrestrictive look is desired.
- To produce a hemline that is free of bulk or ridges.
- On fabrics that will not ravel.
- When a flat look is desired on jersey, silk, wool and crepe.

Pinked Flat Hem

A hem produced by a turned-up fold in which the raw edge has been pinked.

- To prevent raveling.

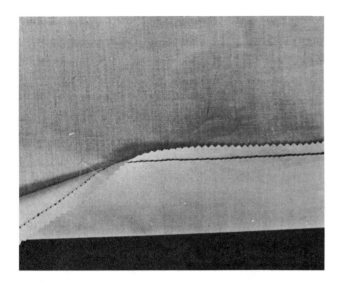

Stitched & Pinked Flat Hem

A hem produced by a turned-up fold which has been pinked and then machine stitched, 1/4 inch (6.4 mm) from the unfinished edge.

- To prevent raveling.
- On garments made of heavier fabrics where other methods of hemming would cause the hemline to show on the face of the garment.

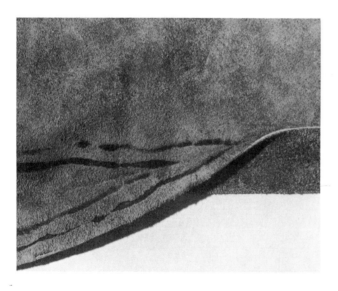

Glued Hem

A hem produced by a turned-up fold with an unfinished edge which is glued to the body of the garment.

- Where hand stitching would be impossible.
- Where machine stitching is undesirable.
- In place of machine or hand stitching.
- On leather, suede and other skins.
- On felt and other matted fabrics.

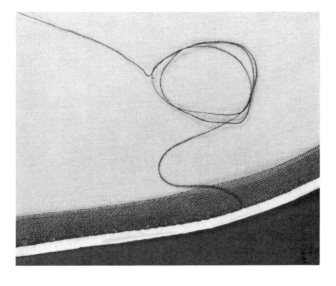

Horsehair Hem

A hem produced when a stiff, transparent woven bias braid, of various widths, which has a heavy thread along one edge to facilitate shaping is placed between fold of hem and garment.

- On a flared hem area of a garment such as the lower edge of sleeves, wide collars, capes and dresses.
- On lightweight or sheer fabrics.
- For bouffant silhouettes.
- In late day or evening wear, formals, bridals and costumes.
- To finish and stabilize hem in heavy fabrics.

Horsehair adds body to the hem producing a billowing affect at the lower edge and allows for controlled fullness.

Interfaced Hem

A hem with an additional strip of reinforcement included for shape retention placed between fold of hem and garment.

- To add body and crispness to hem areas.
- To prevent softening and wrinkling.
- To act as a base for the hem.
- To alter the silhouette of the garment hemline.

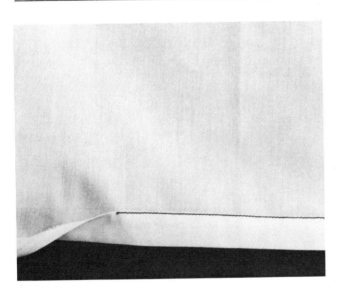

Machine-Stitched Hem

A hem held in place by means of one or more parallel rows of machine stitching, penetrating all plies, and visible on the face of the garment.

- On garments subject to hard wear and frequent washings such as work and playclothes.
- In several rows as a decorative machine trimming.
- On edges of firmly woven fabrics.
- On very full garments such as costumes, where hand hemming is time-consuming.
- On bulky fabrics producing a flat finish.

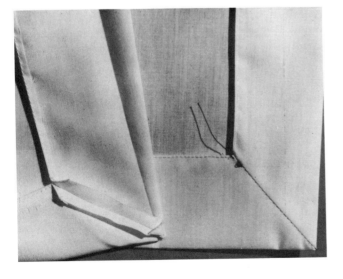

Mitered Hem

A hem which in turning a corner is seamed at an angle bisecting that corner.

- To eliminate bulk at corners.
- To achieve a flat look at corners or points.
- To square the corner of faced and other hems.
- To produce a continuous fitted look when a band or trimming is placed on the outside hem area of garments.
- To form smooth *finished* corners in slashed designs.
- With trimming or bias strips.

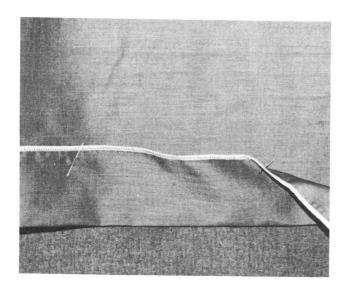

Overedged Hem

A hem made by a machine stitch, which produces a clean finish on a raw edge by means of interlocking thread loops.

- As the final finish of an unturned hem edge.
- To prevent edges from raveling.
- On garments made of cotton, linen or fabric blends where rayon seam tape is not compatible with the fabric.
- To produce a lettuce edge finish on knit and stretch fabrics.

Padded Hem

A hem with an additional piece of thick, soft fabric inserted between the hem and the garment. The additional piece extends beyond the hem area and is doubled at the hem fold.

- To prevent a sharp crease on hem folds.
- On garments where a soft hemline is desired.
- To eliminate ridges on hems of heavy fabrics.
- To produce roundness to lower edges.
- To add weight and body at the lower edges of the garment.

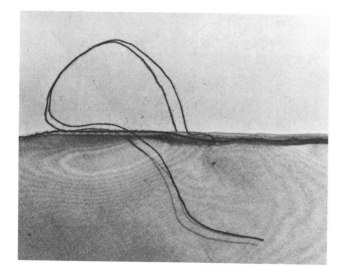

Hand-Rolled Hem

A fine hem, approximately 1/8 inch (3.2 mm) wide, in which the raw edge is rolled under and secured by a slip stitch.

- On lightweight fabrics.
- On wide and circular hems of skirts, capes, sleeves, etc.
- To finish edges of scarfs and handkerchiefs.
- To finish edges of ruffles, trimmings and flounces.

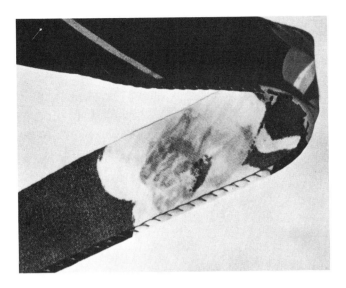

Machine-Rolled Hem

A narrow double-fold hem, 1/8 inch (3.2 mm) depth, in which the raw edge is fed through an attachment which completes the folding and stitching in one operation; or in which the preliminary and final folds have each been machine stitched.

- On very full garments made of sheer fabrics, where hand rolling is impractical or too expensive.
- On sheer and lightweight fabrics such as silk, chiffon, organza, voile, and tricot.

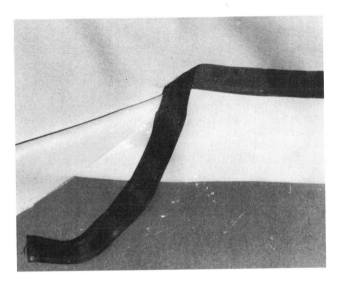

Iron-On Seam Binding / Press-On Tape

Narrow ribbon with a heat-activated bonding agent on two edges of the underside. Ribbon is applied to conceal and fasten hem edge to garment ply in one application.

- When a long edge or fold is to be hemmed quickly.
- Press-on tape is applied by heat to hem and garment to hold hem in place.
- To eliminate the need for hand or machine hemming.

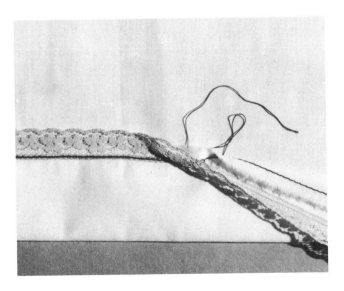

Lace Seam Binding

A stretchable or non-stretchable lace ribbon, in a variety of widths and/or weights, attached to garment edge.

- In place of seam tape or bias binding.
- As a functional or decorative finish on lower edges of garments.
- On lace fabrics.
- On garments made of compatible fabrics such as rayon, silk and cotton, where the care of the garment would be the same as that required for the tape.

Ribbon Seam Tape / Seam Binding

A narrow lightweight ribbon, usually of synthetic yarn, approximately 1/2 inch (12.7 mm) wide, attached to garment edge.

- To conceal the raw edges of fabrics that ravel easily.
- On medium weight and opaque fabrics.
- On garments made of compatible fabrics, such as rayon, silk and nylon, where the care of the garment would be the same as that required for the tape.

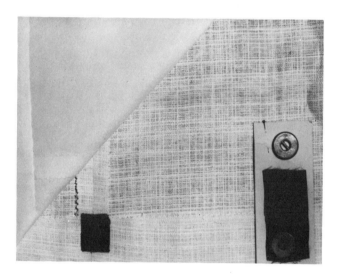

Weighted Hem with Lead Disk

A hem to which a square or round lead disk, which may be fabric covered, has been attached.

- To control the drape of the hem.
- To help the hem fall evenly.
- To keep the hem straight.
- As an anchor to hold hem detail in place.
- On the lower edge of pleats and slashed openings.
- On front corner of hem and facing of coats and jackets.
- To prevent hem areas from shifting.

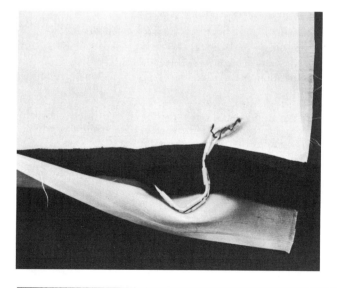

Weighted Hem with Lead Pellets

A hem to which lead pellets, uncovered or encased in fabric, are added and/or attached inside the hem fold of the garment.

- When a uniformly weighted hem is desired.
- To prevent hem from riding upward on body.
- To control the drape of the hem.
- To help the hem fall evenly.
- To keep the hem straight.
- To add body to hem of lightweight fabrics.

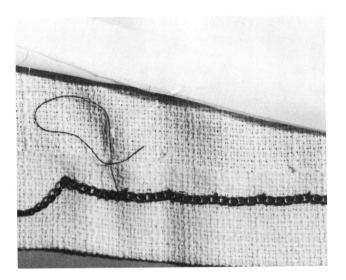

Weighted Hem with Metal Chain

A hem to which a metal chain, in assorted lengths, weights, and metals, has been attached to the face of the lower portion of the finished hem.

- When a uniformly weighted hem is desired.
- To prevent the hem from riding upward on the body.
- To help the hem fall evenly.
- To keep the hem striaght.
- To prevent the hem area from shifting.
- On coat and jacket hemlines.

Known and recognized as the *Chanel jacket* hemline.

Wired Hem

A stiffened edge produced by incorporating a slender plastic or metal wire into the fold of a narrow hem.

- To add body without weight to hem areas.
- To produce hem areas that billow or stand out.
- In hems of ruffles and trimmings.
- On sheer and lightweight fabrics.

Band Placket / Tab Placket
Bound Placket
Continuous Lap Placket
Continuous Lap Placket Placed in a Seam
Dress Placket / Seam Placket
Faced-Slashed Placket
Hemmed-Edge Placket
Tailored Placket / Shirtsleeve Placket

A placket is a finished opening in a garment section.

Plackets should be designed and styled in sufficient length to permit ease and convenience of dressing.

Placket openings are used on sleeves to allow expansion of the narrow end and to provide room when the cuff is opened. They are used on front or back neckline openings instead of a zipper. Plackets are planned as extensions for the placement of buttonholes, snaps and other fasteners.

The type and length of a placket selected depend on:
- Placement of placket
- Function of placket
- Style and design of garment
- Use of garment
- Type and weight of fabric
- Care of garment
- Method of construction

Band Placket / Tab Placket

A placket design utilizing two finished strips of equal width, applied to fill an oblong opening. A lapped closure is produced where the overlap strip is visible on the face of the garment.

- To emphasize an opening in a garment.
- At neck and sleeve openings.
- As an opening in skirts, pants, slacks or shorts.
- On jackets and ponchos designed without full-length openings.

Tab design may be extended to include an all-in-one facing; as a combination neck and placket band.

Tab strip ends may be incorporated into seam allowance of opening to produce a square finish across bottom. Lower end of tab may be planned with a pointed or rounded extension for decorative purposes. Extension may hang freely or may be top-stitched to garment.

Closure may be planned with or without fasteners.

Bound Placket

A non-overlap opening formed by a fabric strip applied, slashed, turned and finished as a welt binding.

- To form an opening where no seam is planned.
- On neck or sleeve openings that will close with a loop fastener or ties.
- To finish slit at lower hem edges of blouses, skirts, pants or shorts to allow ease or as a decorative design detail.
- To form a decorative opening.

Strip may be made of bias or straight grain fabric; or of same or contrasting fabric.

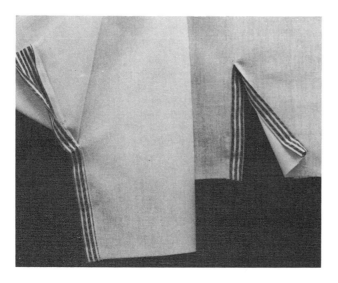

Continuous Lap Placket

A finished opening formed by the application of a strip of bias or straight-grain fabric, in the same or contrasting color, which encases the raw edge of the slash.

- Where placket will be concealed.
- On cuffed sleeve openings to permit hand to fit through sleeve circumference.
- On skirts and trousers where zipper application would detract from appeal of the garment.
- As a neckline opening alternative to other fasteners or closures.

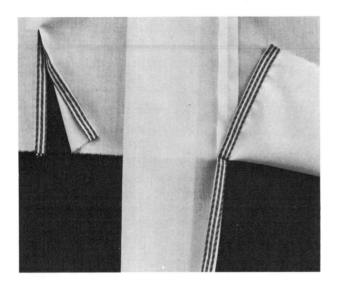

Continuous Lap Placket Placed in a Seam

A finished opening formed by the application of a strip of bias or straight-grain fabric, in the same or contrasting color, which encases the raw edges of the seam at the placket opening.

- In place of a zipper in a seam opening.
- When an opening is needed in a seamed section of the garment.
- To reinforce seams for buttons, snaps, hooks and eye fasteners.
- On infants' and children's wear as an alternative to zipper fasteners or other closures.
- On sleeves, skirts, trousers, and dresses.

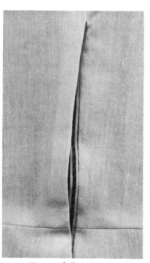 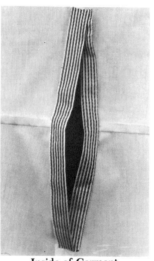

Dress Placket / Seam Placket

An extension which is formed by strips applied to the seam allowance on one or both sides of the opening.

- To strengthen seam areas where fasteners or zippers will be applied.
- On garments made of lightweight, sheer or lace fabrics where the zipper tape would show on the face of the garment.
- When the seam allowance is too narrow or the fabric frays.

Extension strips may be made of self-fabric which has a folded edge, or compatible ribbon.

Face of Garment   Inside of Garment

Faced-Slashed Placket

A clean-finished opening with no overlap which is produced by a facing turned to the face or inside of a garment.

- On sleeves and necklines where no seam is planned.
- On neck or sleeve openings that will close with a loop fastener or by ties.
- Where garment edges meet rather than lap.
- On lower hem edges of blouses, skirts, and shorts to allow ease or as a decorative design detail.

Facing lies flat against garment section.

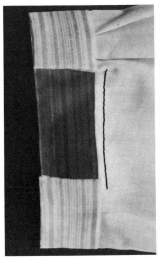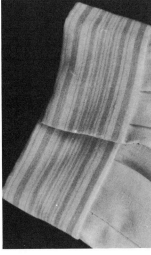

Hemmed-Edge Placket

A horizontally hemmed garment section that lies between the ends of an applied band.

- To provide an economical and simple construction method.
- On bulky or loosely woven fabrics to eliminate bulkiness.

When band is closed, hemmed edge forms a pleat.

Tailored Placket / Shirtsleeve Placket

A tab design consisting of two strips of unequal width which enclose the raw edges of an opening. The wider, top-stitched strip overlaps and conceals the narrower binding strip and unfinished edge.

- When placket is planned as a design detail.
- To emphasize placket opening.
- On sleeve and garment openings with overlap closure.
- On sleeve openings of sport shirts.
- On skirt openings where a zipper is not used.

Top-stitched placket section shows on face of garment. Placket produces a strong, flat-finished opening.

Butted Seam / Abutted Seam
Corded Piped Seam
Eased Seam:
    Eased Seam / Seam with Ease
    Production Eased Seam
Flat-Felled Seam
French Seam:
    French Seam
    False French Seam / Simulated French Seam
Fused Seam
Glued Seam
Hairline Seam
Lapped Seam
Lapped Seam with Raw Edges
Overedged Seam
Padded Seam
Plain Seam
Piped Seam

Safety-Stitched Seam
Seams of Fur
Seams of Lace
Seams of Skins
Slot Seam
Stayed Seam
Strapped Seam
Taped Seam
Tissue-Stitched Seam
Top-Stitched Seam:
    Top-Stitched Seam
    Double Top-Stitched Seam
Tucked Seam / Open Welt Seam
Welt Seam:
    Welt Seam
    Double Welt Seam / Mock Flat-Felled Seam
Zigzagged Seam

Seams are the result of joining together two or more pieces of fabric by means of stitching or fusing. Seams are utilitarian, functional and may be used for decorative purposes.

Lines and design features are expressed through seams in garments.

A *seam line* is the designated line along which the seam is to be joined.

A *seam allowance* is the distance from the fabric edge to the stitching line farthest from the edge. Seam allowance is planned according to the width needed for the type of seam, seam finish or garment design.

Most seams are constructed on the inside or wrong side of the garment. Those constructed on the face or the right side of the garment will be identified in the text.

Under the provision of Federal Standards No. 751, seams are divided into four classes; each class is identified by letters; and seams in each class are subdivided into types. Seam classes are:

SS–Superimposed
LS–Lapped
BS–Bound
FS–Flat

Two or more upper case letters classify the seam; one or two lower case letters identify the type of seam within the class; one or more Arabic numerals indicate number of rows of stitching within the seam.

The type of seam selected depends on:
• Type of fabric
• Use of garment
• Placement or position of seam
• Care of garment

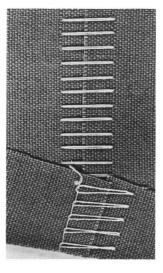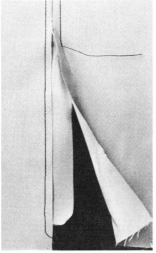

Butted Seam / Abutted Seam

A flat seam joining two plies, edge-to-edge, without overlay or seam allowance.

- For endwise joining of piece goods.
- As a flat finish for joining interfacings of woven or non-woven fabrics where a seam or lapped edge is not desired.
- On garments, such as slickers, that are subsequently coated with opaque waterproofing.
- To join seams of suede, leather, vinyl and felt.
- To join seams of foundation garments where bulk would be irritating to body.
- In conjunction with a flat lockstitch.

Federal Seam Type Classification: FSa-1
  Seams may be abutted by attaching upper plies, edge-to-edge, over an underlay strip.

Corded Piped Seam

A seam stitched with a corded bias strip, of the same or contrasting fabrics, inserted between the plies to show on the face of the garment.

- As a decorative edge to collars, cuffs, pockets, or faced necklines.
- Between the bodice and skirt at waistline of dresses.
- To accentuate yoke or princess line seams.
- To outline openings and hems.
- To add body to seam lines.

Federal Seam Type Classification: SSk-1 (with cord)

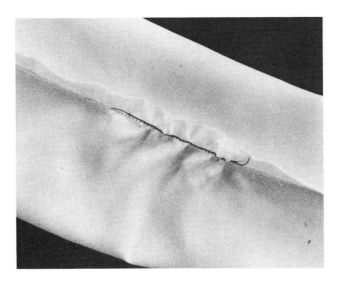

Eased Seam / Seam with Ease

An eased seam entails the drawing in or easing of a longer section of a seam line on one ply to fit a corresponding but shorter section of a seam line on the second ply.

- To replace small darts in necklines, elbows, bustlines, and waistlines.
- On the back sleeve seam at the elbow.
- On the outward curved seam of the side front panel in the princess line garment.
- To shape and mold sleeve caps.
- On waistlines of skirts and bodices to distribute fullness and control fit.
- To match back shoulder to front.

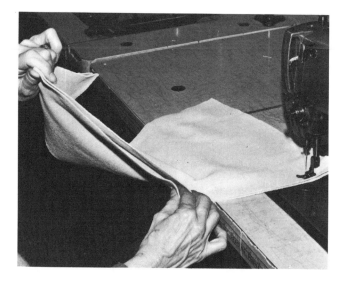

Production Eased Seam

The process of restraining the under ply of a fabric and allowing the upper ply to feed freely while sewing an un-basted seam to compensate for the pull of the feed dog and drag of the presser foot.

- To keep both plies of seam an even length during sewing procedure.
- In mass production sewing.

Both seam plies are cut an even length.

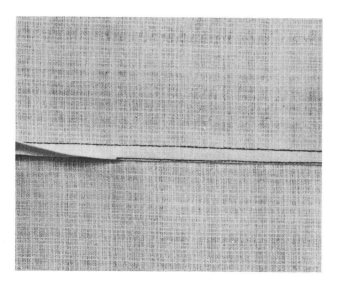

Flat-Felled Seam

A flat-felled seam is the result of enclosing both seam allowances by interlocking opposing folded edges beneath two parallel rows of machine stitching through all plies.

- On garments that are made to take hard wear such as pajamas, play clothes, work clothes, sport clothes, and outerwear.
- On men's shirts, boys' trousers, and women's tailored garments.
- On reversible garments.
- On unlined garments.

Federal Seam Type Classification: LCS-2
   Flat-felled seams may be produced in an all-in-one operation with a felling foot attachment on an industrial machine. In non-industrial production, seam may be made in two or more steps. Method of construction produces a sturdy seam.
   Referred to as the *Jeans Seam.*

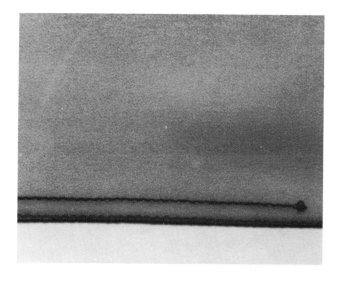

French Seam

A seam constructed so that a narrow seam is contained within a larger one, producing a clean finish.

- To prevent fabrics from fraying.
- When the seam finish will show through garments made of sheer fabrics such as chiffon, organza, georgette, organdy.
- On children's and infants' wear, underwear, and outerwear.
- On straight seams.
- When a seam is to appear as a plain seam on the face of the garment and a clean finish is desired on the inside.

Federal Seam Type Classification: SSe-2 (modified)

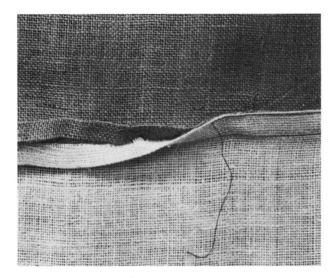

False French Seam / Simulated French Seam

A plain seam made to resemble a French seam by the face-to-face enclosing of the folded seam edges.

- On transparent fabrics that ravel easily.
- In place of a French seam.
- When the fitting and alteration of a garment make the construction of a French seam impractical.
- As a finish on curved seams for armholes and princess line garments.
- As a finish under a lapped seam.
- When a strong finish is desired.

Unclassified

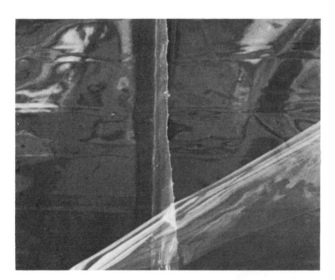

Fused Seam

A seam formed by a melting process, which joins the seam lines of thermoplastic fabrics.

- As a substitute for stitches.
- On plastic clothing such as raincoats, rain hats, slickers.
- On children's protective clothing such as aprons, bibs, smocks.
- On garments made of thermoplastic fabrics and worn for industrial or commercial use such as career clothes, smocks, clothing protectors, aprons, bibs.
- On inside seam of thermoplastic fabrics.
- In interfacing and collars.

Unclassified

Glued Seam

A lapped seam joined by adhesive.

- On garments made of paper or of a temporary nature.
- On suede, leather, and vinyl until the seams are hand- or machine-stitched.
- On skins where seams are not subjected to strain.

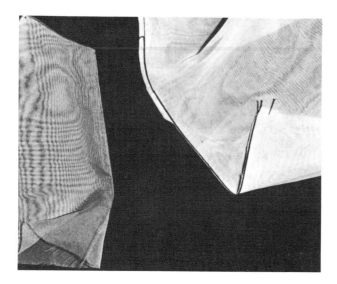

Hairline Seam

A seam with closely stitched rows of machine stitching, zigzagged or overedged, trimmed to remove all excess seam allowance.

- For collars and other seaming where there is no strain.
- To eliminate the raw edges that show through sheer fabrics when sections are joined.
- On silk organza, organdy, lawn, dimity, and other sheer and fine fabrics that fray.

Federal Seam Finish Type Classification: SSa-2

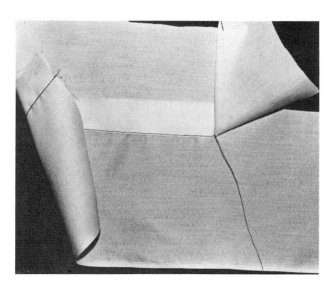

Lapped Seam

A seam joining all thicknesses from the face of the garment and catching the folded edge of the uppermost ply.

- To join garment sections such as a yoke, gusset, or godet to other garment sections.
- On sections of the garment where stitching on the face of the garment aids construction and speeds sewing.
- On seams where the stitching is desired as a decorative finish.
- On fabrics that will not fray.

Federal Seam Type Classification: LSb

Lapped Seam with Raw Edges

A seam formed by two plies overlaid *face-to-back* along the seam line, joined by machine or hand stitching, leaving a raw edge exposed on each surface.

- To produce a flattened finish.
- To join interfacing, buckram or horsehair inside garments.
- To eliminate the bulk of darts on interfacing.
- To eliminate bulk when making buttonholes and joining collars, pockets and flaps to garments made of suede, leather and other skins; vinyl; felt or melton.
- To join seams of suede, leather, and other skins; vinyl, felt or melton.

Federal Seam Type Classification: LSa-1

Overedged Seam

A superimposed seam in which all raw edges have been enclosed within the loops of the overedge stitch used to form the seam.

- To form seams of knit garments.
- To form seams of undergarments and lingerie.
- To prevent fraying and raveling of seam edges.
- On play clothes, work clothes, and sportswear.
- To form an enclosed seam.
- To form a decorative exposed seam.

Referred to as a *Merrow* ® *seam.*

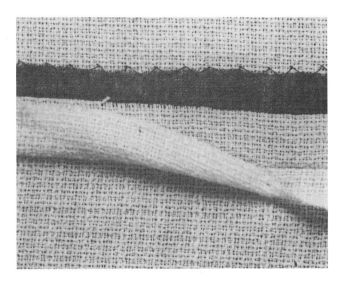

Padded Seam

A seam in which a soft strip has been inserted between the seam allowance and garment ply.

- Where a raised effect for design detail is desired on the face of the garment.
- To accentuate and produce a dimensional surface at the seam line.
- Where nailhead, bead or stone trimmings will be added on the seams.
- In conjunction with top stitching to produce a raised, rolled effect.

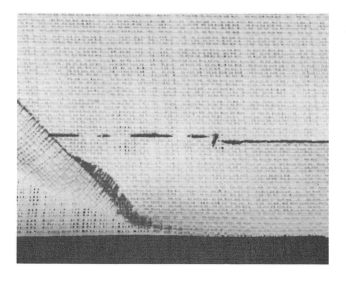

Plain Seam

A commonly used seam joining two sections of fabric. It may be left as is or finished with a seam finish.

- On fabrics that will not ravel.
- On seams of garments that will be covered by a lining.

Federal Seam Type Classification: SSa-1

Piped Seam

A seam stitched with a flat straight grain or bias strip, made with the same or contrasting fabric of suitable texture and thickness, inserted between the plies to show on the face of the garment.

- As a decorative edge to collars, cuffs, pockets or faced necklines.
- Between the bodice and skirt at waistline of dresses.
- To accentuate yoke or princess line seams.
- To outline openings and hems.
- For tailored buttonholes.

Federal Seam Type Classification: SSk-1

Safety-Stitched Seam

A seam stitched simultaneously with two independent parallel rows of stitches, one securing the seam a specified distance from the edge and the other overlapping all plies.

- On seams of knit or stretch garments.
- On play clothes, work clothes, and sportswear.
- To join seams of swimwear.
- To join crotch seam of girdles and undergarments.
- To join and finish seams on fabrics that ravel easily.
- To finish raw edge of seam.

Federal Seam Type Classification: SSa-l; stitch type 301-401, 501-507, 602, 612-619

The formation, size, bite, and spacing of stitches vary according to different machines. An increased seam allowance affords a measure of protection against seam slippage.

Seams of Fur

The joining of skins made with a close overhand stitch or by a special fur sewing machine.

- On skins and animal furs.
- On man-made, high pile fabrics.

Stitches joining the skin penetrate the pelt only.

Seams of Lace

A seam joining two pieces of lace, following the outline of the lace design by means of a machine zigzag stitch or a hand, felling, whip, slip or overhanding stitch.

- To continue the motif design of the lace.
- Where an invisible join is required.

Federal Seam Type Classification: LSa
  A flat-lapped seam is formed when lace is joined.

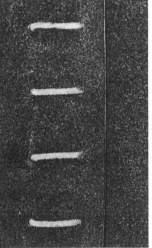

Seams of Skins

The joining of two or more plies of leather in any one of a variety of ways.

Seams of skins may be joined as:

  A plain seam with a glued seam finish;
  A lapped and stitched seam;
  A lapped and double-stitched seam;
  Butted and trimmed as a slot seam;
  Lapped with lacing through punched holes;
  Lapped with lacing through eyelets;
  Lapped with cross-stitched lacing;
  Lapped with parallel lacing.

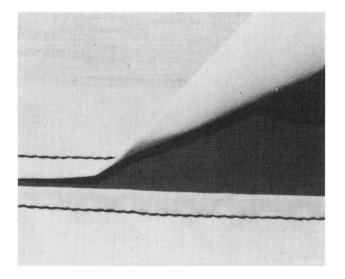

Slot Seam

A decorative seam in which a backing strip, beneath the folded, faced or abutted seam line, holds two sections of the garment in place with stitching parallel to the finished seam line.

- As a decorative seam finish for tailored garments.
- When a contrasting color or textured underlay piece will add interest and decoration to the garment.

Federal Seam Type Classification: SSs-1 (modified)

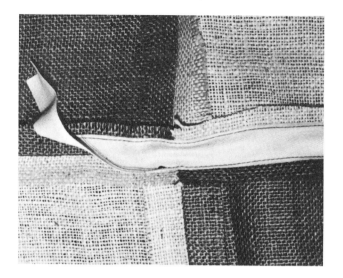

Stayed Seam

A seam on which a reinforcing strip of twill or ribbon tape, bias binding or self fabric spanning the opened seam line, is stitched to each seam allowance ply.

- To support and strengthen a garment seam.
- To relieve strain in the seam section.
- To prevent breakage of seam.
- To reinforce crotch seams.
- To cover seams in fabrics that may cause skin irritation insuring comfort and wearability.
- On seams of leather and vinyl garments.
- On batwing, dolman, kimono sleeves or curved underarm seams.

Strapped Seam

A seam in which the seam allowance on the face or inside of the garment is covered with a stitched-down ribbon or a band made of bias or straight grain fabric.

- As a decorative finish or trimming on the face of coats, jackets, and tailored garments.
- To add strength to the side seam of pants, shorts, and sport clothes.
- As a decorative tailored finish for the inside seams of unlined coats and jackets.

Federal Seam Type Classification: SSad

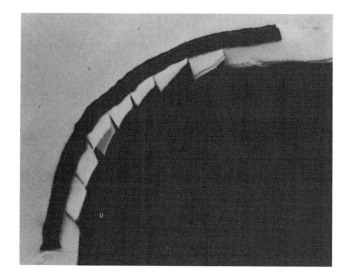

Taped Seam

A seam with twill or ribbon tape, bias binding, net, or a fabric strip included in the line of stitching.

- To add strength and firmness to seams.
- To stabilize seams.
- To prevent:
    Bias and other seams from stretching;
    Shoulder and waistline seams of knitted garments from losing their shape;
    The inside fold of kick pleats from stretching;
    Hip seams from stretching when inserting zippers;
    Gathered seams from stretching and losing their shape;
    The seams on the front openings of coats and jackets from curling.
- On armholes of suits, coats, and tailored garments.
- On necklines, lapels, collars, and closing edges of jackets or coats.
- During the tailoring process.
- To strengthen the curved seams of batwing, dolman, kimono, and raglan sleeves.
- To produce a straight edge where a seam has been eliminated and the garment and facing are cut in one piece.
- To add stability and prevent stretching on neckline seams.

Federal Seam Type Classification: SSa-1

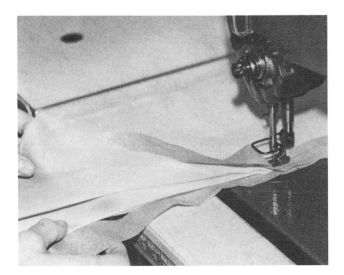

Tissue-Stitched Seam

A seam in which tissue paper is inserted between the fabric plies, and/or fabric and machine parts, then removed upon completion of the stitching.

- To prevent seams from slipping during seaming.
- To eliminate puckering of seams while stitching.
- As a stay during the sewing process.
- To sew bias seams to eliminate stretching.
- To eliminate damage of fabrics from machine parts.
- To protect silk fabrics; soft, sheer fabrics such as chiffon or georgette.

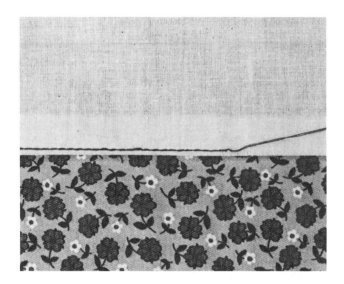

Top-Stitched Seam

A seam which has been pressed to one side and stitched parallel to the seam line, through all plies, from the face of the garment.

- To hold the seam allowance in place.
- To flatten the seams of garment details such as gussets, godets or yokes.
- To hold pleats in place.
- To decoratively stitch pleat lines.
- To emphasize seam and style lines.

Federal Seam Type Classification: LSq-2

Double Top-Stitched Seam

A seam which has been pressed open and stitched parallel to and on both sides of the seam line, through garment and seam plies.

- As decorative stitching.
- To outline seam lines.
- When multiple rows of stitching will accent the seam line.
- To hold intersecting seam areas flat.
- To strengthen seams.

Federal Seam Type Classification: LSq-3

Tucked Seam / Open Welt Seam

A seam in which the edge of the upper ply, folded along the seam line, forms a tuck when top stitched to the lower ply.

- As a decorative seam.
- To add interest and accent seam lines.
- On yokes, midriffs, and bands of garments.

Federal Seam Type Classification: LSd-1
    Used in various tuck widths according to style and design of garment.

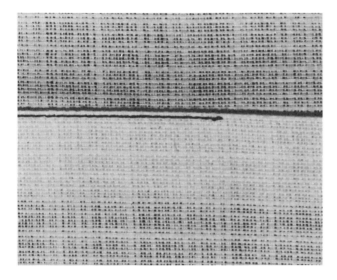

Welt Seam

A flat inside seam, graded and pressed to one side; the larger seam allowance being top-stitched to the garment thereby enclosing the smaller.

- For sportswear made of heavy fabrics wherever a strong flat seam is desired.
- On women's tailored shirtwaist dresses, tailored blouses, and yokes of garments.
- To reduce bulk on the inside of garments when joining seams.
- On work clothes and garments made of bulky fabrics where a flat-felled seam would be too heavy.
- To accent seam and/or style lines.

Federal Seam Type Classification: LSq-2 (modified)

Double Welt Seam / Mock Flat-Felled Seam

A welt seam with an additional row of top-stitching, through all plies, parallel to the original seam line fold.

- To strengthen the seam.
- To make the seam more compact.
- As decorative stitching.
- To accent seam and/or style lines.
- When planning a raised effect between the two rows of machine stitching.
- Instead of a flat-felled seam on garments made of bulky fabrics.

Federal Seam Type Classification: LSq-3 (modified)

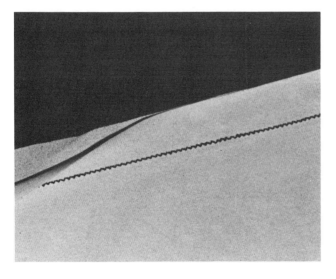

Zigzagged Seam

A seam joined by utilizing the short stitch length and small bite of a zigzag pattern.

- To produce a seam with give.
- As a lingerie seam.
- To join lace.
- On knit and stretch fabrics.
- For spandex undergarment construction.
- To apply appliqué.

Federal Seam Type Classification: SSa-1; stitch type 304-404

30~Seam Finishes

Book Seam Finish
Bound Seam Finish:
　Net-Bound Seam Finish
　Self-Bound Seam Finish /
　　Rolled Seam Finish
　Single-Ply Bound Seam Finish
　Double-Ply Bound Seam Finish
Double-Stitched Seam Finish
Double-Stitched & Overcast Seam Finish
Double-Stitched & Trimmed Seam Finish
Edge-Stitched Seam Finish / Turned Under
　Edge Seam Finish
Glued Seam Finish

Overcast Seam Finish:
　Single-Ply Overcast Seam Finish
　Double-Ply Overcast Seam Finish /
　　Whipped Seam Finish
Pinked Seam Finish
Pinked & Stitched Seam Finish
Pinked & Double-Stitched Seam Finish
Serging / Single-Ply Overedged Seam Finish
Untreated Seam Finish / Plain Seam Finish
Zigzag Seam Finish:
　Single-Ply Zigzag Seam Finish
　Double-Ply Zigzag Seam Finish

Seam edges are finished to prevent the fabric from raveling, strengthen the seam, and improve the appearance of the seam.

　Seam finishes are applied to the seam allowances.
　The type of seam finish selected depends on:
• Type of fabric
• Position of seam
• Use of the garment
• Care of the garment
• Life of the garment

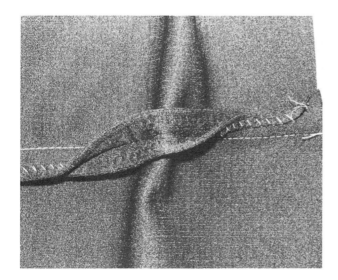

Book Seam Finish

A seam finish in which the raw edge of each seam allowance is folded under and secured to the garment ply by a concealed blind stitch, prior to stitching the seam.

- To hold the seam allowance ply to the garment.
- To prevent the raw seam allowance ply from fraying.
- On garments where the seams will take hard wear.
- To finish seams of unlined jackets and coats.
- On seams of trousers.

Federal Seam Finish Type Classification: SSb a-3

Blind stitch may be made with thermoplastic thread which bonds the seam allowances to garment when activated by heat, steam, and pressure.

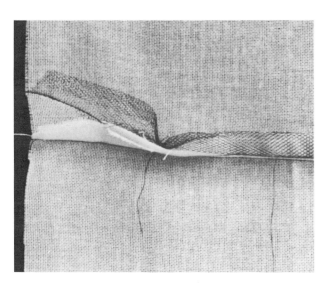

Net-Bound Seam Finish

A seam finish in which the raw edge of the seam allowance is encased within a folded net strip.

- As a binding to finish the raw edge of seams.
- On fabrics that fray easily.
- On delicate and sheer fabrics such as silk velvet, chiffon, or lace.
- On raw edges of metallic fabrics which irritate the skin.
- For edges or seam finishes where other bindings would add bulk.

Federal Seam Finish Type Classification: Lace Binding BSA-1 (no-fold edge)

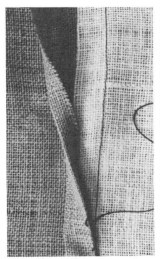 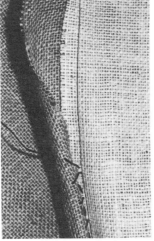

Self-Bound Seam Finish / Rolled Seam Finish

A clean finish in which a folded- or rolled-over ply of a seam allowance, hand- or machine-stitched, encloses a trimmed ply and gives a bound appearance.

- To reduce size of seam allowance.
- On sheer or transparent fabrics.
- When a strong, sturdy seam is desired.
- When the seam allowance would show on the face of the garment.

Unclassified

Self-Bound Seam Finish   Rolled Seam Finish

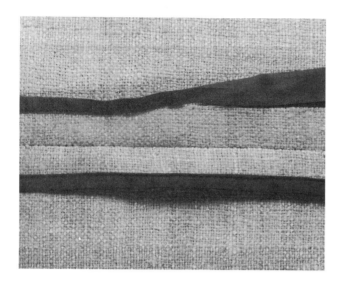

Single-Ply Bound Seam Finish

A seam finish in which the raw edge of the seam allowance is covered with a folded ribbon tape or bias binding.

- On heavy fabrics which ravel easily.
- On the seams of unlined coats, jackets, and vests.
- When the inside or wrong side of the clothing may show.
- To reduce the abrasion of seam edges.
- To cover the raw edge of fabric that may chafe the skin.
- To protect the raw edge of easily frayed fabrics.
- On fabrics that are too thick to be turned under and edge stitched.

Federal Seam Finish Type Classification: Ribbon—BSa-1; Bias—BSc-1

Double-Ply Bound Seam Finish

A seam finish in which both raw edges of the seam allowances are bound together with a folded ribbon tape or bias binding.

- On garment seams that are pressed in the same direction.
- On seams of soft or lightweight garments.
- To reduce the abrasion of seam edges.
- To protect the raw edge of easily frayed fabrics.
- When the inside or wrong side of the clothing may show.

Federal Seam Finish Type Classification: Ribbon—BSd-2; Bias—BSc-2

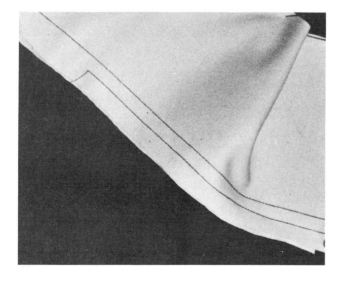

Double-Stitched Seam Finish

A plain seam with a parallel row of stitches, through all plies, placed 1/4 inch (6.4 mm) from the first.

- To reinforce a plain seam.
- On sheer and transparent fabrics; laces.
- To eliminate bulk in soft and embroidered fabrics.
- When additional seam finishes are not needed.
- In conjunction with a seam finish.
- To prevent the seam edge from curling on knits, jerseys, and tricot.

Federal Seam Finish Type Classification: SSa-2; stitch types 301 or 401

Double-Stitched & Overcast Seam Finish

A seam joined through all plies by two parallel rows of stitching, 1/4 inch (6.4 mm) apart, finished with a series of loose, slanting hand stitches encircling the raw edges of the seam allowance.

- Around armholes.
- At waistlines.
- On the underlay seams of pleats on fabrics that fray easily.

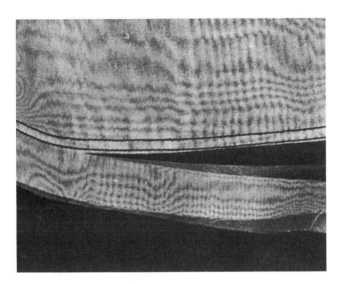

Double-Stitched & Trimmed Seam Finish

A seam joined through all plies by two closely spaced parallel rows of stitching, in which the remaining seam allowance is removed.

- On fabrics that require a flat narrow seam.
- On lace and eyelet fabrics.
- On georgette, chiffon and silk organza.
- To prevent seams of sheer or jersey fabrics from rolling.

Federal Seam Finish Type Classification: SSa-2

Edge-Stitched Seam Finish / Turned Under Edge Seam Finish

A seam finish in which the raw edge of the seam allowance is turned under, stitched, and concealed.

- To prevent the seam edges from fraying.
- On straight-edged seams.
- On garments where the seam allowance will not show on the face of the garment.
- On plain weave fabrics.
- On soft, medium, and lightweight fabrics.
- On unlined coats, jackets, or vests.

Federal Seam Finish Type Classification: Seam—SSa-1; Stitching—EFa-1

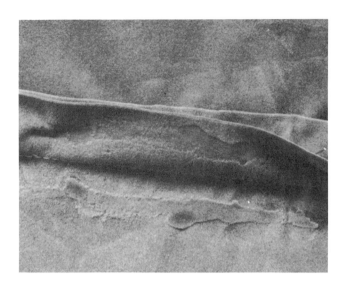

Glued Seam Finish

A seam allowance ply held in place against the garment ply by means of an adhesive.

- On the underside of seams to join seam allowance to the garment.
- To flatten seams of garments made of suede, leather, and other skins; vinyl and felt.
- To hold seam in an open position.

Glued seam allowance is finger pressed, pounded, or rolled to compress the layers.

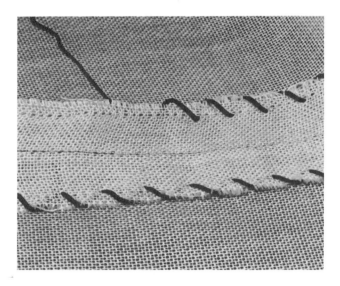

Single-Ply Overcast Seam Finish

A hand stitched seam finish in which a series of loose, slanting stitches encircle the raw edges of each seam allowance individually.

- To prevent the raw edge of a seam allowance from raveling.
- On fabrics that ravel and fray easily.
- On soft and medium weight fabrics.
- Where a soft, pliable finish is required.
- To join the backing and face fabric plies at the free edge of the seam allowance.
- On fabrics that are too thick to be turned under.
- On fabrics where bound seams are impracticable.

In conjunction with:
- Plain seam;
- Double-stitched seam;
- Pinked seam;
- Stitched and pinked seam.

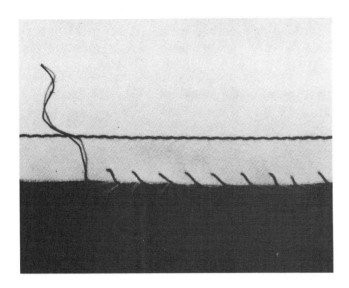

Double-Ply Overcast Seam Finish / Whipped Seam Finish

A hand-stitched seam finish in which a series of loose, slanting stitches encircle and join together both raw edges of the seam allowance plies.

- Around armholes, at waistlines, and behind lapped seams.
- On the underlay seams of pleats.
- On straight or curved edges.

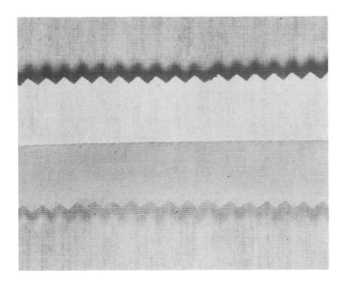

Pinked Seam Finish

A saw-toothed edge produced by a power machine equipped with a special disc or by the action of a pinking shears.

- On fabrics that do not fray easily.
- On fabrics where the seam will not be visible on the face or right side of the garment.

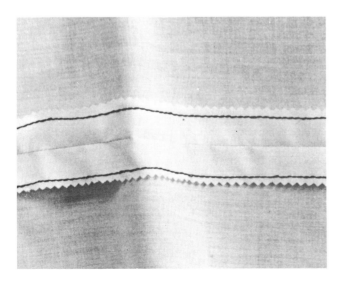

Pinked & Stitched Seam Finish

A seam finish in which a line of machine stitching is made 1/4 inch (6.4 mm) from the raw cut edge before pinking.

- To prevent the pinked edge from raveling.
- To prevent the seam from curling.
- On fabrics which ravel slightly.

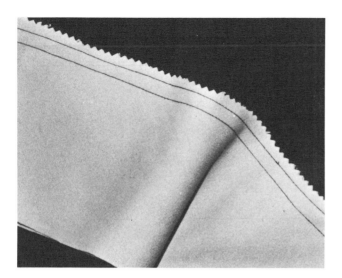

Pinked & Double-Stitched Seam Finish

A seam finish in which a line of machine stitching, through both plies of the seam allowance, is made 1/4 inch (6.4 mm) from the raw cut edge before pinking.

- To reinforce the plain seam.
- To prevent the fabric from fraying.
- On lightweight or medium weight fabrics.

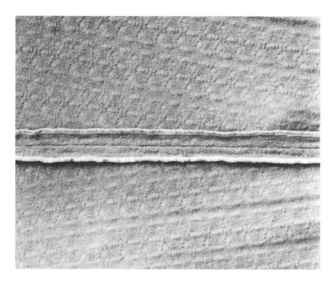

Serging / Single-Ply Overedged Seam Finish

A machine finish covering flat, raw seam edges with a series of interlocking loop stitches.

- To prevent fraying and raveling of seam edges.
- On knit fabrics.
- On play clothes, work clothes, and sportswear.

Federal Seam Finish Type Classification: Seam—SSa-1; Machine Stitching—EFd-1

Untreated Seam Finish / Plain Seam Finish

A plain seam in which the seam allowances are pressed open to lie on either side of the line of stitching.

- On fabrics that do not fray or curl.
- On fabrics that do not ravel such as knits and felt.
- On bonded fabrics.
- On garments that will be worn infrequently.
- On inexpensive garments in order to keep the construction costs down.
- On coats or garments that will be fully lined.

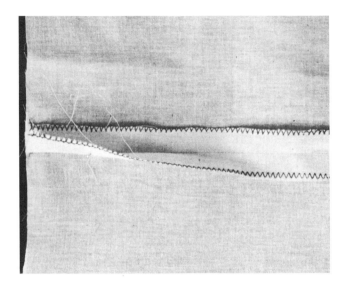

Single-Ply Zigzag Seam Finish

A machine-stitched seam finish in which a series of alternately angled stitches are applied to the raw edges of each seam allowance ply.

- To prevent seam edges from rolling.
- On fabrics that do not fray, such as jersey.
- In place of overedging.

Federal Seam Finish Type Classification: EFd-1

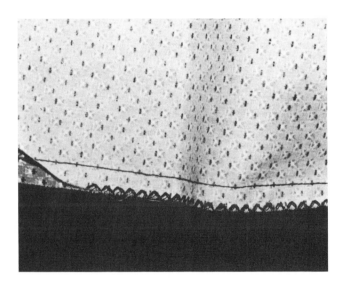

Double-Ply Zigzag Seam Finish

A machine-stitched seam finish in which a series of angled stitches are applied through both plies of the seam allowance.

- On loosely woven fabrics.
- On fabrics that fray easily.

Curved Seam:
  Inside Curved Seam
  Outside Curved Seam
Enclosed Seam
Exposed Seam
Extended Seam Allowance / Extended Seam Edge
Intersecting Seam / Crossed Seam
Rolled Seam Edge

Seam terminology describes the intrinsic and/or visual results that are part of the seam or seam finishing process.

They refer to the results that take place during the initial design of a pattern for the garment section; during construction, or as a consequence of subsequent construction procedure.

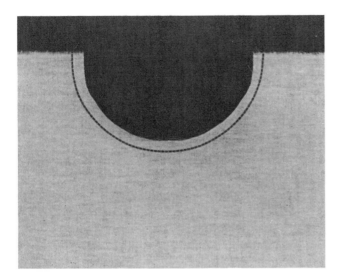

Inside Curved Seam

A seam in which the fabric to be stitched or seamed lies on the farther side of an arc, *away* from the center of the circle of which the arc is a segment.

- To produce inside curves of necklines, armholes, and front panels of princess line seams.
- To produce inside curves found on faced hems of sleeves, skirts, jackets, coats, and appliqués.

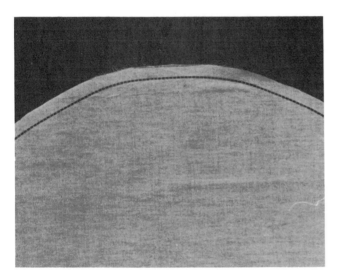

Outside Curved Seam

A seam in which the fabric to be stitched or seamed lies on the inner side of an arc, *towards* the center of the circle of which the arc is a segment.

- To produce the rounded and shaped lines of jacket and coat edges and the curve of wrap-around skirt hems.
- To produce the outer edges of Peter Pan, choir-boy, Bertha, capelet and shawl collars.
- To produce the curved outer edges of scallops, rounded patch pockets, rounded flaps, and rounded appliqués.
- To construct a faced circular hem.
- To establish the curve of the side front panel of the princess line dress.

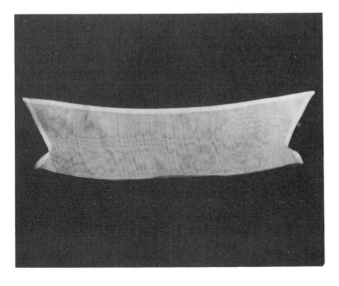

Enclosed Seam

A construction process that conceals seam allowances between garment plies when they are turned to form a clean finish.

- On reversible garments.
- On fully lined garments where edges of garment and lining meet.
- On collars, cuffs, facings, lapels, pockets and pocket flaps.

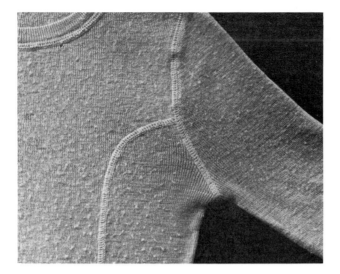

Exposed Seam

A seam in which the seam allowances are visible on the inside or outside of the garment.

- When the seam is overedged and exposed on the face of the garment for decorative and styling detail.
- Where a frayed edge is a design detail.
- On suede or heavy skins to eliminate bulk.

Extended Seam Allowance / Extended Seam Edge

That portion of a seam allowance where additional width is provided.

- Instead of a facing on a slit seam opening of sleeves or hems; on straight edges.
- To form a pocket in a seam.
- As an underlay for top stitching.
- As an extension for zipper plackets.
- On seams of jacket and coat vents.

Inside of Garment   Face of Garment

Intersecting Seam / Crossed Seam

The point where two or more seams meet and cross each other.

- To describe the crossing of the following seams:
    Center back and waistline seams;
    Center front and waistline seams;
    Yoke and bodice seams;
    Princess line and waistline seams;
    Bodice and skirt side seams;
    Bodice and sleeve underarm seams.

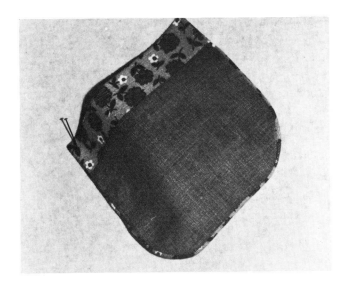

Rolled Seam Edge

An enclosed seam edge where the seam line has been brought slightly to the underside of the garment ply.

- Where the face of the garment should roll at the seam edge to hide the seam line.
- To conceal the seam edge of collars, lapels, pockets, and fully lined garments.

32 ~ Hand Stitches

Back Stitch:
  Back Stitch
  Half Back Stitch
  Modified Back Stitch / Prick Stitch
Blanket Stitch
Blind Stitch
Buttonhole Stitch
Catch Stitch:
  Catch Stitch
  Blind Catch Stitch
Crochet Chain Stitch
Felling Stitch
Overcasting Stitch
Overhand Stitch

Overhanding Stitch / Napery Stitch / Damask Stitch
Padding Stitch
Pick Stitch / Picking Stitch
Running Stitch
Saddle Stitch
Shell Stitch
Slip Stitch
Tack Stitch:
  Tack Stitch
  Arrowhead Tack Stitch / Triangular Tack Stitch
  Bar Tack Stitch
  French Tack Stitch
Whip Stitch

Hand stitches are produced and named according to the upright or slanting sewing action which alternates between plies or penetrates one ply before the other. The sewing motion of this action is from right to left, or left to right.

Hand stitches anchor and finish parts of the garment. They are either visible or invisible. They may be applied to one or more plies along seam or style lines, within the body of the garment or at the garment edge.

The type and method of hand stitches selected depends on:
• Style and design of garment
• Type of garment
• Use of garment
• Life of garment
• Care of garment
• Type of fabric
• Placement of stitch
• Size of stitch

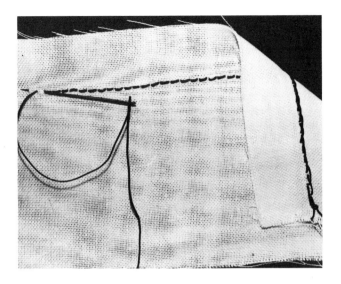

Back Stitch

A stitch produced in a series, simulating machine sewing, with no space between stitches on the face ply and overlapping stitches on the under ply.

- A permanent stitch for joining seams and garment sections.
- Where firm hand sewing is necessary.
- To replace machine stitches that have broken.
- To begin and end a permanent row of hand stitching.

The stitch is formed by inserting the needle behind the point where thread emerges from the previous stitch.

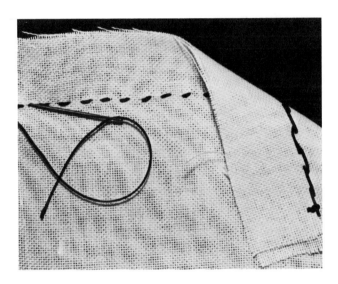

Half Back Stitch

A stitch produced in a series in which a backward or reverse sewing motion produces overlapping stitches on the underply and equidistant stitches and spaces on the face ply.

- To make or repair seams.
- To understitch facing and lining.
- To hold undercollar and lapel in place.

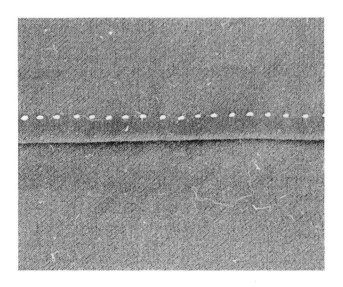

Modified Back Stitch / Prick Stitch

A stitch which penetrates all plies and produces a widely spaced, small stitch, spanning only two fabric threads, on the uppermost ply and an overlap stitch on the under ply.

- A permanent stitch to hold two or more pieces of the garment or trimming together.
- For hand application of zipper.
- An understitch to hold and prevent facing or lining from rolling to the face of the garment.

Blanket Stitch

An interlocking stitch produced in a series at 1/2 inch (12.7 mm) or less intervals, formed to lie on the edge of the ply. The edge of the ply is encased to a depth of 1/2 inch (12.7 mm) or less.

- As an edge finish on garments made of felt fabric.
- As a decorative hem edge for infants' and children's wear.
- To cover edge of fabric.
- As an alternative to a buttonhole stitch for buttonholes, eyelets, and bar tacks.
- To attach hook, eye, and snap fastener.

Stitch is formed by the action of the thread passing behind the needle. Stitch size and space can be the same or varied. Stitches may encase raw or finished edge of garment.

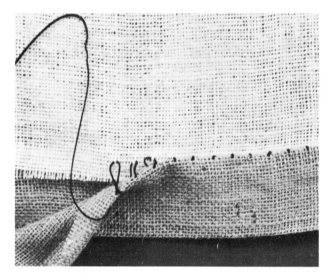

Blind Stitch

A 1/8 inch (3.2 mm) or smaller stitch produced in a series. Each stitch alternates between the folded seam edge of one ply and the stitching line or folded seam edge of another ply.

- To secure zipper tape to folded seam line of garment.
- To secure and finish inside fold of waistbands in slacks, skirts and aprons.
- To join and attach lining.
- To join garment section on the right side or face of the garment.
- To attach pockets and trimmings on garments.
- To apply strapping or banding on the face of the garment.
- A stitch for hems where there is a fold or turned under edge.

Stitching and thread do not show on face of the garment.

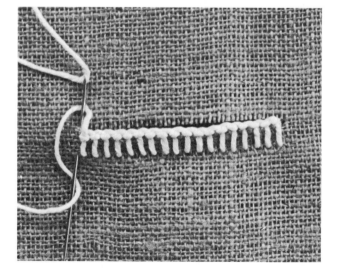

Buttonhole Stitch

A closely worked series of parallel, interlocking stitches formed by a looping of the thread around the needle, producing with each stitch a purl or knot which lies on the cut edge.

- For hand-worked buttonholes, eyelets or openings.
- To form a thread loop or belt carrier when worked around suspended thread.
- To form a bar tack at the ends of buttonholes, pockets or pleats.
- To attach hook, eye, and snap fasteners.

Stitch bite is guided by the size of buttonhole.

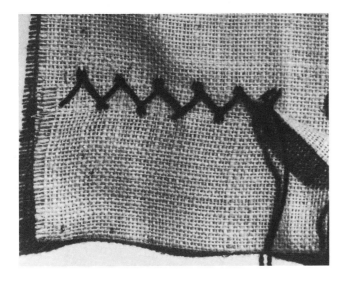

Catch Stitch

A stitch, taken alternately from ply to ply, with the point of the needle facing away from the direction of the work as it progresses from left to right, producing a loose cross stitch.

- To maintain flexibility in the fastening of two plies.
- To attach and hold facing edge to interfacing or garment.
- To hold:
    Interfacing in place;
    Facing to seam allowance.
- To attach raw seam edge to garment surface ply.
- To join abutted seams of interfacings.
- To fasten lining to garment.
- To tack lining fold in place.
- To secure pleats and tucks.
- As a hem stitch for loosely woven, stretch and knit fabrics.
- To secure hems of bulky and non-frayable fabrics.

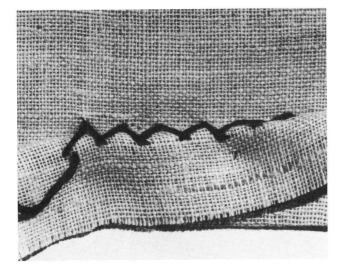

Blind Catch Stitch

A stitch taken alternately between plies, with the point of the needle facing away from the direction of the work as it progresses from left to right, producing a loose cross stitch which does not show on the face of either ply.

- To maintain flexibility in the fastening of two plies.
- To attach and hold facing edge to interfacing or garment.
- As a hem stitch for loosely woven, stretch and knit fabrics.
- To secure hems of bulky fabrics.
- When hem of garment is heavy and two rows of catch stitching are needed to prevent hem from sagging.
- To prevent ridge or impression of under ply from showing on the face of a garment.

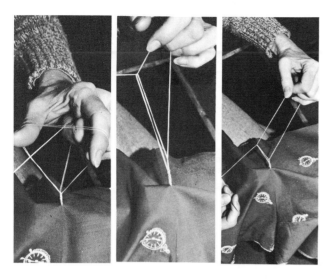

Crochet Chain Stitch

A chain represented by a series of interlocking stitches. Chain is produced by looping each successive stitch through the proceeding one.

- A carrier to hold belt in position.
- To attach belt, sash and ribbon to garment.
- To hold lining to garment hemline.
- A lingerie strap holder in a garment.
- To form button loops; thread eye for hooks.

Chain worked to desired length. May be made in button-hole twist or garment sewing thread.

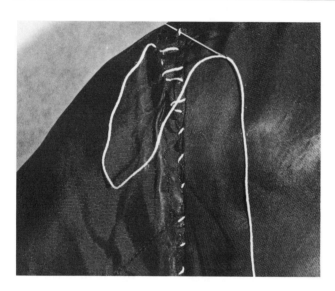

Felling Stitch

A stitch through the folded edge of one ply attaching it to the seam line of another.

- To stitch lining in coats and jackets.
- To stitch sleeve lining into lined garments.
- To stitch down collars in tailoring process.
- To secure and finish inside fold of waistbands in slacks, skirts, and aprons.
- To attach tape on seam edges.

According to U.S. Government specifications, a felling stitch is a term describing hand or machine stitches used in the finishing process.

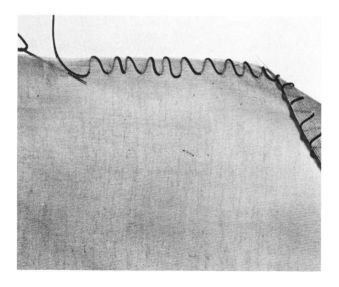

Overcasting Stitch

An evenly spaced, slanting stitch loosely encircling the raw edge of a ply or plies to a depth of 1/16 inch (1.6 mm).

- On raw or unfinished edges to prevent fraying.
- On raw edges of seams and hems.
- A finish for raw edges of facings where a turned edge would produce bulk.

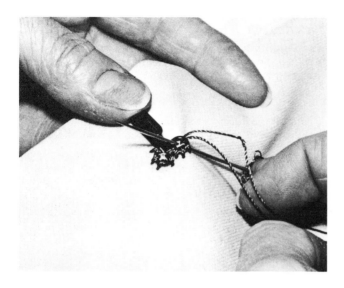

Overhand Stitch

A series of closely worked stitches penetrating the fabric ply or plies and encasing a portion of the fastener or edge to be attached or joined.

- To attach hooks, metal eyes, and snaps to garments.
- To attach tape of taped fasteners to garment.
- To join two finished edges as in ties, belts, and sashes.
- To hold a raw edge to a flat surface.
- To hold a folded edge to a flat surface.

Single- or double-ply thread may be used for stitching.

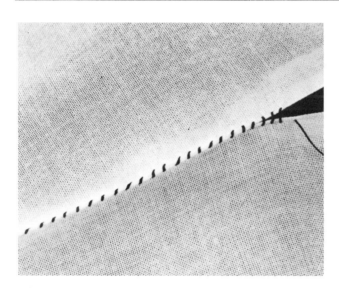

Overhanding Stitch / Napery Stitch / Damask Stitch

A series of closely worked stitches joining and encircling two raw or folded edges to a depth of 1/32 inch (0.8 mm).

- To join two flat pieces of material.
- To hold two finished edges together.
- Where a strong, secure visible seam is desired.
- To hem table linen.
- To sew on or appliqué lace.
- To join lace edgings and to attach edgings or trimmings to garments.
- For patching.

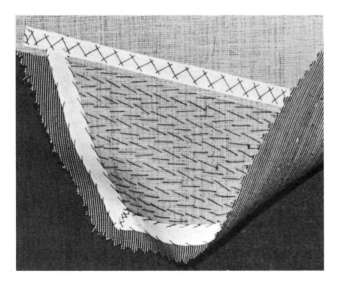

Padding Stitch

A series of permanent stitches penetrating the interfacing and picking the underside of the garment ply, worked at an angle to the direction of the grain or seam line, producing a pattern of parallel, slanting lines.

- To attach interfacing to under collars, lapels, and front sections in the tailoring process.
- To permanently attach at least two layers of fabric.

Two plies being joined are molded as the stitch is worked. Effect is to produce a contraction of the underlay of fabric thereby shaping the roll in a collar or lapel. Stitches may be of even or uneven length and do not show through on face of garment.

Pick Stitch / Picking Stitch

A series of stitches penetrating the uppermost ply or plies in which the length and spacing of the stitch are 1/8 inch (3.2 mm) or more.

- As a face or surface decorative stitch on collars, lapels, cuffs, and pockets.
- As an edge finish in tailoring.
- When only the top part of the stitch should be seen.

Stitching does not penetrate or show on the under ply or back of garment. Each stitch picks up a thread of the interfacing. Buttonhole twist, embroidery floss, or tightly twisted yarn may be used for stitching.

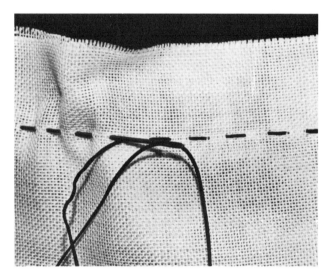

Running Stitch

A stitch produced in a series and taken in a forward progression, in which the length and spacing of the stitches are each 1/8 inch (3.2 mm) or less.

- A permanent stitch on seams of garments that do not receive strain.
- To ease a seam length.
- To ease sleeve cap.
- To stitch tucks of varying widths.
- To stitch pin tucks to retain softness of fabric.
- To produce shirring or French shirring.
- A preliminary stitch for smocking.
- To mend and patch.
- To join patchwork.
- A quilting stitch.
- To apply braid and embroidery.
- To sew hems and facings flat, allowing stitch to show on the face of the garment.

Saddle Stitch

A stitch produced in a series, in which the length and spacing of the stitches are each 1/8 inch (3.2 mm) or more.

- For hand top stitching.
- To accent edge of collars or lapels.
- To accent princess line, yoke, tab, and midriff seam lines of garments.
- As a decorative stitch on collars, pockets, and cuffs.

Stitch penetrates all plies and appears the same on both sides of the garment part. Buttonhole twist, embroidery floss, or tightly twisted yarn may be used for stitching.

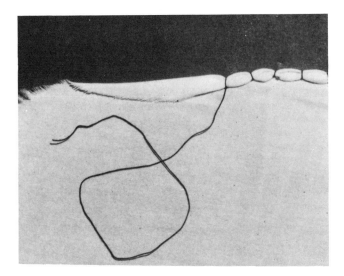

Shell Stitch

A stitch produced in a series of stitches worked to compress a folded edge producing a decorative scalloped effect.

- As a decorative edge finish for collars, cuffs, infants' wear, and lingerie.
- As an edge finish for narrow hems.
- To produce shell tucking.
- To finish the edges of ties, belts or sashes.

May be referred to as the *lingerie hem* by some production personnel.

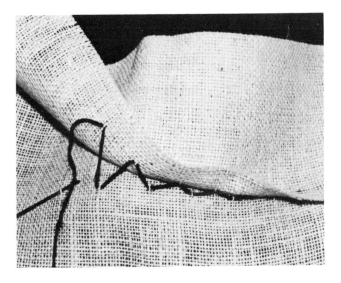

Slip Stitch

A stitch produced in a series of loose flexible, evenly spaced stitches of 1/4 inch (6.4 mm) or less, worked alternately between two plies so as not to show on the face of either ply.

- To join two folded edges or a folded edge to a flat surface.
- To attach a lining to garment.
- To fasten and hold lining at lower edge of hems and sleeves.
- To attach pocket or trimming to garment.
- To mend a seam on the face of the garment.
- To secure facing edge to zipper tape or seam allowance.
- As a hemming stitch.
- As a hem stitch on fabrics such as jersey, knit and crepe avoiding hem imprint from showing on face of garment.

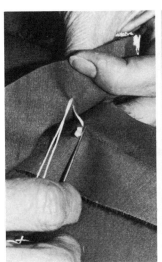 

Tack Stitch

A group of several stitches, 1/4 inch (6.4 mm) or less in length, taken between two points.

- To fasten one section of a garment to another.
- To link together any two or more parts of a garment.
- To fasten waistline stay to garment seam.
- To hold:
    Facing to garment at seams and darts;
    Shoulder pads in place;
    Belt to garment.
- At the beginning or end of a sewing line to hold the stitching securely.

May be referred to as a *fastening stitch*.

Arrowhead Tack Stitch / Triangular Tack Stitch

A triangular pattern formed by the placement of diminishing parallel stitches worked alternately from two sides and gradually filling in the triangle.

- To reinforce strain points of pockets, slashes, seams, and buttonholes.
- As a decorative detail.
- To accentuate openings of garment detail.
- At release point of action pleat or vent.

Bar Tack Stitch

A group of parallel stitches, worked so that each stitch touches the next, spanning a garment detail to a width of 1/2 inch (12.7 mm) or less.

- As a decorative thread reinforcement on the face of the garment at the ends of pleats, pockets, buttonholes, and seams.
- To strengthen ends of seams, plackets, and slashes.
- To strengthen release points of kick or action pleats and vents.

French Tack Stitch

A group of several long, loose stitches taken between two garment sections and strengthened by winding thread over the suspended stitches.

- As a connection between two surfaces where ease and distance are desired.
- As a suspension tack to join belt to garment at a desired distance.
- To hold hem edge of lining in position.
- To link two separate garment sections.
- To hold collars and turned-up cuffs in position.
- To attach belt to garment.
- To join buttons to form cuff links.

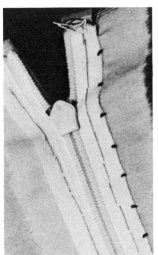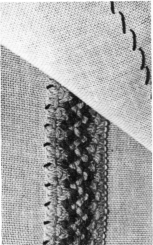

Whip Stitch

A stitch produced in a series of parallel stitches, 1/16 inch (1.6 mm) or less, formed by inserting the needle into the lower ply directly opposite the advanced stitch on the upper ply.

- To hold:
    - Two edges together;
    - Raw edge to a flat surface.
- To catch a folded edge to another ply.
- To join:
    - Edges of straps, belts, and ties;
    - Facing corners or edges at coat hems;
    - Two folded edges or selvages together.
- To attach:
    - Taped edges and straps;
    - Lace edging or trimming to garment;
    - Taped edge of fastener closing to garment;
    - Hooks and eyes, and snaps to garment.
- To secure inside fold of waistbands in slacks, skirts or aprons.
- To appliqué:
    - Lace seam joinings;
    - Lace and fabric motif.

Only short parallel stitches joining the two parts are visible.

Blind Stitch
Chain Stitch
Double-Needle Machine Stitch
Hemstitch
Lettuce Edging
Lockstitch Zigzag Machine Stitch
Overedge Machine Stitch
Purl Edging
Picot Edging
Pull-Out Overedge Machine Stitch
Safety Stitch:
   Safety Stitch

Mock Safety Stitch
Scallop Overedge / Scallop Edging
Machine Shell Stitch
Shirring / Gathering:
   Shirring Stitch / Gathering Stitch
   Elasticized Shirring
Simulated Hand Stitch (New Stitch 801)
Single-Needle Lockstitch
Smocking Stitch

Machine stitching is a process forming a series of stitches which may be concealed within or may show on the face of the garment. Machine stitching may be used for functional purposes as well as decorative purposes, or to finish an edge.

Types of stitches are referred to in terms that describe their configuration or effect. However, production engineers require a numbered specification to avoid confusion in production operations.

Under the provision of Federal Standard No. 751a, machine sewing stitches are divided into eight classes. Each class is identified by the first digit of a three digit number, 100 through 800. Federal Standard stitch classes are:

100—Chain Stitch
200—Hand Stitch
300—Lockstitch
400—Multi-Thread Chainstitch
   (or Double-Locked Stitch)

500—Overedge Stitch
600—Flat Seam Stitch
700—Single Thread Lockstitch
800—Simulated Hand Stitch

Individual stitches are further identified by a second and third digit denoting their concatenation.

Industrial sewing machines are usually designed to produce one type of stitch. With minor adjustments, some machines may produce more than one stitch configuration.

Home sewing machines are designed to produce a variety of stitches compatible for use in a wide range of construction techniques.

Machines are equipped with lettered or numbered stitch size regulators that can be set to sew a selected number of stitches per inch. The set number is an approximate indicator of stitches per inch. Type and weight of fabric, number of plies being sewn, size of thread, and type of machine are factors influencing the final result or stitch performance. Setting can be taken as a starter point and tested for accuracy and performance.

Zigzag, buttonhole and hemstitch machines as well as special attachments that operate with a side-to-side motion of the needle, produce stitch bite. Bite indicates the width of the track or stitching pattern.

Different machine stitches are designed to duplicate the stitch, appearance, and process of hand stitching. Blind stitch machines, attachments or cams produce a variety of stitch configurations which hold garment plies together without visible stitching on the face of the garment.

The type and size of machine stitches selected depends on:
• Design and style of garment
• Use or function of garment
• Care of garment
• Life of garment
• Type and weight of fabric
• Placement of stitch
• Availability of machine and/or attachments
• Technique of construction
• Method of production
• Quantity of garments produced

Blind Stitch

A stitch that attaches one portion of a garment to another through one or more plies without penetrating the full depth of the face ply.

- As a hemming stitch.
- When constructing a book hem or book seam.
- As the stitch to hold a machine rolled hem.
- To apply interfacing to collars, lapels, and coat fronts.
- To fasten free edge of facing to garment.
- For hemming raw edge finishes.
- For hemming where seam binding is utilized.
- For felling turned under hems eliminating need for serging.
- For felling bottom of unlined suits, jackets, coats, skirts, pants and other garments.
- For felling hems of linings.

Unclassified

The type of stitch used is determined by the type of fabric, use of garment, type of thread, and count of loop stitch required. Zigzag stitch may be used as blind stitch. Finished garment shows no threads on the outer surface of the face fabric.

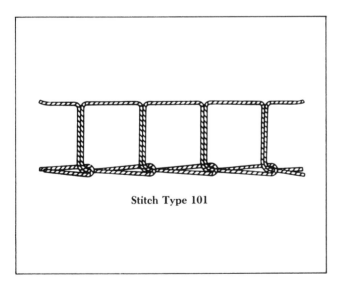

Stitch Type 101

Chain Stitch

A type of stitch in which a single thread passes through a ply or plies of fabric and interloops with itself on the opposite surface.

- For permanent stitching.
- As temporary stitches for basting.
- For construction guide lines.
- For stay stitching.
- To attach trimming.
- To make a stay chain to anchor linings, make loops and belt carriers.
- To sew knit and other loosely woven or bulky fabrics.

Designated by Federal Standards: Class 100; Stitch Type 101

Stitching can be removed with a pull on unlocked thread end. Loop formation produces a flexible stitch. Stitch length can be regulated.

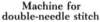

Machine for
double-needle stitch

Double-Needle Machine Stitch

Two parallel, independent rows of stitches sewn simultaneously by a machine equipped with two needles and two concatenating devices.

- To stitch double topstitched seams.
- To reinforce joined seams by topstitching.
- In conjunction with an attachment to make flat-felled seams.
- To finish hem edges.
- To apply bias stripping.

Produced by a lockstitch or chainstitch machine. Double needles may be spaced from 1/16 to 1/2 inch (1.6 to 12.7 mm) apart.

Concatenating devices may be eye loopers or bobbin hooks. Machines equipped with split bar to allow one needle to remain stationary while other needle continues to move a given amount of stitches and after corner, first needle re-engages.

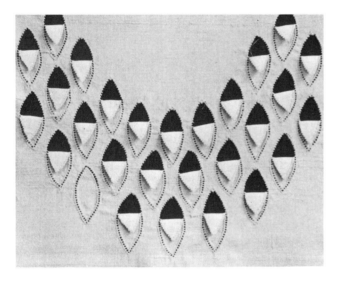

Hemstitch

A finished edge produced by a lockstitch, on each side of patterned openings, formed by the action of two vibrating needles operating in unison with a piercer and the feeding mechanism.

- On a single fabric ply as a decorative effect.
- To hold and finish a hem which is visible on the face of the garment.

Unclassified

Adjustable needle holders allow a wide range of vibration giving a wider stitch when necessary.

Hemstitching, when cut, produces a picot edge finish.

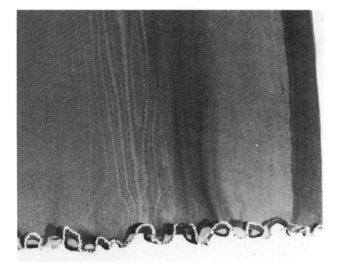

Lettuce Edging

A frilled, unturned finished edge, similar in appearance to lettuce leaves, produced by stretching a knit fabric as it feeds into an overedge machine.

- To finish the lower edges of knit garments.
- As a decorative hem finish.
- To finish edge of collars, pockets, scarfs, and ruffles.

Designated by Federal Standards: Class 500

Width of bite and density of stitch may vary depending on type of fabric or effect desired.

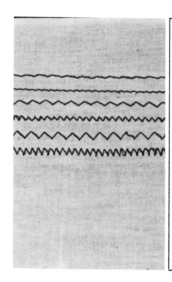

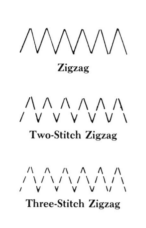

Zigzag

Two-Stitch Zigzag

Three-Stitch Zigzag

Lockstitch Zigzag Machine Stitch

A stitch formed through the combined action of the needle, moving from side to side, and the fabric feeding through the machine whereby the needle and bobbin threads interlace midway between the surface and fabric ply or plies.

- On knit and stretch fabrics.
- To finish raw edges.
- To apply elastic to garment edge.
- To apply elastic for casing application.
- To join elastic fabric.
- To hold seams, elastic and trimming on swimwear.
- To join or attach lace application.
- To attach trimming.
- As a decorative feature.

Narrow bite for sewing seams; deep bite for raw edge finishes. Lockstitch zigzag machine can be adjusted to produce zero bite or, in effect, a single-needle lockstitch.

Different industrial machines produce a wide variety of stitch patterns. Different cams or dials on home machines produce a variety of stitch patterns.

Two-stitch zigzag formed by two stitches in same direction and two stitches in opposite direction.

Three-stitch zigzag formed by three stitches in one direction before reversing itself.

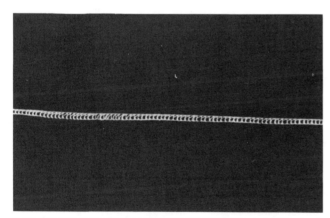

Overedge Machine Stitch

A stitch produced by interlocking one or more threads whereby threads enclose the raw edges of fabric ply or plies.

- To produce a seam.
- To finish an edge.
- To prevent fraying, raveling or rolling of seam edge.
- To prevent raveling hem edge.
- As a hem finish.
- To join garment seam of knit and stretch fabric.
- To join elastic fabric.
- To join elastic to garment edge.
- To join and finish exposed seams made on the face of the garment for decorative or styling purposes.

Designated by Federal Standards: Class 500; Stitch Type includes all Overedge, Overlock, Serging Overcast and Merrow®

Stitch formation, size, bite, and spacing varies according to different machines. Overedge machine stitch may be used for purl edging and lettuce edging.

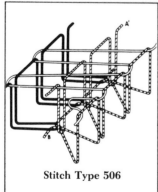

Stitch Type 506

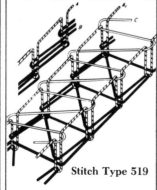

Stitch Type 519

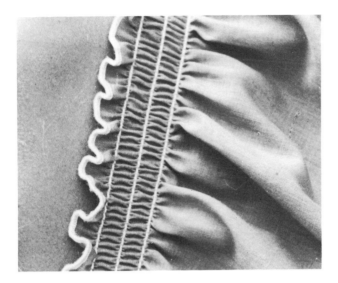

Purl Edging

A clean finish produced on the edge of a fabric ply by means of closely spaced, shallow bite overedge stitches.

- As a decorative hem finish.
- As a finish on collars, cuffs, pockets, ruffles and jabots.
- As a hem finish for lingerie.
- As a hem finish for garments made of silk or satin.
- On sheer and lightweight fabrics.
- As a finish on shawls, scarfs and sashes.

Designated by Federal Standards: Class 500
Width of bite and density of stitch may vary, depending on type of fabric or effect desired.

Picot Edging

An unturned machine finish edge characterized by a series of small points which is the end result of cutting in half a line of machine hemstitching.

- As a decorative hem finish.
- As a finish on collars and cuffs of children's and infants' wear.
- As an imitation of the decorative hand-stitched hemstitching.
- On lightweight, soft and sheer fabrics.

Unclassified
Picot edging produced by the same action, time and speed at which hemstitching is formed. Each hemstitch bar is cut the same length producing the picot edging.

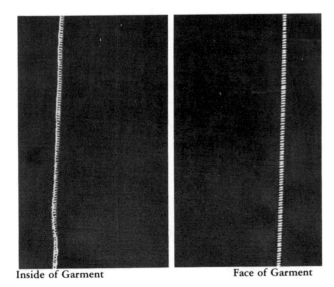

Inside of Garment   Face of Garment

Pull-Out Overedge Machine Stitch

A stitch formed by using a loose tension on the needle thread of a two-thread overedge machine. Result is a flat seam showing different thread configurations on face and back of finished seam when sections are opened and pulled flat.

- To produce a smooth flat decorative seam on foundation garments with great elasticity.
- With a contrasting thread to produce a decorative stitch on face of garment when seams are joined inside.

Designated by Federal Standards: Class 500, Stitch Type 502
Stitch formation, size, bite and spacing may be planned with regard to type and placement of seam and effect desired.
Accepted as the most elastic face stitch in the 500 class.

Safety Stitch

A machine stitch produced by the simultaneous sewing of two parallel independent rows of stitches; a specified distance from edge one row of overedge, the other a row of lockstitch or multi-thread chain stitch.

- To join:
    Seams of stretch or knit garments;
    Seams of swimwear;
    Crotch seams of girdles and undergarments.
- To join and finish seams of sportswear and work clothes.
- To join and finish seams of garments that ravel easily.
- To finish raw edges of seams.

Designated by Federal Standards: Class 500; Stitch Types, 515 through 520; 520 is two rows of multi-thread chain-stitch
Stitch formation, size, bite and spacing varies according to different machines. An increased seam allowance affords a measure of protection against seam slippage.

Mock Safety Stitch

A stitch produced on a multiple needle overedge machine in which the top surface appears to have two independent rows of stitches and the bottom surface shows the two rows to be a totally integrated single stitch.

- Instead of a safety stitch when a more elastic stitch is desired.
- To join:
    Seams of stretch or knit garments;
    Seams of swimwear.
- To join and finish seams of sportswear and work clothes.
- To join and finish seams of garments that ravel easily.

Designated by Federal Standards: Class 500; Stitch Type 507, 508, 510, 512
Stitch formation, size, bite and spacing varies according to different machines.

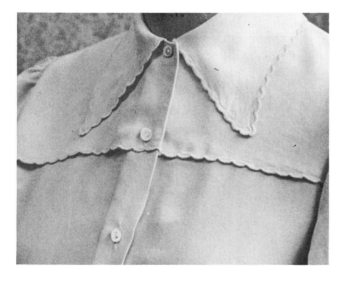

Scallop Overedge / Scallop Edging

A decorative finish on the edge of fabric ply or plies forming a scalloped pattern produced by means of a closely spaced shallow bite purl stitch.

- As a decorative hem or edge finish.
- As a finish on collars, cuffs, pockets, ruffles, belts, and jabots.
- As a hem finish for lingerie.
- As a finish on sheer and lightweight fabrics.
- As a finish on shawls, scarfs, and sashes.

Designated by Federal Standards: Class 500
Shape of scallop, width of bite and density of stitch may vary depending on type of fabric or effect desired.

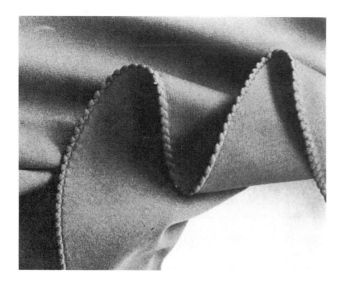

Machine Shell Stitch

A rolled edge crimped by the bite of a long-length, wide-pattern zigzag stitch producing a decorative scallop shell stitch resembling hand-stitched shell stitching.

- As a decorative finish for collars and cuffs; infants' wear; lingerie.
- To finish edges of necklines, sleeves, and hems on garments.
- To finish edge of belts, ties, and sashes.
- As a design feature on tucks and cross tucks.

Stitch pattern may be set to produce shell scallop from 1/8 to 1/2 inch (3.2 to 12.7 mm).

Two rows of machine stitches pulled to gather or shirr fabric

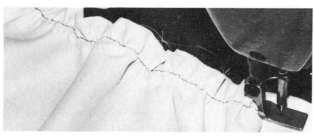

Shirring with shirring foot attachment

Shirring Stitch / Gathering Stitch

The process of decreasing a given length of fabric to a predetermined shorter length by any one of the following processes:

1. One or more parallel rows of unbalanced stitches with bobbin threads pulled and tied;
2. A shirring foot attachment that decreases fabric length;
3. Differential feed mechanism (feed dogs moving at different stitch lengths);
4. A dynamic attachment with a feeder blade pushing fabric beneath needle.

- Whenever gathering or intended fullness is desired.
- To create fullness in garments or garment parts such as dirndl or peasant skirts and blouses, puff sleeves, ruffles, jabots, and flounces.

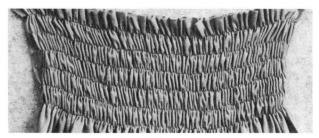

Face of Garment

Inside of Garment

Elasticized Shirring

A process of decreasing a given length of fabric to a predetermined shorter length by any one of the following means:

1. Elastic thread in the bobbin only;
2. Chainstitch utilizing elastic as needle thread;
3. Woven elastic, or "live" rubber stitched to ply in stretched position;
4. Elastic cord enclosed in a zigzag stitch pattern.

- In single, grouped or multiple rows.
- On cuff, midriff and bands.
- At waistline.
- On bodice section.
- On skirts from waist to hip area to form a fitted yoke effect.
- At neckline and shoulder of garments.
- For tube tops.
- On lightweight fabrics such as voile, batiste, crepe or jersey.

Elasticized shirring expands and contracts; stretches to conform to body shape and size. Flexibility of elastic stitching allows freedom of body movement.

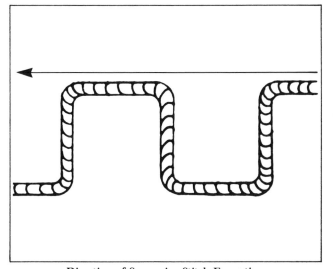

Direction of Successive Stitch Formation

This type of stitch shall be formed with one needle thread which is passed completely through the material and returned by another path after the material has been moved forward one stitch length.

Simulated Hand Stitch (New Stitch 801)

A series of stitches formed with one or more threads in a double-pointed, center-eye needle passing through ply or plies of fabric to show alternately on face and reverse of garment.

- To simulate a hand saddle stitch.
- To simulate a hand running stitch.
- As a decorative stitch which shows on the face of the garment.

Designated by Federal Standards: Class 800; Stitch Type 801

This type of stitch is formed with one needle thread which is passed completely through the material and returned by another path after the material has been moved forward one stitch length.

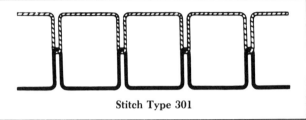

Stitch Type 301

Single-Needle Lockstitch

A stitch formed when the needle thread and bobbin threads interlace midway between the surface of fabric ply or plies as they feed through the machine and give the same appearance on top and bottom surfaces.

- For straight sewing.
- To join two or more plies of fabric.
- To stitch a single ply of fabric.
- For embroidery.

Designated by Federal Standards: Class 300; Stitch Type 301

Considered by some to be the standard or regular machine stitch. Length of stitch can be regulated from 4 to 30 per inch depending on individual machine.

Smocking Stitch

A patterned design of decorative cover threads included in a multiple needle operation which decreases a given length of fabric to a predetermined shorter length.

- On yokes, cuffs, midriff and bands.
- At waistline releasing fabric above and below.
- To create a hip yoke effect from waist to hipline.
- At neckline and or shoulder of garments.

Fabric folds may vary in size up to 1/2 inch (12.7 mm) depth. Decorative patterns vary according to stitch or group of stitches used.

Multiple rows of machine-stitched pattern, referred to as smocking, may be applied to elasticized shirring, non-elastic shirring or flat fabric.

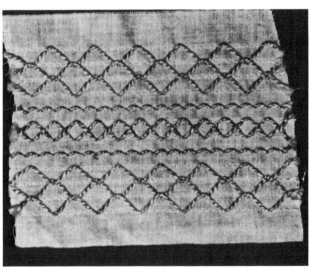

Face of Garment without Shirring

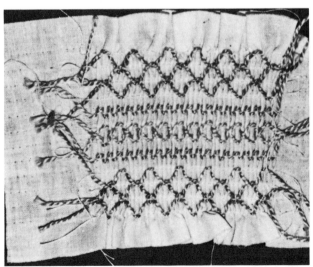

Face of Garment with Shirring

Belt:
  Belt
  Half Belt
  Tie Belt
Built-Up Waistline
Elasticized Waistline
Faced Waistline:
  Faced Waistline
  Bias-Faced Waistline
  Ribbon-Faced Waistline
Insert Waistline / Inset Waistline
Seamed Waistline
Stayed Waistline with Tape or Binding
Stayed Waistline with Ribbon

Unseamed Waistline
Waistband:
  Contoured Waistband
  Ribbon Waistband
  Straight Waistband
  Straight Waistband Reinforced with
    Commercial Backing
  Elastic-Backed Straight Waistband
  Non-Slip-Belting-Backed Straight Waistband /
    Rubberized-Belting-Backed Straight Waistband
  Ribbon-Backed Straight Waistband
  Stretch Waistband
  Trouser Waistband / Curtain Waistband
Waistline with Casing

Waistline finishes with no waistband or visible band complete a garment which covers either the upper or lower torso. Waistbands and waistline finishes hold garments in proper position on the body.

Style ease, which is part of the design, and wearing ease are included in the development of the pattern for waistbands and waistband finishes.

Waistlines on garments may be designed without an opening or may be planned with a lapped or centered opening at center front, center back, side seam, or princess line according to design and function of the garment.

Garments designed with horizontal seams joining upper and lower portions of the garment are designated as having seamed waistlines or inserts.

Waistlines may be established on an all-in-one garment by the use of casing, elastic or puckering to draw in the excess fabric to fit the body.

The type of waistband or waistline finishes selected depends on:
• Design and style of garment
• Purpose and use of garment
• Care of garment
• Type and weight of fabric
• Design of fabric
• Procedures of construction and production

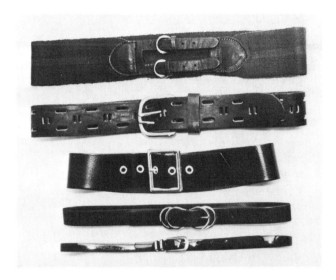

Belt

A clean-finished strap, with or without a fastener, designed in a variety of widths, lengths, and materials.

- To support trousers, pants, shorts, and skirts.
- To hold a garment in place.
- As a design feature at empire, long torso, or natural waistline-styled garments.
- To hold a garment closed.

Belt may be soft or reinforced for strength; held in position with belt carriers. Sash or scarf may be substituted for belt.

Half Belt

A clean-finished strap of one or more sections, with or without a fastener, designed in a variety of widths, lengths and materials. Each section is attached to the side seams of garment.

- As a design effect.
- To fit a front or back garment to the figure.
- On vest, tabard, aprons, and pinafores when designed as ties.

Half belt may be straight or contoured, soft or reinforced, attached, suspended from seam-to-seam or applied as ties.

Tie Belt

A clear-finished strip or strap designed in a variety of widths, lengths, and materials.

- When a restrictive fastener would interfere with the design of garment.
- On garments spanning more than one size.
- Where a rigid belt would interfere with body movement.

Tie belt may be made of cord, braid, trimming, or leather.
   Fabric belt may be of self or contrasting fabric, cut on the straight grain or bias.

Built-Up Waistline

An integral part of the garment pattern which rises above the natural waistline and is shaped by darts or panels to fit the body.

- As a design feature.
- To enhance geometric fabric patterns.
- To avoid the horizontal seam line produced by an added waistband.

Built-up section is strengthened by interfacing and/or boning and is finished with a shaped facing or lining.

Elasticized Waistline

Elastic applied in any of a variety of methods to a waistline edge or a waistline area.

- To draw in an unfitted waistline.
- On waistlines of garments spanning more than one size.
- Instead of stable waistbands to eliminate restriction.

A variety of elastic webbing widths and degree of elasticity produce differences in flexibility and/or design effect.

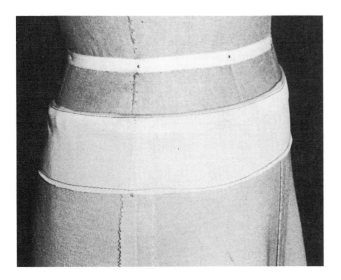

Faced Waistline

A garment component of the same shape as the waistline area and edge applied to produce a flat finish which does not extend beyond the waistline edge.

- On garments where a visible waistband is not desired.
- Where other waistline applications would interfere with the design element of garment.
- Where a waistband is considered restrictive of body movement.

Facing usually applied to lie flat on the inside of the garment but may be applied to lie on the face of the garment as a decorative finish.

Bias-Faced Waistline

A self- or commercially prepared bias strip of the same, contrasting or lighter weight fabric, shaped to fit contour of the garment waistline; does not extend beyond the waistline edge.

- To produce a flat finish.
- Instead of other facing to reduce bulk.
- Where shaped or other facing would detract from the appearance of the garment.
- In mass production of garments to reduce yardage requirements and production costs.

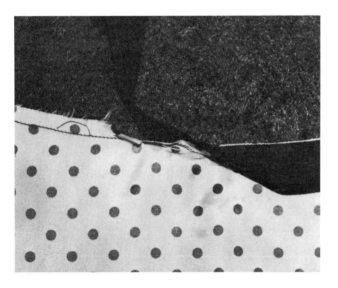

Ribbon-Faced Waistline

Grosgrain, twill or satin ribbon shaped to fit contour of garment waistline producing a flat finish which does not extend beyond the waistline edge.

- Instead of facing when imprint of facing would detract from appearance of the garment.
- On garments made of eyelet, openwork or lightweight fabrics where facing would show through to the face of the garment.
- On designs of knit or jersey fabrics where width of facing would restrict flexibility of garment.

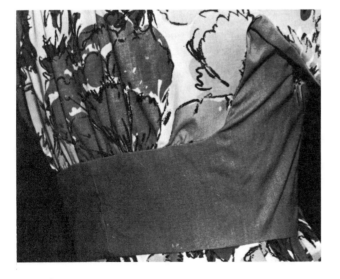

Insert Waistline / Inset Waistline

A shaped or straight band, made of self or contrasting fabric or ribbon, attached between the bodice and lower garment sections.

- As a design feature to emphasize waistline area.

Width and shape of insert varies depending on design. Insert can be designed to imitate a belted garment; to lie above or below the natural waist or to span the waistline.

Seamed Waistline

A horizontal seam or seams joining the upper and lower sections of a garment.

Horizontal design lines designating waistlines are identified as:

Natural Waistline—At the actual body waistline.
Raised Waistline—Slightly above the natural waist.
Lowered Waistline—Slightly below the natural waist.
Long Torso—Approximately at hip area.
Empire—Just below bust or breast level.

Joined seam may have insert of corded piping, piping or trimming; may be covered with decorative band, ribbon or trimming. Joined seam may be strengthened with ribbon tape, ribbon, belting and/or a stay on inside of garment.

Seam finish applied according to design of garment, care and use of garment, and type of fabric.

Stayed Waistline with Tape or Binding

A firmly woven tape or binding cut to a predetermined length and applied to inside of waistline seam during construction of the garment.

- To prevent stretching and distortion of waistline.
- To stabilize waistline of skirt to facilitate subsequent construction operations.

Binding or tape may be applied to skirt portion at waistline seam prior to joining bodice. Stay may be applied while joining waistline seam of bodice or skirt.

Stayed Waistline with Ribbon

A firmly woven ribbon, 1/2 to 1 inch (12.7 to 25.4 mm) in width, measured to fit waistline, and attached to inside of waistline of finished garment.

- To prevent:
    Tension or strain on closure in fitted garments;
    Waistline of garment from sliding up on body;
    Stretching and distortion of waistline.
- When skirt is heavier than bodice.
- On garments made of stretch or knit fabrics.
- To stabilize waistline of sheath and princess line garments.

Unseamed Waistline

A waistline on a garment which spans the body above and below the waist area, and is not delineated by seams or bands.

- Where no waistline seam is necessary in the design of the garment.
- Part of sheath, shift, A-line, or tent silhouette.
- When other methods of drawing in fullness would restrict body movement.

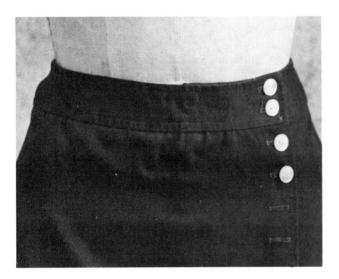

Contoured Waistband

A band formed to fit the body's curve accommodating differences in measurement between waist and hip, waist and midriff, or both; attached to the waistline.

- To provide a finish to the garment edge.
- To provide a band finish for special design features such as hip-hugger pants, or lowered or raised waistlines.
- To provide a band finish for garments that span the waistline from hip to midriff.
- To add interest to a garment.

Contoured waistband may be interfaced, stiffened or boned according to support desired; may be decoratively shaped along either or both edges, and of uniform or graduated width. Contoured waistband requires a separate facing shaped to match.

Ribbon Waistband

A grosgrain, twill or satin ribbon forming a straight band, 2 inches (5.1 cm) or less in width, attached to the waistline.

- To provide a finish to the garment edge.
- Instead of a self-fabric waistband.
- As a decorative waistband.
- To avoid bulk when a belt will cover the waistband.

Ribbon waistband may extend to form ties for garments such as pinafores, overskirts, or aprons.

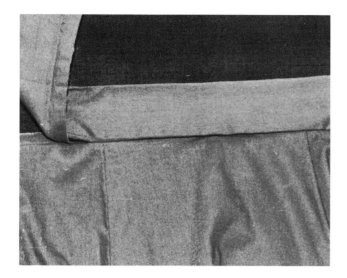

Straight Waistband

A band, 2 inches (5.1 cm) or less in finished width, of two or more plies attached at the waistline.

- To provide a stable finish to the garment edge.
- To support garments covering lower torso such as trousers, shorts, or skirts.
- To anchor garments covering upper torso such as jackets or blouses.

Band may have a seamed or fold-over upper edge and may be finished flush with one end of garment concealing an extended underlay. Planned with pointed or rounded extension for lapped openings. May open at center front, center back side seam or princess line and provided with belt carriers.

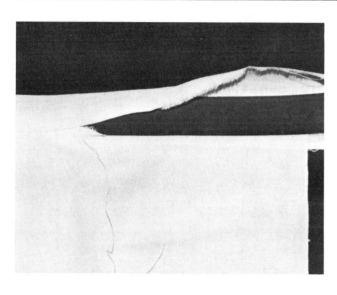

Straight Waistband Reinforced with Commercial Backing

A band, 2 inches (5.1 cm) or less in finished width, of two or more plies with commercial backing inserted, and attached at the waistline.

- To provide a stiffened, stable finish to the garment edge.
- To prevent rolling or creasing of waistband.
- To support garments covering lower torso such as trousers, shorts, or skirts.
- To anchor garments covering upper torso such as jackets or blouses.

Waistband may have a seamed or fold-over upper edge; may be provided with belt carriers; may be finished flush with one end of garment concealing an extended underlay. Planned with pointed or rounded extension for lapped openings. Band may open at center front, center back side seam or princess line.

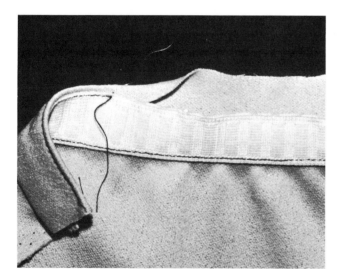

Elastic-Backed Straight Waistband

A single-ply band of self-fabric, 2 1/2 inches (6.4 cm) or less in finished width, utilizing non-roll or ribbed elastic to complete the inside of a waistband.

- On knit fabrics.
- As a waistband support comparable to or compatible with the stretchability of knit fabrics.
- To provide a non-roll waistline.

Weight and construction of elastic eliminates need for interfacing in waistband.

Non-Slip-Belting-Backed Straight Waistband / Rubberized-Belting-Backed Straight Waistband

A grosgrain belting with applied rubber banding or woven with rows of rubber yarn on one surface, attached to complete the inside of a single ply of self-fabric waistband.

- To produce a non-slip waistband.
- To hold tuck-in blouses and shirts in place.

Weight and construction of belting eliminates need for interfacing in waistband.

Belting available in widths of 2 inches (5.1 cm) or less.

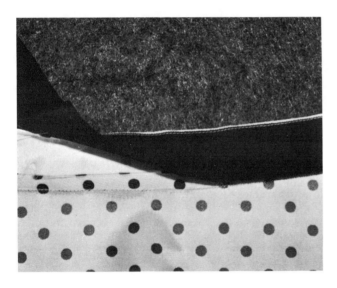

Ribbon-Backed Straight Waistband

A self-fabric band, 2 inches (5.1 cm) or less in width, of two or more plies, attached at the waistline. Grosgrain or twill ribbon is used to complete the inside of the waistband.

- To eliminate bulk on garments made of heavy, coarse or nubby fabrics.
- To eliminate bulk of fold-over fabric band.
- To add body and stability to garments made of sheer and loosely woven fabrics.
- To prevent garment fabric from coming into direct contact with body.

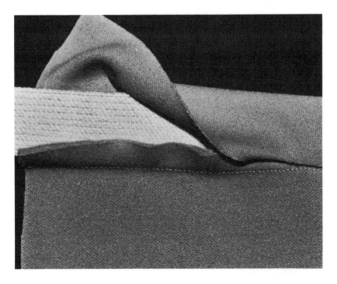

Stretch Waistband

A separate waistband or casing enclosing an applied elastic.

- On knit garments.
- On slip-on pants, skirts and shorts.
- On garments spanning more than one size.

Separate waistband is cut the same length as the garment waist seam.

Placket may be needed on garments made of a limited stretch knit fabric.

Trouser Waistband / Curtain Waistband

A waistband with a self-fabric face supported by a reinforced, commercially prepared bias strip which is constructed with an additional bias strip designed to hang below waistline seam.

- On tailored slacks and men's trousers.
- As a support for waistbands.

Waistband support attached to self-fabric ply at upper edge only.
  Band may be designed with belt carriers.
  Available in 3/4 to 2 inch (1.9 to 5.1 cm) widths.

Waistline with Casing

A fabric strip applied to a waistline edge, or to span a waistline area, or a folded edge constructed to enclose an elastic or drawstring.

- As a means of drawing in an unfitted waistline allowing for individual control of circumference adjustment.
- On waistline of garments spanning more than one size.

Casing which encloses elastic or drawstring may be applied to the face of the garment for decorative purposes. Width of casing and elastic affects the silhouette of the garment.

  Width of elastic, degree of elasticity, and method of application produces difference in flexibility and/or design effect.

Arrowhead
Band:
  Band / Banding
  Ribbing Band / Knit-Ribbed Band
Belt Carriers / Belt Loops
Camisole
Eye Slit
Foundation Support
Godet
Gusset
Interfacing
Lingerie Strap Holder
Lining:
   Backing / Underlining

Interlining
Lining
Partial Lining
Patch:
  Applied Patch
  Reinforcing Patch
Stay:
  Collar-Pocket Stay
  Fabric Stay
Strapping
Underlay
Weights in Garments

Various construction details are those essential parts applied to or incorporated into the body of the garment during construction, not already described under a particular heading within this volume. They include garment components, self-prepared details, or purchased notions and findings.

Garment components are interior construction and finishing units which influence the wear and appearance of the finished garment.

Interfacing and underlinings are separate fabric plies applied as integral parts of the construction process. They support and reinforce garment sections and are used with regard to silhouette and effect desired.

Linings and partial linings are separate units attached to provide a clean finish to the interior of the garment.

Interlinings are utilized to provide warmth.

Arrowhead

1. A triangular pattern of hand embroidery or machine stitches worked directly on the garment. 2. A commercially prepared triangular appliqué simulating hand stitches.

- To reinforce:
    Strain point on pocket, slash, seam and buttonhole;
    Release point of action pleat or vent;
    Release point of inverted or box pleat.
- To accentuate openings of garment detail.
- As a decorative design detail.

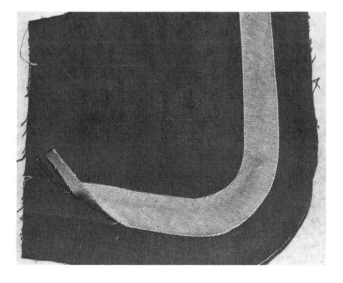

Band / Banding

Ribbon, lace or fabric strip made of straight grain, bias or shaped, inserted or top stitched to garment ply.

- As a decoration on face of garment.
- As a finish for edge of garment sections.
- As an extention of a garment edge such as on a hemline of jacket, blouse, sleeve, dress, skirt or pants.

Also, may be used as a facing.

Ribbing Band / Knit-Ribbed Band

A flexible strip knitted in a rib pattern, in a variety of types, weights and widths; one, both or neither edge is finished.

- To finish necklines, armholes, sleeves and waistlines on knit garments.
- To produce crew, mock turtle and turtleneck styles.
- At the waist or sleeve edge to draw circumference on garments of woven fabrics.
- At the neckline, waistline, sleeve and pants ends to provide close-to-the-body fit.
- On the neckline, sleeve and pants leg of balbriggan pajamas.
- On waistlines of garments spanning more than one size.
- On unfitted waistlines as a means of drawing in fullness.
- To finish waistlines on both upper and lower torso garments.
- On knitted garments where other waistline treatments are not applicable.
- As a waistline insert.
- On ski wear and snow suits.
- To form windbreaker cuff when attached to garment sleeve lining.
- As a decorative design detail.

Degree of flexibility and stretchability varies with the yarn, knit pattern, and manufacturing method.

Maximum stretch bands are pulled to fit garment edge during application.

Bands cut from limited stretch knits are pulled and steamed to match garment edge before application. Width of band determined by location and style of garment.

Ribbing available by the yard (meter), in prepackaged quantities, or tubular units cut and finished to specific width.

Belt Carriers / Belt Loops

One or more strips, bands, or loops attached to face of garment, belt or trimming.

- To hold belt in position.
- In a series of three or more on the waistband of skirts, pants or shorts.
- On waistline at side seam of dresses, tunics, blouses, jackets, and coats.
- To hold belt, sash or ribbon in position at empire or long torso style line.
- Individually, on a belt near closure, to hold free end in place.
- At lower section of belted sleeve designs such as trench coat, safari jacket, and sportswear garments.

Belt carriers are made in a variety of widths and lengths depending on the type or width of the belt and the style of the garment; of self or contrasting fabric, ribbon, braid, cord, elastic, or thread.

They may be planned as decorative features. Applied during garment construction or added to finished garment or may be attached spanning an area or as a closed loop.

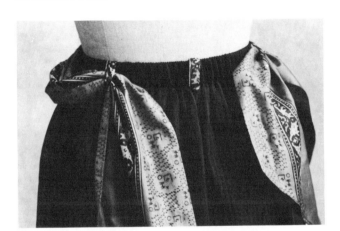

Camisole

A loose or semi-fitted finished bodice, of lightweight fabric, seamed to skirt portion of a garment.

- Worn or sewn under overblouse, blouson top, or tunic.
- As a support for skirt section of garment to eliminate waistband.
- To prevent skirt from shifting.

Eye Slit

A clean-finished vertical or circular opening on a garment made by the application of a stitched, slashed, and turned patch or strip.

- On face of garment, to allow drawstring, belt or slash to emerge.
- On inside or outside casing to allow drawstring to emerge.
- In the process of making open-slit buttonholes.
- To finish facing side of bound buttonholes.
- To hold a decorative scarf.

An open seam, buttonhole, eyelet or grommet may be utilized as an eye slit.

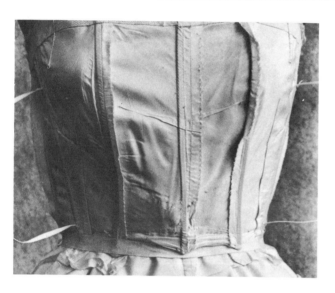

Foundation Support

A finished interior component, constructed of supporting material, and fitted to the body shape. Spanning the torso anywhere from bust to hip area.

- To hold a strapless garment in place.
- Where an undergarment would add bulk or detract from the appearance of the garment.
- To eliminate the need for a separate bra or waist cincher.
- In design where part of the garment is shaped to the figure.

Foundation support may be boned, elasticized or padded; may be made of spandex fabric.

Godet

A triangular or rounded piece designed to be inserted into a slashed opening or seam in garment section or sections.

- Singly or in multiples to create fuller circumference.
- At lower portion of skirts, pants, sleeves, tops, jackets, coats, and capes; petticoats, slips, lingerie, robes, and aprons.
- To create:
    A fuller silhouette in fitted evening gowns;
    A flounce effect on sheaths or fitted garments;
    A trumpet silhouette.

Length, width, and shape of godet varies according to garment style or desired effect.

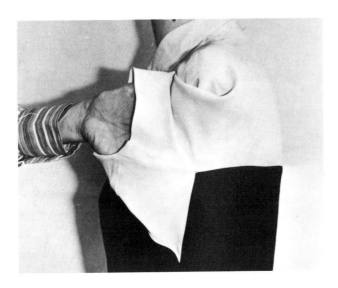

Gusset

A diamond-shaped unit of one or more pieces designed to be inserted into a slashed opening on a larger garment section or sections.

- Set into a kimono or dolman sleeve design to allow freedom of arm movement.
- To ease restrictiveness of fitted bodice and sleeve for freedom of arm movement.
- In crotch of pants or trousers; thermal underwear.
- In slips and intimate apparel; actionwear clothes; dance clothing.

Gusset may be planned using one, two or four pieces. One-piece gusset may have a vertical or horizontal double dart.
May be incorporated into garment bodice section.

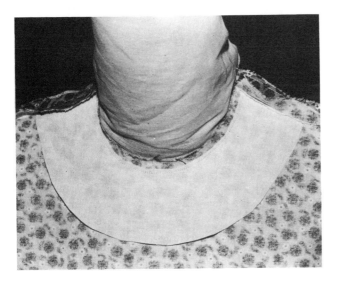

Interfacing

A separate fabric ply lying between the facing and outer fabric ply of a finished garment.

- To maintain shape and prevent stretching and wrinkling of the area to which it is applied, such as necklines, sleeveless armholes, and lapped closures.
- To give support and crispness to collars, lapels, reverse, cuffs, pockets, and flaps.
- To define shape and give support to body sections of tailored suits and coats.
- To span shoulder area of tailored jackets and coats.
- To reinforce button and buttonhole areas.
- To add body to hemlines and sleeve edges.
- To add firmness to belts and waistbands.

Weight of interfacing is selected to be compatible with the fabric of the garment area in which it is used and to give effect desired.

Interfacings are available in woven, nonwoven or fusible fabrics, of natural or synthetic yarn, in assorted widths of various weights and hand.

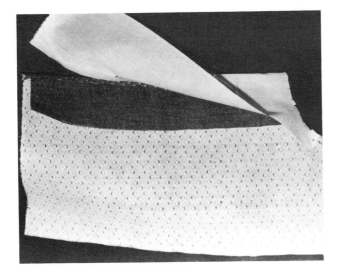

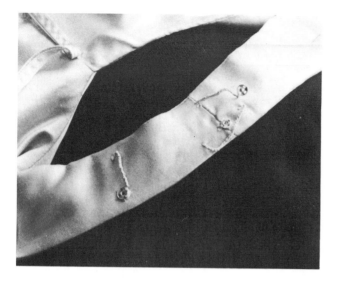

Lingerie Strap Holder

A narrow strip of tubing, ribbon or thread chain completed with a snap closure.

- To hold a lingerie strap in position underneath garment.
- On garments designed with narrow shoulder straps.
- On garments designed with wide or deep necklines.
- On sleeveless garments.

Strap holder may be self-prepared or purchased commercially. Snap closure may be substituted by a no-sew snap, covered snap, nylon snap, Velcro fastener, or safety pin.

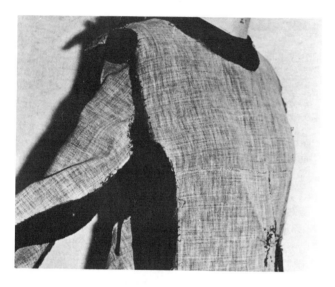

Backing / Underlining

An underply of fabric, cut to duplicate a garment section, applied to the back of the outer ply where outerply and underply are handled as one ply during garment construction.

- To prevent stretching or sagging of a loosely woven outer fabric.
- To strengthen and support outer fabric.
- To change drapability quality of garment fabric.
- To accentuate silhouette of garment.
- To back a section of the garment or the complete garment.
- To lend opacity to sheer or lightweight fabrics.

Underlining fabric may be comparable to, crisper, or softer than outer fabric depending on effect or fashion silhouette desired.

Underlining is cut from the same pattern as the garment.

Interlining

A fabric ply, with insulating properties, placed between the outer fabric ply, and lining of the garment.

- To add warmth to outer garment.

Interlining ply may be applied to back of outer fabric or lining fabric during garment construction. Completed interlining unit may be attached between finished garment and lining units. Interlining unit may be made as a detachable unit for multiseason outerwear garments.

Lining

A unit assembled in the same or similar silhouette as the garment unit.

- To provide a clean, inside finish when attached.
- To conceal raw edges and inside construction details.
- To facilitate putting on and taking off of garment.
- To prevent a garment from stretching or sagging.
- To prevent the outer fabric from coming in direct contact with the body.
- To prolong life of garment.

Type and quality of lining fabric selected with regard to type of fabric and garment. Lining can be made with free hanging or fully attached hem edge. Pattern for lining unit is planned or drafted as a separate cutting guide. Lining is assembled separately and then attached by hand or machine.

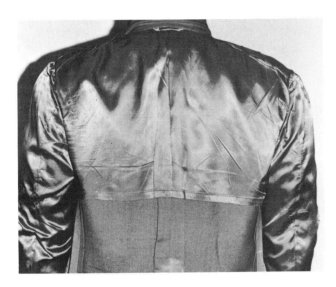

Partial Lining

A unit assembled in the same or similar silhouette as a portion of the garment unit.

- To maintain shape of garment area such as seats of skirts, slacks and trousers; knees of slacks and trousers.
- To conceal construction detail at shoulder area of tailored jackets.

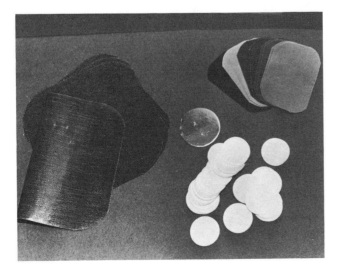

Applied Patch

A piece of fabric or leather shaped and measured to accommodate an area to be reinforced.

- On the face or inside of a garment.
- To reinforce areas subject to hard wear:
    At the elbow of sweaters, jackets and coats;
    At the knee of sportswear garments.
- Inside the trouser hem at the heel to prevent fraying.
- As a decorative design element.

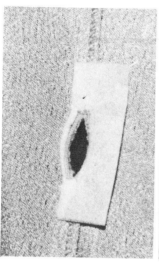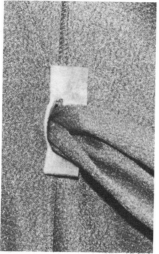

Reinforcing Patch

A piece of lightweight fabric shaped and measured to accommodate seam portion or slash point.

- To reinforce:
    A seam or slash at point of strain;
    Corners or angles;
    Inside of garment behind patch pockets, trimmings and appliqués;
    Seam or body of garment made of lightweight, loosely woven, stretch and knit fabrics.
- To strengthen:
    Tapered end of slash neckline or placket;
    Buttonholes and button areas of lightweight, loosely woven, stretch and knit fabrics.

Reinforcing patch may be made on the straight grain or bias.

Collar-Pocket Stay

A stitched pocket or casing on the underside of a collar which accommodates a supporting strip.

- On tailored collars to maintain shape of point.
- To keep collar end from twisting, turning or curling.
- To support and maintain shape of stand-up collar.
- To support pointed cuff.

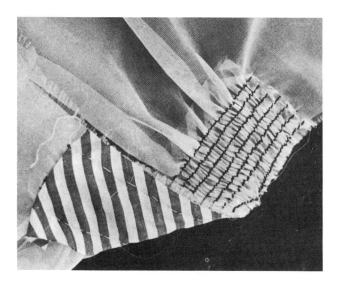

Fabric Stay

A strip of tape, ribbon or fabric, of a predetermined length and width, measured to accommodate a seam length or garment area.

- To reinforce seams subject to strain preventing tears and breakage.
- On curved crotch seam of pants, trousers, and shorts.
- On curved seam of sleeves such as dolman, batwing and raglan.
- To cover seams in fabrics that may cause skin irritation insuring comfort and wearability.
- To stabilize and hold French shirring in place.
- To prevent bias seams or edges from stretching.
- To stabilize fold line where facing and garment are cut in one.
- To reinforce corners of slashes, plackets, gussets and godets.
- To prevent stretching and distortion of waistlines.
- To stabilize waistline of skirt to facilitate subsequent construction operations.

Stay may be made of straight grain or bias fabric, or may be cut from ribbon or commercially prepared bias.

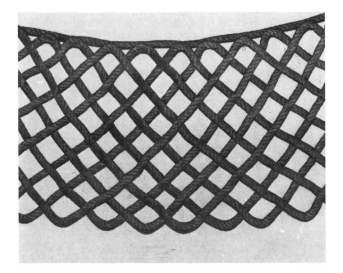

Strapping

A clean-finished, flat tubing produced by a variety of construction methods.

- In the development of strapwork and lattice designs on garments.
- For drawstrings; lacing; ties; belts or bows; belt carriers; carrier for boning; shoulder straps; lingerie straps; appliqués.

Width is planned with regard to the design of fabric and type of fabric. May be made of bias or on the straight grain of fabric.

Underlay

A strip of self or contrasting fabric or ribbon measured to accommodate the area to be backed and constructed to lie beneath a folded, faced, or abutted seam.

- When contrasting color or texture underlay will add interest or decoration to a garment.
- As part of a folded, faced or abutted slot seam construction.
- As a separate ply to complete a pleat.
- As underportion of pleat where panels of princess line or gored garments are joined.
- As underportion of inverted pleat when planned at center front or center back.
- To introduce color or fabric contrast to inverted or kick pleat.
- As underportion of pleat for fabric economy.
- As a free hanging strip behind slashed opening at lower edge of shirts or pants.
- Behind a butted placket or seam.
- Behind laced or hooked openings.
- Behind a frog or loop, and button placket or opening.
- Behind a zipper to protect undergarment or body from zipper teeth.

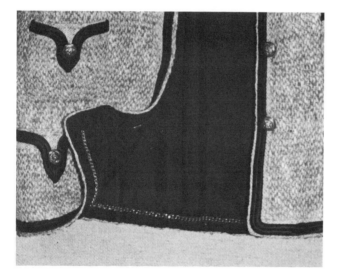

Weights in Garments

Square or round, covered or uncovered lead disks; lead pellet string encased in fabric or uncovered; or various types of metal chains.

- To prevent garment hems from shifting; riding upward on body.
- To anchor or hold hem detail in place.
- To add weight and body to hem of lightweight garments.
- At lower edge of pleats or slashed openings.
- At front corner of hem and facing of coats and jackets.
- To establish and hold drape of cowls.
- On trains and free flowing panels of evening and bridal wear.
- At edge of exaggerated bell and kimono sleeves.

Chevron / Mitering
Clipping / Snipping
Crack Stitching / Stitching in the Crease
Directional Stitching
Easing
Easing by Crowding
Easing by Manipulation
Edge Stitching
Foot Space
Frayed Edge
Layering / Grading (Blending / Beveling)
Notching
Pivot / Pivoting
Raw Edge

Reinforcing
Roll / Rolling
Slashing / Slash
Stay Stitching
Tack:
   Back Tack / Back Tacking
   Bar Tack / Bar Tacking
   Pin Tack
Top Stitching
Trimming
Understitching:
   Hand Understitching
   Machine Understitching

Construction terminology describes techniques, manipulations, and methods that are part of the construction procedure.

They include stitching processes that are applied to structural seams to help stabilize and strengthen garment sections prior to construction, or specific techniques and manipulations applied during various stages of construction to facilitate subsequent sewing operations.

The techniques or methods of construction selected depend on;
- Specific functional purpose
- Construction procedure
- Type and placement of seam
- Type and weight of fabric
- Type and style of garment
- Care of garment

Chevron / Mitering

The "V" design produced at the seam line when adjoining pattern pieces of geometric design fabric or trim are cut and sewn at the same angle.

- As a design feature.
- On square necklines, armholes, and slashed openings.
- On seams of flared skirts.
- On bias-cut garments.
- On kimono sleeves.

Chevrons are formed by joining balanced or reversible fabrics of geometric design or trim. Patterns are placed for cutting so that sizes and colors of bands will produce identical chevrons.

Clipping / Snipping

Making a single or series of short cuts into a seam allowance from the free edge towards the stitching line.

- To eliminate rippling and pulling of enclosed seams.
- To relieve straining when curved seams are pressed flat.
- To reduce strain on rounded seams.
- To allow freedom and spread of seam allowance in areas such as the inside curved seams of princess line garments, necklines, shaped facings, pivot points, or under-arms of dolman and raglan sleeves.
- To allow one edge to be spread in order to fit another section of the garment.

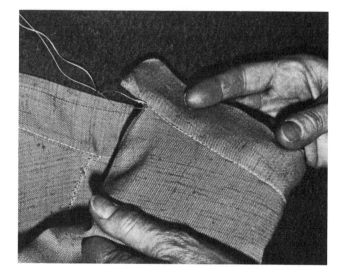

Crack Stitching / Stitching in the Crease

A stitch produced by a row of straight machine stitches in a finished seam line. Applied from the face of the garment, the stitch penetrates all plies and fastens the under ply or plies to garment.

- To complete application of:
  Waistbands, cuffs, collars and faced yokes;
  French piping, binding and bands;
  Plackets and tabs.

| With the grain | Against the grain |

Directional Stitching

Stitching with the grain or from the wider portion of a garment towards the narrower portion, close to the seam line or cut edge.

- As a preliminary stitch.
- When stitching seams.
- To prevent:
    Garment section from changing shape;
    Grain distortion of curved or angled seams;
    Seams and edges from stretching;
    Edges from raveling;
    Pile fabrics from slipping.
- On loosely woven and stretch fabrics.
- When top stitching napped or pile fabrics to prevent distortion.

At the cut edge, yarn moves together with the grain when motion is with the grain and separates or frays when motion is against the grain.

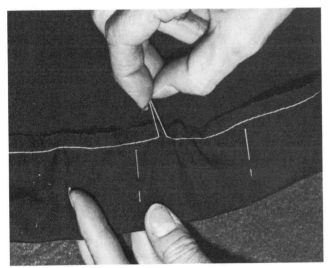

Easing by pulling a line of stitching

Easing

A process producing an even distribution of fullness by drawing in the bobbin thread of machine stitches applied to a seam line or edge.

- To enable the longer section of one ply to fit a corresponding but shorter section of a second ply.
- To control a slight amount of fullness in a seam line.
- At back neck and sleeve elbow areas instead of darts.
- To join shoulder seams.
- On sleeve cap to fit sleeve into armscye.
- On seams of princess line garments.
- At waistline of skirts or pants before applying waistband, facing or bodice.
- On curve of patch pocket, band or trimming before application to garment.
- On top edge of hem for flared and circular garments.
- On top collar or lapel.

Stitch length is selected with regard to type and weight of fabric.

Easing by Crowding

A manual process producing an even distribution of fullness by restraining fabric with the finger behind the presser foot as fabric is fed through the machine.

- To enable the longer section of one ply to fit a corresponding but shorter section of a second ply.
- To control a slight amount of fullness in a seam line.
- At back neck and sleeve elbow areas instead of darts.
- To join shoulder seams.
- On sleeve cap to fit sleeve into armscye.
- On seams of princess line garments.
- At waistline of skirts or pants before applying waistband, facing or bodice.
- On curve of patch pocket, band or trimming before application to garment.
- On top edge of hem for flared and circular garments.
- On top collar or lapel

Crowding manipulation may be performed with or without thread. Length of stitch need not be adjusted.

Easing by Manipulation

The process of restricting or pulling the upper ply of fabric allowing the lower ply to feed freely while sewing an unbasted seam.

- To enable the longer section of one ply to fit a corresponding but shorter section of a second ply.
- To control a slight amount of fullness in a seam line.
- At back neck and sleeve elbow areas instead of darts.
- To join shoulder seams.
- On sleeve cap to fit sleeve into armscye.
- On seams of princess line garments.
- At waistline of skirts or pants while applying waistband, facing or bodice.
- On curve of patch pocket, band or trimming during application to garment.
- On top edge of hem for flared and circular garments when applying binding.
- On top collar or lapel.

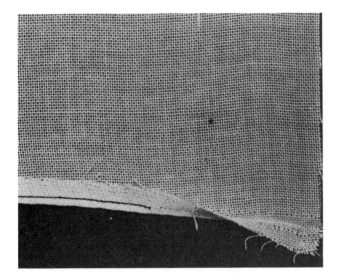

Edge Stitching

A line of machine stitching through a folded edge, 1/32 inch (0.78 mm) away from, and parallel to the edge.

- As a preliminary stitch for hems.
- As a seam finish.
- On inside and outside of folds of pleats to produce a sharp crease and maintain fold line.
- To make pin tucks.

Foot Space

A term stipulating a unit of measure using the presser foot as a guide.

- To space:
    Parallel rows of decorative stitching;
    Parallel rows of stitching for shirring;
    A row of stitching which is a uniform distance from a fold, edge, or seam line.

Foot space measurements differ with regard to the make of machine and the style of foot.

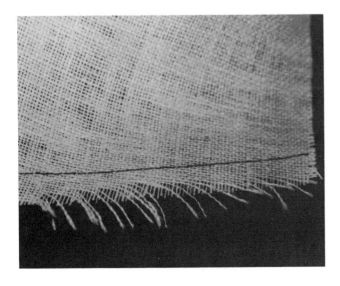

Frayed Edge

The result of abrasion on a raw edge whereby the weave separates.

A frayed edge occurs on loosely woven and satin fabrics; multifilament yarn fabrics; on interior unfinished seams subject to hard wear.
    May be produced on the outside of unfinished seams or hems as a design detail.

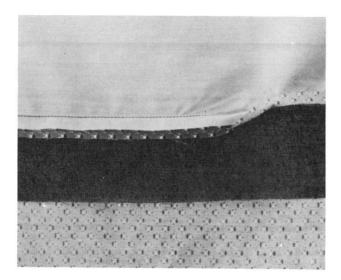

Layering / Grading (Blending / Beveling)

Trimming to different widths all plies of the seam allowance in a completed seam.

- To reduce thicknesses of different plies.
- On enclosed seams to avoid a ridge from forming on the face of the garment.
- To taper the edges of multiple plies such as facing, interfacing and garment sections to reduce bulk.
- To eliminate bulk in seams on heavy fabrics.
- During the finishing of curved seams.
- To trim and thin an enclosed seam.

Notching

The process of clipping to remove a small wedge of fabric from seam allowance plies.

- To eliminate bulk.
- To reduce strain and produce a smooth seam.
- To reduce bulk created from overlapping excess fabric when seams of garment are turned to the face of the garment.
- On piping or cording when inserted between curving edge of two plies.
- To eliminate fullness on an enclosed seam.
- On outwardly curved seams of rounded collars, pockets, lapels, scallops, capes, facings, and princess lines.

Pivot / Pivoting

A method of changing direction of a continuous line of machine stitching.

- To stitch:
    Around a square neckline corner;
    A placket;
    Sharply pointed collars, cuffs, lapels, flaps, or pockets;
    Angled design detais.
- To insert a gusset or godet.

Raw Edge

The cut edge on the length- or crossgrain or bias of a piece of fabric.

Raw edge occurs around perimeter of cut-out garment section; in the process of slashing; as part of a plain seam; as part of a flat, turned-up hem.

Reinforcing

A portion of a seam in which a single ply of a garment section before assembling has been strengthened with a preliminary row of stitching in the seam allowance, adjacent to the seam line.

- On seams with a corner edge.
- To strengthen pivot points of kimono sleeves, shawl collars, and slashed openings.
- When an inner corner needs clipping on details such as square necklines, gussets, and godets.
- As additional stitching across acute angled corners on collars, lapels, pockets, flaps, and cuffs.

Roll / Rolling

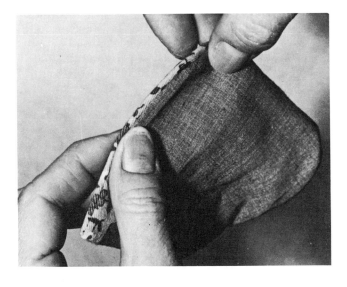

The process of manipulating a finished seam line to the underside of a garment ply.

- Where the face of the garment should roll at the seam edge to hide seam line.
- To conceal the seam edges of collars, lapels and pockets; fully lined garments.

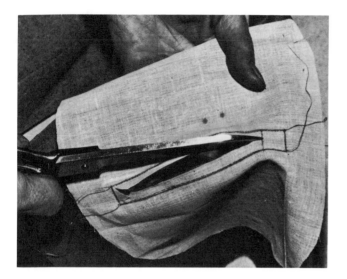

Slashing / Slash

A cutting, from the free edge to a designated point, in the body of a garment section or from two designated points within the garment.

- In order to achieve a design detail.
- To produce a sharp corner.
- To allow insertion of a gusset or godet.
- To prepare for continuous placket application.
- In the process of:
    Making bound- or faced-slashed plackets;
    Opening tailored or bound buttonholes, or pockets;
    Opening eye- and open-slit buttonholes;
    Opening a patch-slit buttonhole finish;
    Opening darts in interfacing or in skins for overlapping;
    Opening the fold of a dart in heavy fabrics to reduce bulk.
- To continue subsequent operation of garment construction.

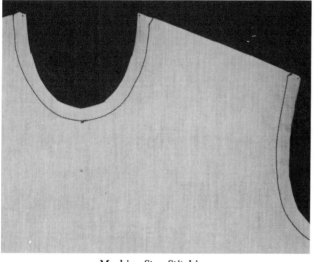

Machine Stay Stitching

Stay Stitching

A line of machine or hand stitching applied to the seam allowance on the single ply of a garment section before garment is assembled, adjacent to the seam line.

- To prevent stretching in the curved seam of armholes; neck-, waist-, shoulder-, and princess lines.
- To prevent shaped edges from stretching when fitting and handling garments.
- As a guideline for clipping and joining.
- As a reinforcement of seams.
- To strengthen curves, corners and bias lines of garments.
- On the seam lines of knits and loosely woven fabrics.
- To preserve seam, style and detail lines on muslin pattern.
- As a reinforcement and guide for design details which are turned under and top-stitched to garment.

Selection of the stitch length will vary with the type of fabric and subsequent sewing operations.

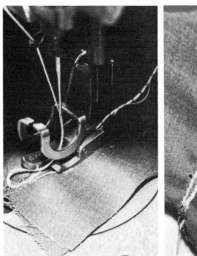

Back Tack / Back Tacking

Two short rows of stitches superimposed in a continuous sewing motion at either end of an original line of stitches.

- To secure start and finish of a row of machine stitching.
- Instead of tying thread ends.
- To reinforce points of strain.

Stitches are produced by raising the presser foot and re-stitching ends, or by utilizing the reverse stitching mechanism of a home machine.

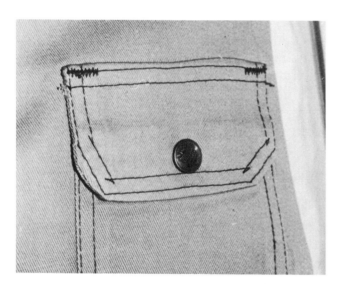

Bar Tack / Bar Tacking

A group of stitches worked so they overlap or touch one another; formed by the action of a zigzag stitch, special cam insert or dial control on home machines, or by specialized industrial machines.

- To reinforce small areas of strain.
- On fly-front zipper applications.
- At the end of pockets, buttonholes, pleats, and slashes.
- At stress points of pants, jeans, overalls, and work clothes.
- To fasten facings, shoulder pads, and belts to garments.

Configuration of tack can vary from wide to narrow, long to short, and includes arrowhead pattern.

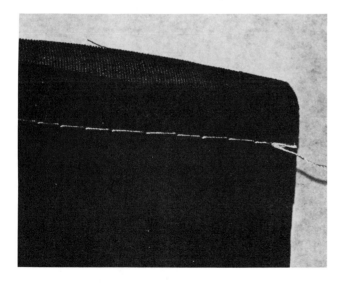

Pin Tack

One or two stitches superimposed at either end of an original line of stitching.

- To secure the start and finish of machine stitching on fine or sheer fabrics.
- Instead of tying thread ends.
- Where a longer back tack would detract from the appearance of finished seam, dart, or detail.

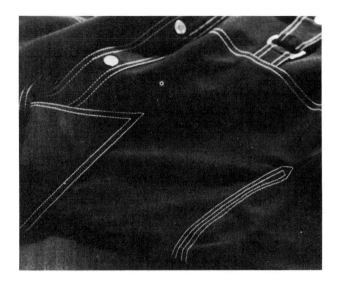

Top Stitching

One or more rows of functional and/or decorative machine or hand stitching, penetrating all plies, worked from the face of the garment parallel to a finished edge or seam line.

- To hold seams, facings, or pleats flat; and in place.
- To construct welt and tucked seams.
- To accentuate seam lines.
- To emphasize the structural lines of the garment.
- As a second operation when constructing a seam with a decorative stitch.
- On collars, lapels, cuffs, flaps, and pockets.
- On pleats, yokes, and midriffs.
- As a second operation when constructing a seam to prevent distortion and twisting of seams.

Thread color may match or contrast. Silk buttonhole twist, heavyweight thread, or two strands of needle thread may be used.

Length or type of stitch used varies according to type of thread and design feature.

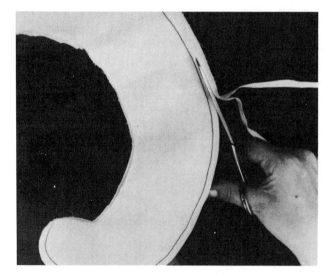

Trimming

Cutting away excess fabric after the seam has been stitched.

- To reduce or eliminate bulk in seams.
- To remove excess fabric in corners of collars, revers, lapels, pockets, flaps, and cuffs.
- To reduce thickness of crossed or intersecting seams.
- To produce an even hem width.
- When interfacing should be narrower than facing.

Seam allowance surface of high piled fabrics may be trimmed to remove depth of pile prior to machine stitching.

Hand Understitching

A line of hand stitching on the top *facing* ply close to the seam; secures facing to all plies in the seam allowance, but does not include the *garment* ply.

- In place of machine understitching.
- On sheer and fine fabrics where machine stitching would mar the face of the fabric.
- On fine fabrics where machine stitching detracts from the appearance of the garment.
- To prevent facings, linings, and the underside of garment sections from rolling to the face of the garment.
- Where or when machine stitching could distort shape of garment.

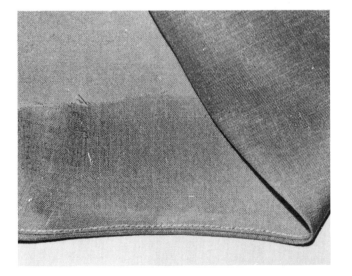

Machine Understitching

A line of machine stitches applied close to the seam, which secures the top ply of the garment underpart to all plies of the seam allowance but does not include the face garment ply.

- To prevent facings, linings, and the underside of garment sections from rolling to the face of the garment.
- To produce a delineated seam edge without pressing.
- To hold seam slightly to the underside so that it will not show when the garment is turned.
- On undercollars, necklines, facings, armholes of sleeveless dresses, and lower edges of faced hems.

37 ~ Aids, Tools & Equipment for Pressing

Brush
Canvas Shelf
Foot Press / Steam Press / Pressing Buck
Iron:
    Electric Puff Iron
    Portable Steam Presser
    Steam Iron
    Steam Iron, Pressure Tank
    Temperature Regulated Iron
Ironing Board:
    Home or Small Shop Ironing Board
    Industrial Ironing Board
    Pressing Form
Iron Shoe

Iron Stand / Iron Rest
Needle Board / Velvet Board
Paper Strips / Brown Paper
Point Presser / Collar Board
Pounding Block / Clapper / Spanker
Press Mitt
Pressing Cloth
Pressing Pad
Seam Stick
Sleeve Board
Sleeve Roll
Sponge
Tailor's Ham

Appropriate pressing equipment is essential to properly finish a garment. Pressing smooths the surface; shrinks fullness; and shapes the fabric at darts, curved seams, and caps of sleeves.

    Fiber content determines the temperature of the pressing tool. *Fiber texture* determines how the fabric is to be handled.

    Pressing tools selected depend on:
- Type of fabric
- Type of fabric finish
- Type of garment
- Construction of garment
- Technique of pressing

Brush

A device composed of natural, synthetic, or wire bristles set in a suitable back or handle.

- To raise nap of fabrics.
- To remedy overpressing of fabrics.
- To remove threads and lint after final pressing.

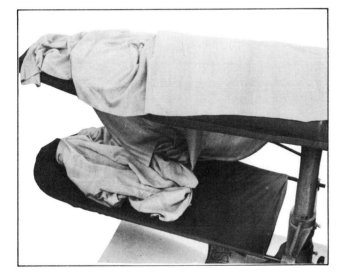

Canvas Shelf

A soft, hammock-like sling attached approximately 20 inches (50 cm) beneath the ironing board.

- To prevent garments and fabric from touching the floor.
- To prevent knit or loosely woven garments from stretching while pressing.
- To lend support to full garments while pressing.

Foot Press / Steam Press / Pressing Buck

A two-piece flat or curved padded form which applies heat, moisture, and pressure when the upper and lower opposing beds are activated by foot pedal and/or handle.

- To facilitate the pressing of a particular garment part such as a collar, shoulder or body of a coat.
- To shape and smooth the final garment.
- To smooth and shape garment parts making it possible for the tailor or machine operator to perform a variety of subsequent operations of garment assembly.
- To improve the fit of the garment.
- To steam and press woolen fabrics.
- To shrink wool fabrics before they are used.
- To press creases and pleats in garments.
- To press face and underside of garments at the same time.

Flat beds are used to press knit fabrics.

Padded surfaces are covered with silicone-treated fabric, heavy canvas, or drill cloth.

Externally generated steam may pass through top, bottom, or both surfaces.

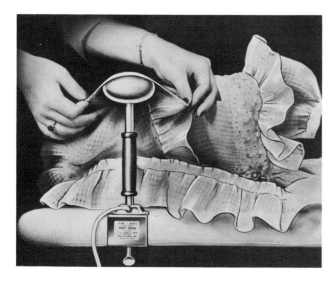

Electric Puff Iron

An ovoid, metal ironing head fixed to a metal stand and provided with an adjustable clamp for attachment to a stable base.

- To press or shape contoured seams.
- To press puffed sleeves; ruffles; pocket details.
- To block and shape millinery.

Portable Steam Presser

An electrically operated pressing aid consisting of a lightweight, flat, nonmetallic plate, approximately 5 inches (13 cm) long and 3 inches (8 cm) wide; tapering to a point at one end. Constructed with a handle and a chamber to hold a limited measure of water, which when heated emerges as steam through perforations in the bottom of the iron.

- To steam garments on model form.
- To steam garments while on a hanger.
- To open darts and seams during construction process.
- On lightweight and sheer fabrics where pressure of iron would mar the garment.
- On pile and napped fabrics where pressure of the iron would crush or flatten the fabric surface.

Steam Iron

A weighted, flat, polished metal plate, approximately 8 inches (20 cm) long by 5 inches (13 cm) wide, and tapering to a point at one end. Provided with a handle and constructed with a chamber to hold a limited measure of water, which when heated emerges as steam through perforations in the bottom of the iron.

- To smooth or crease fabrics.
- To set blocked muslin.
- To aid in the blocking of muslin.

Steam Iron Pressure Tank

A weighted, flat, polished metal plate, approximately 8 inches (20 cm) long by 5 inches (13 cm) wide, and tapering to a point at one end, furnished with a handle and steam release thumb control. Operates with steam supplied through a hose from a separate chamber where heat and pressure can be adjusted to accommodate use.

- To smooth or crease fabrics.
- To provide a steady source of steam for sustained operation.
- When heat and pressure must be adjusted for various fabrics.

Temperature Regulated Iron

A flat, weighted, polished metal plate, approximately 8 inches (20 cm) long by 5 inches (13 cm) wide, and tapering to a point at one end, furnished with a handle. Electric iron provided with a rheostat which when set holds the temperature at a chosen constant heat.

• To smooth or crease fabrics.

Home or Small Shop Ironing Board

A flat, perforated metal board, about 54 inches (1.4 meters) long by 15 inches (38 cm) wide tapering to 6 inches (15 cm) at one end, supported at table height; with a padded top usually covered with a silicone-treated, fitted cover. Board is portable.

• To provide a stable, soft surface on which to iron or press.

Industrial Ironing Board

A flat board, about 54 inches (1.4 meters) long by 15 inches (38 cm) wide tapering to 6 inches (15 cm) at one end, supported at table height. Board is permanently fixed to a table or stand, padded and covered with canvas, wool, or silicone-treated fabric depending on garment fabric or section of work pressed.

• To provide a soft surface on which to iron or press.

Pressing Form

A collapsible fabric structure simulating a garment shape which inflates and applies heat and steam when activated.

- As a means of avoiding flat pressing.
- To press total garment in one operation.
- To set shape of knit garments.
- When other methods of pressing would distort or mar garment fabric or shape.
- On knit and loosely woven goods when other methods would stretch garments.
- On garments where hard pressing and flattened seams are not necessary or desired.

Shape of pressing form is planned to conform to garment category such as shirts, evening gowns, knit garments. May be made of natural or synthetic fabrics.

Planned with zippers at strategic points for increased or decreased diameters and changing shapes.

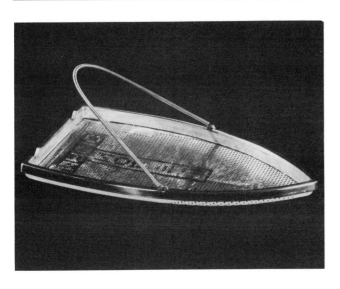

Iron Shoe

A metal fitting with a thick, teflon sheet laminated to the bottom surface, perforated and shaped to fit and strap on to the sole of a steam iron.

- To prevent shine and scorching of fabric.
- To distribute evenly steam from iron over the entire ironing surface.
- In place of a pressing cloth.
- To press the face of garments made from taffeta, gabardine, and synthetic fabrics.

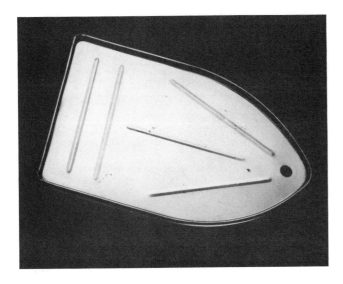

Iron Stand / Iron Rest

A flat, metal, asbestos or transite piece approximately the size, and sometimes the shape, of a hand iron. Metal type contains an asbestos insert on the bottom.

- In the home or industry.
- To rest a heated iron.
- To prevent the ironing surface from scorching.

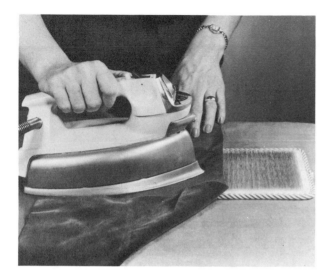

Needle Board / Velvet Board

A flat board consisting of a rigid top nap formed by short, blunt wires imbedded upright in a base.

- To avoid crushing the pile or nap of the fabric which is placed face down against the needle board during pressing or steaming.
- To prevent pile fabrics from matting and flattening.
- To prevent the impressions of a seam ridge from appearing on the face or right side of pile fabrics when pressed.
- To press velvet, velveteen, corduroy, fleece, Ultrasuede, fake fur, pile and napped fabrics.

Available in a variety of lengths and widths; and a rigid or flexible base.

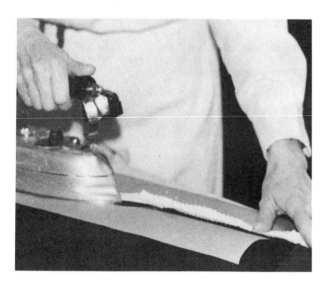

Paper Strips / Brown Paper

Heavy, uncoated paper strips.

- Slipped under seam allowances and darts before pressing to prevent their impressions from appearing on the face or right side of the garment.
- Slipped between hem and garment during pressing to prevent the impression of a hem ridge from showing on the face or right side of the garment.
- To cushion the pressure of pressing.

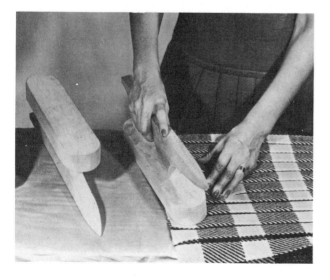

Point Presser / Collar Board

A narrow, wooden form with acute angled edges and a tapered point, and supported by a stand. The base is 13 inches (33 cm) long by 3 inches (7.6 cm) wide; the ironing surface is 13 inches (33 cm) long by 1 inch (2.5 cm) wide; the stand is 4 inches (10 cm) high.

- To press and form sharp corners.
- To press open the seams of points on collars, lapels, pockets, facings, and waistbands before they are trimmed and turned.
- To press open seams without pressing the surrounding garment.
- To produce proper profile or shape to corners of collars, lapels, bands, and cuffs.

The base or wider portion may be used as a clapper.

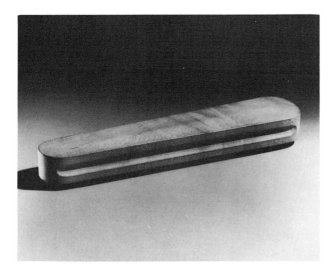

Pounding Block / Clapper / Spanker

A smooth wooden block about 12 inches (30.5 cm) long, 4 inches (10 cm) wide, and 2 inches (5 cm) thick; rounded at one end and grooved along the sides to provide a handhold.

- To flatten seams and darts during or after pressing process.
- To flatten pleats during pressing process.
- On hard-to-press fabrics.
- On woolen and heavy fabrics:
    To pound edges and seams flat;
    To obtain sharp edges without a shine on the outside of garments.
- To flatten faced edges on lapels, collars, buttonholes, and hems.

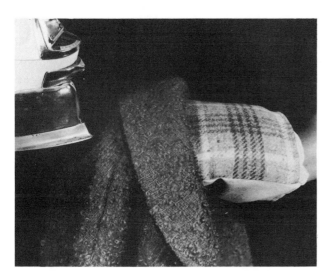

Press Mitt

A soft, hollow, padded "mitten-like" form that covers and protects the hand; permitting the wearer to hold the fabric directly beneath the iron.

- To mold and shape hard-to-get-at curved areas.
- To press small details.
- To press sleeve caps.
- To press rounded seams or style areas.

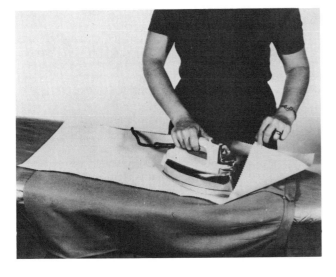

Pressing Cloth

An oblong or square piece of cotton, linen, or wool cloth. The weight may vary from sheer gauze to heavy canvas.

- To protect the surface of fabrics.
- To prevent the shine produced by direct contact of an iron on the surface of a fabric.
- To eliminate damage when pressing construction details such as zippers, closings, pockets, buttonholes, and hems.
- To protect monograms, appliqués and lace.

Muslin or *cheesecloth* is used on cotton, linens, and fiber blends.

Wool is used on woolen fabrics to prevent flattening texture.

Drill cloth or *heavy canvas* is used on woolens, worsted, gabardine and fiber blends.

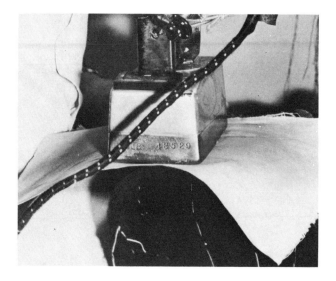

Pressing Pad

A soft blanket-like pad of cotton, felt or foam available in assorted sizes.

• To protect, while pressing, dimensional designs such as beading, embroidery, eyelet, lace, monograms, and appliqués.

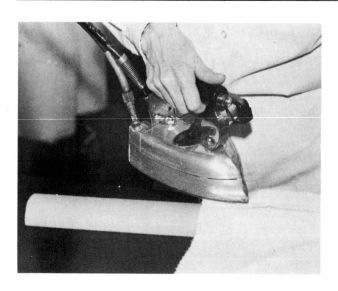

Seam Stick

A half-rounded block of wood, about 30 inches (76 cm) long by 3 inches (7.6 cm) wide, covered with cotton, felt, or silk.

• To prevent the impressions of a seam ridge from appearing on the face or right side of the garment.

Provides a limited surface on which to press.

Sleeve Board

A small-scale, wooden ironing board with rounded ends measuring about 21 inches (53 cm) long, tapering from a width of 5 inches to 2 1/2 inches (12.7 to 6.4 cm), and standing 5 inches (12.7 cm) high. The surface is padded and covered with silicone-treated cotton or canvas fabric.

• To press:
    Sleeves;
    Short seams;
    Hard-to-get-at areas;
    Areas that do not fit over a regular-sized board.
• To avoid the crease which results from pressing sleeves on a larger flat surface.

Sleeve board rests on top of ironing surface or table.

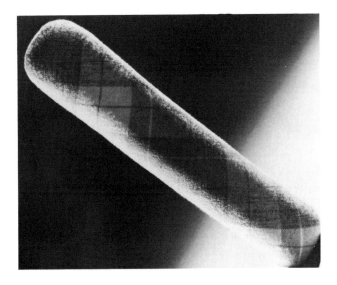

Sleeve Roll

A firm, cylindrical cushion covered with tightly woven fabric.

- To prevent the impressions of a seam ridge from appearing on the face or right side of garments when seams are pressed.
- To press sleeves, cuffs, and pants legs.
- To avoid misshaping or wrinkling the rest of the garment.

Constructed to offer a choice of wool or cotton as a pressing surface.

Sponge

A round or block, soft, compressible, porous form which retains water.

- To dampen:
    Fabrics while pressing;
    Cottons and linens directly;
    The press cloth when pressing silk, rayon, and wool.
- To moisten seams while pressing.

Tailor's Ham

A firm, rounded cushion, shaped somewhat like a ham, covered with tightly woven fabric.

- To mold shaped areas.
- To shape lapels and collars.
- To press areas that need shaping such as curved or shaped darts, curved seams, shoulders, bust, hip, and details in rounded areas.
- When shrinking out fullness of sleeve cap.

Constructed to offer a choice of wool or cotton as a pressing surface.

Pressing
Ironing
Set
Steam
Shrink
Underpress
Finger Pressing
Sponging

Pressing
The process of alternately pressing down and lifting up a heated iron on fabrics or newly stitched seams, darts, and other parts of the garment to "set" them.

Ironing
The process of sliding a heated iron back and forth over a wrinkled fabric or garment to render it smooth.

Set
The process of flattening or creasing a section of fabric or garment by means of pressing with or without steam.

Steam
The process by which steam is passed through fabric, usually downward, by means of a steam iron, pressing buck, pressing form, or dampened press cloth. An alternate method is to permit the steam to rise up through the fabric from below.

Shrink
The steaming process whereby an area of a garment or fabric is caused to draw in or contract in size.

Underpress
The process of pressing small units of work such as finished collars, cuffs, pockets, yokes, seams, darts, and tucks, as construction of garment proceeds.

Finger Pressing
The process of using one's fingers in place of an iron to open a seam or to crease a fold.

Sponging
The process of dampening the surface of a fabric or garment by means of a wet sponge.

Adhesive / Mucilage / Glue
Awl / Stiletto
Beeswax
Belting:
   Non-Slip Belting / Rubberized Belting
   Waistband Belting / Trouser Waistband
Bias Binding:
   Single-Fold Bias Binding
   Double-Fold Bias Binding
Bias Hemming / Hem Facing
Binding:
   Iron-On Seam Binding / Press-On Tape
   Lace Binding
   Ribbon Seam Binding / Seam Binding
Bodkin
Bonding Strip / Fusible Adhesive
Bra Cup
Buckle:
   Buckle
   Clasp / Interlocking Buckle
   Concealed Hook Buckle
   Covered Buckle
   Hook and Eye Buckle / Anchor Buckle
   Overall Buckle
   Spring-and-Hook Buckle / Ratchet Buckle
Buttons:
   Covered Button
   Corded Button
   Sew-Through Button
   Shank Button
Coat and Jacket Hanger
Cord:
   Cord / Cable Cord
   Cording / Corded Piping
   Tubular Cording
Elastic:
   Elastic Braid
   Elastic Ribbon / Ribbed Elastic
   Elastic Cord
   Elastic Edging
   Elastic for Lingerie
   Elastic for Pajamas
   Elastic Thread
   Elastic Webbing
   Non-Roll Elastic
Eyelet
Eyelet Setter / Grommet Setter
Grommet
Grosgrain Ribbon
Hole Punch
Hook:
   Hook and Bar (Prong)

Hook and Bar (Sew-On)
Bra and Swimsuit Hook
Hook and Eye
Gimp-Covered Hook and Eye / Fur Hook and Eye
Hook and Eye Tape
Hook and Loop Fastener / Velcro® Fastener
Hook and Loop Tape / Velcro® Tape
Horsehair Braid
Lingerie Strap Holder
Magnet
Needles:
   Hand Needles
   Machine Needles
Needle Threader
Paired Rings
Pins:
   Ball Point Pin
   Large Head Pin
   Straight Pin
   T-Head Pin / "T" Pin
Pin Cushion:
   Pin Cushion
   Emery Bag
Powdered Chalk
Ribbing Band / Knit Band
Shoulder Pads
Snaps:
   Covered Snap
   Nylon Snap
   No-Sew Snap / Hammer-On Snap
   No-Sew Snap Tape / Hammer-On Snap Tape
   Snap
   Snap Tape
   Punch Snap Setter / No-Sew Snap Setter
Stay / Support:
   Boning / Feather Boning
   Collar Pocket Stay
   Foundation Stay
Suspender Clip
Tape:
   Double-Faced Tape
   Self-Stick Tape
   Tissue Tape
   Transparent Tape
   Twill Tape
Thimble:
   Tailor's Thimble
   Thimble
Toggle
Turner:
   Crease Turner
   Loop Turner

Point and Tube Turner
Weights:
    Chain Weights
    Lead Disk Weights
    Lead Pellet Weights
Zippers:
    Decorative Zipper / Industrial Zipper

Dress Zipper
Invisible Zipper
Reversible Zipper
Separating Zipper
Skirt or Neckline Zipper
Two-Way Zipper / Dual Opening Zipper
Zipper Lubricant

Thread

COMMON YARDAGE PUT-UPS	EXACT METRIC CONVERSION (METERS)	NEW METRIC PUT-UPS (METERS)	CUSTOMARY YARDAGE EQUIVALENT
10	9.14	9	9.8
50	45.72	45	49
70	64.01	60 or 65	66 or 71
75	68.58	65 or 70	71 or 77
80	73.15	70 or 75	77 or 82
100	91.44	90	98
125	114.30	100 or 115	109 or 126
150	137.16	135 or 140	148 or 153
200	182.88	180 or 185	197 or 202
225	205.74	200	219
250	228.60	225	246
275	251.46	250	273
300	274.32	270 or 275	295 or 301
325	297.18	295 or 300	323 or 328
400	365.76	365	399
425	388.62	385 or 390	421 or 427
475	434.34	430 or 435	470 or 476
500	457.20	450 or 455	492 or 498

Tapes & Braids (Packaged)

COMMON YARDAGE PUT-UPS (YARDS)	EXACT METRIC CONVERSION (METERS)	NEW METRIC PUT-UPS (METERS)	CUSTOMARY YARDAGE EQUIVALENT (YARDS)
2	1.83	1.8	1.97
2 1/2	2.29	2.2 or 2.3	2.41 or 2.52
3	2.74	2.7	2.95
4	3.66	3.6 or 3.7	3.94 or 4.05
4 3/4	4.34	4.3	4.70
5	4.57	4.5 or 4.6	4.92 or 5.03
COMMON WIDTHS (INCHES)	**EXACT METRIC CONVERSION (MM)**	**NEW METRIC WIDTH (MM)**	**(CUSTOMARY EQUIVALENT (INCHES)**
1/8	3.18	3	.12
3/16	4.76	5	.20
1/4	6.35	6	.24
3/8	9.52	10	.39
1/2	12.70	13	.51
5/8	15.9	16	.63
3/4	19.0	19	.75
7/8	22.2	22	.87
1	25.4	25	.98
1 3/4	44.4	44	1.73
2	50.8	51	2.01

Zippers

COMMON ZIPPER LENGTHS (INCHES)	EXACT METRIC CONVERSION	NEW METRIC LENGTH (CM)	CUSTOMARY (INCH) EQUIVALENT
4	10.16	10	3.9
5	12.7	12	4.7
6	15.24	15	5.9
7	17.78	18	7.1
9	22.86	23	9.1
10	25.4	25	9.8
11	27.94	28	11.0
12	30.48	30	11.8
14	35.56	35	13.8
16	40.64	40	15.7
18	45.72	45	17.7
20	50.8	50	19.7
22	55.88	55	21.7
24	60.96	60	23.6
26	66.04	65	25.6
27	68.58	68	26.8
28	71.12	70	27.6
30	76.2	75	29.5
34	86.36	85	33.5
36	91.44	90	35.4

Bibliography

Allen, Vivian. *Beyond the Pattern.* Spinning Spool Publications, 1975.

The Art of Sewing (series). New York: TIME-LIFE Books, 1976.
    Basic Tailoring
    Boutique Attire
    The Classical Technique
    Creative Design
    The Custom Look
    Delicate Wear
    The Personal Touch
    Separates That Travel
    Short Cuts to Elegance
    Traditional Favorites

Bancroft, Vivian S. *It's So, Sew Easy.* Minneapolis, Minnesota: Burgess Publishing Company, 1970.

Bane, Allyne. *Creative Clothing Construction.* New York: McGraw-Hill, Inc., 1973.

_____. *Flat Pattern Design.* New York: McGraw-Hill, Inc., 1972.

Bath, Virginia C. *Lace.* Chicago, Illinois: Henry Regnery Company, 1974.

Besserman, Harry. *5 Sources of Design.* Brooklyn, New York: Harry Besserman, 1971. (Available through Fashion Institute of Technology, New York.)

Bishop, Edna Bryte, and Marjorie Stotler Arch. *Super Sewing: The New Bishop-Arch Book.* Philadelphia, Pennsylvania: J.B. Lippincott Company, 1974.

Brockman, Helen. *The Theory of Fashion Design.* New York: John Wiley & Sons, Inc., 1967.

Calasibetta, Dr. Charlotte. *Fairchild's Dictionary of Fashion.* New York: Fairchild Publications, 1975.

The Clothing Factory. London: Clothing Institute of London, 1972.

Coats and Clark Educational Department. *Coats and Clark's Sewing Book: Newest Methods from A to Z.* New York: Coats and Clark Inc., 1971.

Complete Guide to Sewing. Pleasantville, New York: Reader's Digest Association, 1977.

Corbman, Bernard P. *Textiles: Fiber to Fabric.* New York: McGraw-Hill, Inc., 1975.

Courtney, Gretel. *The Butterick Sewing Machine Handbook.* New York: Butterick Publishing Co., 1977.

Craig, Hazel T. *Clothing: A Comprehensive Study.* Philadelphia, Pennsylvania: J.B. Lippincott Company, 1973.

Dictionary of Textile Terms, A. 12th ed., New York: Dan River Inc., 1976.

Duncan, Ida R. *American Woman's Complete Sewing Book.* Rev. ed., New York: Liveright Publishing Company, 1961.

Ein, Claudia. *How to Design Your Own Clothes and Make Your Own Patterns.* Garden City, New York: Doubleday & Co., Inc., 1975.

Hillhouse, Marion, and Evelyn Mansfield. *Dress Design Draping and Flat Patternmaking.* New York: Houghton Mifflin Company, 1948.

Hollen, Norma R. *Patternmaking by the Flat Pattern Method.* Minneapolis, Minnesota: Burgess Publishing Company, 1975.

How to Tailor A Woman's Suit. The Department of Agriculture. Washington: Government Printing Office, 1968.

Hutton, Jessie, and Gladys Cunningham. *Singer Sewing Book.* New York: Golden Press, 1972.

Ironside, Janey. *The Fashion Alphabet.* London: Michael Joseph Ltd., 1968.

Jaffe, Hilde. *Children's Wear Design.* New York: Fairchild Publications, 1972.

Jaffe, Hilde, and Nurie Relis. *Draping for Fashion Design.* Virginia: Reston Publishing Co., 1973.

Joseph, Marjorie. *Essentials of Textiles.* New York: Holt, Rinehart & Winston, 1976.

Kawashima, Masaaki. *Fundamentals of Men's Fashion Design: A Guide to Tailored Clothes.* New York: Fairchild Publications, 1974.

_____. *Men's Outerwear Design.* New York: Fairchild Publications, 1978.

Kleeberg, Irene Cummings, editor. *The Butterick Fabric Handbook.* New York: Butterick Publishing Co., 1975.

Kopp, Ernestine, Vittorina Rolfo, and Beatrice Zelin. *Designing Apparel through the Flat Pattern.* 5th ed. New York: Fairchild Publications, 1979.

_____. *How to Draft Basic Patterns.* New York: Fairchild Publications, 1975.

_____. New Fashion Areas for Designing Apparel through the Flat Pattern. New York: Fairchild Publications, 1972.

Kramer, Rose. *Fundamentals of Garment Machine Operating.* New York: New York State Vocational Teachers Association.

Lewis, Virginia S. *Comparative Clothing Construction Techniques.* Minneapolis, Minnesota: Burgess Publishing Company, 1976.

Ley, Sandra. *America's Sewing Book.* New York: Charles Scribner's Sons, 1972.

Linton, George E. *The Modern Textile and Apparel Dictionary.* 4th ed. Plainfield, New Jersey: Textile Book Service, 1973.

Lippman, Gidon, and Dorothy Erskine. *Sew It Yourself: How to Make Your Own Fashion Classics.* New Jersey: Prentice-Hall, Inc., 1976.

Loeb, Jo. *The Leather Book.* New Jersey: Prentice-Hall, Inc., 1975.

Mactaggart, Ann. *Complete Book of Dressmaking.* New York: Van Nostrand Reinhold Company, 1975.

Man-Made Fiber Fact Book. Washington: Man-Made Fiber Producers Association, Inc., 1974.

Margolis, Adele P. *Fashion Sewing for Everyone.* Garden City, New York: Doubleday & Co., Inc., 1974.

_____. *How to Make Clothes That Fit and Flatter.* Garden City, New York: Doubleday & Co., Inc., 1969.

Mauck, Francis. *Modern Sewing Techniques.* New York: Macmillan, Inc., 1963.

Moores, Dorothy. *Patterndrafting and Dressmaking.* Sydney, Australia: Golden Press Pty., Ltd., 1971.

Morris, Ben, and Elizabeth Morris. *Making Clothes in Leather.* New York: Taplinger Publishing Co., Inc., 1976.

Musheno, Elizabeth, editor. *The Vogue Sewing Book.* New York: Vogue Pattern Co., 1975.

Nordquist, Dr. Barbara. *Guide to Patternmaking.* New York: Drake Publishers, Inc., 1973.

Palestrant, Simon S. *Tailoring and Dressmaking.* New York: Wehman, 1952.

Parker, Xenia Ley. *Working with Leather.* New York: Charles Scribner's Sons, 1972.

Perry, Patricia, editor. *Butterick Sewing Book: Ready Set Sew.* New York: Butterick Publishing Co., 1971.

Picken, Mary B., editor. *The Fashion Dictionary: Fabric, Sewing, and Apparel As Expressed in the Language of Fashion.* New York: Funk and Wagnalls, Inc., 1972.

Pizzuto, Joseph J. *Fabric Science.* 4th ed., revised by Arthur Price, Allen C. Cohen. New York: Fairchild Publications, 1979.

Pizzuto, Joseph J. *101 Weaves in 101 Fabrics.* Pelham, New York: Textile Press, 1961.

Price, Jeanne, and Bernard Zamkoff. *Grading Techniques for Modern Design.* New York: Fairchild Publications, 1974.

Rhinehart, Jane, and B.J. Shewbart. *How to Make Men's Clothes.* Garden City, New York: Doubleday & Co., Inc., 1975.

Roberts, Edmund B. *Fundamentals of Men's Fashion Design: A Guide to Casual Clothes.* New York: Fairchild Publications, 1975.

Robinson, Julian. *The Penguin Book of Sewing.* New York: Penguin Books, 1974.

Roxanne. *The Secret of Couture Sewing.* New York: McGraw-Hill, Inc., 1972.

Silverstein, Morton, Saul Smilowitz, and Jack Walfish. "A Research Project on Seam Performance." Apparel Research Foundation, 1971.

Simplicity Education Department. *Simplicity Sewing Book.* New York: Simplicity Pattern Company, 1975.

Simplified Clothing Construction. The Department of Agriculture. Washington: Government Printing Office, 1967.

Singer Education Department. *Singer Dressmaking Course.* New York: Grosset & Dunlap, Inc., 1961.

Solinger, Jacob. *Apparel Manufacturing Analysis.* Columbia, South Carolina: Needle Trades Publishing Corp., 1969.

Stitches, Seams and Stitchings. Federal Standard #751a. Washington: Government Printing Office, 1965.

Tanous, Helen N. *Designing Dress Patterns.* Peoria, Illinois: Chas. A. Bennett Co., Inc., 1971.

Unit Method of Clothing Construction. 6th ed. Iowa Home Economics Association, 1976.

Warch, Constance. *Illustrated Guide to Sewing.* Plycon Press, 1975.

Wilson, Violet. *Sewing without Tears.* New York: Charles Scribner's Sons, 1972.

Wingate, Dr. Isabel B. *Fairchild's Dictionary of Textiles.* 6th ed. New York: Fairchild Publications, 1979.

_____. *Textile Fabrics and Their Selection.* New Jersey: Prentice-Hall, Inc., 1976.

abutted seam, 239
accordion pleat, 6
adhesive, 140, 323
    fusible, 143, 323
adjustable L-square, 18
all-in-one shaped facing, 180
anchor buckle, 184, 323
animal skin, 59
    opening, 208
    pattern layout, 76
    seams, 245
apex
    of dart, 31
    of model form, 38
applied patch, 297
arrowhead, 291
arrowhead tack stitch, 270
awl, 140, 323

back stitch, 263
    half, 263
    modified, 263
    prick stitch, 263
back tack, 309
backing, 296
balance
    of muslin, 38
    patternmaking lines, 31
balanced stripe
    pattern layout, 82
balancing of muslin, 38
balancing patternmaking lines, 31
ball point needle
    hand sewing, 107
    sewing machine, 113-14
        Machine Needle/Fabric Selection Guide, 113-14
ball point pin, 149, 323
ball-tipped shears, 95
band, 291
band hem, 223
band knife, 86
band placket, 235
banding, 291
bar tack, 309
bar tack stitch, 270
basic pattern, 25
basting, 160-63
    diagonal, 161
    even, 161
    machine, 161
    pin, 162
    press, 162
    slip, 162
    tailor, 161
    uneven, 163
beading needle, 107
beeswax, 140, 323
belt, 285. *See also* waistline
    half, 285
    tie, 285
belt carriers, 293
belt loops, 293
belting, 141, 323
    non-slip, 141, 323
    rubberized, 141, 323
    trouser waistband, 323
    waistband, 323
bent handle dressmaker's shears, 95
bent trimmers, 95

betweens needle, 107
beveling, 306
bias, 68, 164-70
    application methods
        with binder attachment set, 169
        with binder foot attachment, 170
        without attachment, 170
    binding, 165-66
    commercially prepared, 169
    facing, 165
    forty-five degree, 68
    hemming, 165
    self-prepared, 169
    true bias, 68
bias application methods, 169-70
bias binding
    double-fold, 166, 224, 323
    single-fold, 165, 224, 323
bias cut, 2
bias-faced waistline, 187
bias facing, 165, 180
bias fold, 224
bias hemming, 165, 323
bias preparation methods, 168-69
bias tape, 224
bias tubing, 167
binding, *See also* bound hem
    iron-on seam, 141, 231, 323
    lace seam, 142, 231, 323
    press-on tape, 141, 231, 323
    ribbon seam, 142, 232, 323
    seam, 142, 232, 323
blanket stitch, 264
blend, 45
blending, 306
blind stitch, 264, 273
    hand sewing, 264
    sewing machine, 273
blind catch stitch, 265
blind-stitched hem, 223
block pattern, 25
blocking, 68
bodkin, 142, 323
bonded fabric structure, 60
bonded hem, 224
bonded invisible thread (Nymo®), 126
bonding strip, 143, 323
boning, 155, 323
book edge finish, 167
book hem, 223
book seam finish, 251
border design fabric
    pattern layout, 76
border fabric
    pattern layout, 76
bound hem, 225
    bias fold, 224
    bias tape, 224
    double-fold bias binding, 224
    Hong Kong finish, 225
    net binding, 225
    single-fold bias binding, 224
bound placket, 235
bound seam finish
    double-ply, 252
    net-bound, 251
    rolled, 251
    self-bound, 251
    single-ply, 252
box pleat, 7

bra cup, 143, 323
bra and swimsuit hook, 189, 323
braid
  elastic, 175
  horsehair, 147
  ribbon, 175
  rib-type, 175
braid loop, soutache, 206
break point, 38
break point line, 31
brown paper, 318
brush, 313
buckle, 183, 323
  anchor, 184, 323
  clasp, 184, 323
  concealed hook, 183, 323
  covered, 183, 323
  hook and eye, 184, 323
  interlocking, 184, 323
  overall, 185, 323
  ratchet, 185, 323
  spring-and-hook type, 185, 323
built-up waistline, 283
bundle, 102
butted seam, 239
button attaching clip, 200
button and carpet thread, 123
buttonhole, 203-10. See also loop
  corded bound, 204
  eye slit, 204, 294
  hand-worked, 205
  hand-worked with cord, 205
  in seam, 209
  keyhole, 209
  machine-fused, 207
  machine-worked, 207
  machine-worked with cord, 208
  open slit, 208
  opening in skins, 208
  patch slit, 205
  slot, 209
  tailored, 209
  welt bound, 204
  worked, 203
buttonhole machine, 209
  attachment (non-industrial), 210
buttonhole scissors, 93
buttonhole stitch, 264
buttons, 198-202
  attaching clip, 202
  corded, 200, 323
  covered, 200, 323
  jet clip, 202
  sew-through, 201, 323
  shank, 201, 323

cable cord, 144, 323
calyx-eyed needle, 107
camel hair, 64
camisole, 293
canvas shelf, 313
carbon tracing paper, 28
cardboard gauge, 145
carpet thread, 123
casing, 171-73
  elastic in, 172, 177
  inside applied, 173
  outside applied, 173
  self, 173
  with drawstring, 172
  with heading, 172

catch stitch, 265
  blind, 265
center finding rule, 23
centered zipper insertion, 218
centimeter stick, 24
chain stitch, 273
chain-thread loop, 206
chain weights, 158, 323
chalk
  powdered, 152, 323
  tailor's, 26
chalked marking, 52
chalked thread, 52
chalking pencil, 148
Chantilly lace, 63
check fabric
  pattern layout, 77
chenilles needle, 108
chevron, 302
Chinese ball button, 200
circle template, 15
clam-shaped dart, 5
clamp, 86
clapper, 319
clasp, 184, 323
clear plastic ruler, 24
click press, 86
clipping, 302
closed end zipper, 213
cloth measuring and inspection machine, 87
cloth notcher. See also notcher
  electrical, 87
  manual, 88
cloth point needle, 113, 117
coat and jacket hanger, 143, 323
collar board, 318
collar-pocket stay, 298, 323
color coding, 52
combination ruler and curve, 15
combination shaped facing, 180
commercial pattern, 55
compass, 15
compromise, 33
concealed hook buckle, 183, 323
continuous lap placket, 235
  placed in a seam, 236
conventional zipper, 213
converge, 45
contoured waistband, 286
cord, 144, 323
  elastic, 176, 323
cord-filled bias tubing, 167
cord loop, 206
corded bound buttonhole, 204
corded button, 200, 323
corded piped seam, 239
corded piping, 166, 323
cording, 166, 323
cording foot, 221
corduroy, wide wale, 65
cotton basting thread, 123
cotton-covered polyester core thread, 127
cotton darners needle, 108
cotton thread, 123
  Thread/Fabric Selection Guide, 133-35
covered buckle, 183, 323
covered button, 200, 323
covered snap, 194, 323
crack stitching, 302
crease, 39
crease turner, 157, 323
crewel needle, 109

crochet chain stitch, 266
crochet loop, 206
crossed seam, 260
crossgrain, 69
crossmarks, 39
crystal pleat, 7
cupping, 45
curtain waistband, 289
curve
    combination ruler and, 15
    curve rule, 16
    Dietzgen #17, 16
    French, 16
    hip, 16
    irregular, 16
    neckline, 16
    sleigh, 17
    vary form, 16
curve rule, 16
curved needle, 108
curved seam
    inside, 259
    outside, 259
cut of garment
    bias cut, 2
    flare, 3
cutter. *See also* knife
    circular, 89
    portable rotary knife, 89
    rotary, 89
    round, 89
    straight knife, 88
cut-off machine, 98
cutting, 40, 101-05
    procedure guide, 101
    tools and equipment, 84-100
cutting board, 90
cutting guide line, 32, 103
cutting line, 103
cutting room thread marker, 90
cutting table, 90
cutting table triangle, 91

dacron thread
    Thread/Fabric Selection Guide, 137
damask stitch, 267
darners needle
    cotton, 108
    yarn, 108
darning thread, 124
dart, 3
    apex of, 31
    clam-shaped, 5
    decorative, 4
    diamond-shaped, 5
    double, 5
    double-ended, 5
    flange, 4
    French, 3
    temporary, 36
    working, 36
dart manipulation, 46
dart slash, 4
dart substitution, 46
dart tuck, 5
dart variation, 46
decorative dart, 4
decorative elastic band, 175
decorative zipper, 213, 324
diagonal basting, 161

diagonal design fabric
    pattern layout, 77
diagonal weave fabric
    pattern layout, 78
diamond-shaped dart, 5
die cutting press, 86
Dietzgen #17, 16
directional design fabric
    pattern layout, 78
directional seam line, 48
directional stitching 303
dog leash fastener, 186
dots, 40
double dart, 5
double-ended dart, 5
double-faced tape, 156, 323
double-fold bias binding, 224
double fold hem, 225
double-needle machine stitch, 274
double-ply layout, 73
double-stitched hem, 226
double-stitched seam finish, 252
    overcast, 253
    trimmed, 253
double top-stitched seam, 248
double welt seam, 249
draft, 32
drafted pattern, 55
drafting, 30-36, 43-50
drape, 40
draped pattern, 55
draping, 37-50
    tools, 14
drawstring, 186
    casing with, 172
dress placket, 236
    zipper insertion, 217
dress zipper, 213
dressmaker's gauge, 146
dressmaker's shears, 95
dressmaker's tracing paper, 28
drill, 91-92
dual opening zipper, 216, 324

ease, 5, 41
    in a hem, 226
eased seam, 239, 240
easing, 303
    by crowding, 304
    by manipulation, 304
edge-stitched hem, 226
edge-stitched seam finish, 253
edge stitching, 305
elastic, 174-78
    braid, 175, 323
    casing with, 172, 177
    cord, 176, 323
    decorative elastic band, 175
    edging, 176, 323
    lingerie, 178, 323
    non-roll ribbed, 176, 323
    pajamas, 323
    ribbed, 323
    ribbon, 176, 323
    ribbon braid, 175
    rib-type braid, 175
    sewn to garment, 178
    swimwear, 178
    thread, 177, 323
    webbing, 177, 323

elastic-backed straight waistband, 287
elasticized shirring, 10, 279
elasticized waistline, 283
electric puff iron, 314
electrical cloth notcher, 87
embroidery floss, 124
embroidery needle, 109
embroidery scissors, 94
embroidery thread, 124
emery bag, 152, 323
enclosed seam, 259
end catcher, 98
end guide rail, 98
equalize, 33
eraser, 17
even basting, 161
exposed seam, 260
exposed zipper insertion
    decorative, 217
    industrial, 217
    in a slash, 217
extended facing, 181
extended seam allowance, 260
extended seam edge, 260
eye slit, 204, 294
eyelet, 144, 323
    hand-worked, 187
    metal, 187
eyelet setter, 152, 323

fabric, 58-66, 67-70
    bonded, 60
    excess, 41
    face of fabric, 69
    felt, 60
    fold layout. See fold layout
    flocking, 60
    fused, 61
    knit, 62
    lace, 63
    laminated, 60
    layout. See fold layout
    napped, 64
    net, 64
    nonwoven, 61
    pattern layout. See pattern layout
    pile, 65
    plastic, 66
    right side, 69
    spreading. See spreading
    woven, 66
fabric excess, 41
fabric loop, 206
fabric stay, 299
face-to-face spreader, 98
faced hem, 227
faced-slashed placket, 236
faced waistline, 283
facing, 179-81
    all-in-one shaped, 180
    bias, 165, 180
    extended, 181
    one-piece, 181
    outside, 180
    self, 181
    shaped, 181
false French seam, 241
fasteners, 182-97. See also buttons and zippers
fastening stitch, 269
feather boning, 155, 323
Federal standard stitch classes, 272-80

felling stitch, 266
felt fabric structure, 60
fiber board, 20
final pattern, 33
finger pressing, 322
fitting platform, 145
flange dart, 4
flare, 3
flat-felled seam, 240
    mock, 249
flat hem, 227
    pinked, 227
    plain, 227
    stitched and pinked, 228
    turned flat, 227
flocking fabric structure, 60
fly-front concealed zipper insertion, 218
fold, 41
fold layout, 72-74
    bifold, 73
    combination, 72
    crosswise, 72
    double lengthwise, 73
    double-ply, 73
    lengthwise, 72
    multi-ply, 73
    open-ply, 74
    partial lengthwise, 73
    single-ply, 74
    spreading. See spreading
fold line, 46
foot press, 314
foot space, 305
forty-five degree bias, 68
foundation pattern, 25
foundation support, 294, 323
frayed edge, 305
French binding, 167
French curve, 16
French dart, 3
French gathering, 11
French piping, 167
French seam, 240
    false, 241
    simulated, 241
French shirring, 11
French tack stitch, 270
frog, 187
fur hook and eye, 191, 323
fur seams, 244
fur tack, 188
fused fabric structure, 61
fused seam, 241
fusible adhesive, 143, 323

garment section, 47
gathering, 10
    French gathering, 11
gathering stitch, 278
gauge
    cardboard, 145
    dressmaker's, 146
    hem, 146
    hemline, 145
    hemline marking, 145
    scallop, 146
    sewing, 146
    sleeve, 146
gauging, 6
gimp-covered hook and eye, 191, 323
glazing, 121

glovers needle, 109
glue, 140, 323
glued hem, 228
glued seam, 241
glued seam finish, 254
godet, 294
graded pattern, 56
grading, 306
grainline indicator, 33
grainlines, 42
granite tag, 20
graph paper, 20
grommet, 188, 323
grommet setter, 323
grosgrain ribbon, 147, 323
guide line
   cuttin, 32, 103
   on muslin, 42
gusset, 295

hairline seam, 242
half back stitch, 263
half belt, 282
hammer-on snap, 194, 323
hammer-on snap tape, 195, 323
hand smocking, 12
hand-stitched zipper application, 216
hand stitches, 262-73. *See also* machine stitches
   arrowhead tack, 270
   back, 263
   bar tack, 270
   blanket, 264
   blind, 264
   blind catch, 265
   buttonhole, 264
   catch, 265
   crochet chain, 266
   damask, 267
   felling, 266
   French tack, 270
   half back, 263
   modified back, 263
   napery, 267
   overcasting, 266
   overhand, 267
   overhanding, 267
   padding, 267
   pick, 268
   prick, 263
   running, 268
   saddle, 268
   shell, 269
   slip, 269
   tack, 269
   triangular tack, 270
   whip, 271
hand understitching, 311
hand-worked buttonhole, 205
   with cord, 205
hanger, coat and jacket, 143, 323
heading, casing with, 172
hem, 222-33
   band, 223
   blind-stitched, 223
   bonded, 224
   book, 223
   bound, 225
   double fold, 225
   double-stitched, 226
   ease, 226
   edge-stitched, 226
   faced, 227

   flat, 227
   glued, 228
   hand-rolled, 230
   Hong Kong finish, 225
   horsehair, 228
   interfaced, 229
   iron-on seam binding, 231
   lace seam binding, 231
   lingerie, 269
   machine-rolled, 231
   machine-stitched, 229
   mitered, 229
   net binding, 225
   overedged, 230
   padded, 230
   pinked flat, 227, 228
   plain, 227
   press-on tape, 231
   ribbon seam tape, 232
   seam binding, 232
   stitched and pinked, 228
   sweep of, 49
   turned flat, 227
   weighted, 232, 233
   wired, 232
hem facing, 323
hem gauge, 146
hemmed-edge placket, 237
hemline gauge, 145
hemline marking guide, 145
hemstitch, 274
hip curve, 16
hole punch, 153, 323
Hong Kong finish, 225
hook, 188, 323
   bra and swimsuit, 189, 323
hook and bar, 189, 323
hook and eye, 190, 323
   covered, 190
   fur, 191, 323
   gimp-covered, 191, 323
hook and eye buckle. 184, 323
hook and eye tape, 191, 323
hook and loop fastener, 191, 323
hook and loop tape, 192, 323
horsehair braid, 147, 323
horsehair hem, 228

in seam buttonhole, 209
Industrial Cutting Procedure Guide for Fabric Spreading, 101
industrial thread, 125
   needle sizes, 138
   physical properties, 138
   ticket numbers, 138
industrial zipper, 213, 324
inset waistline, 284
insert waistline, 284
inside applied casing, 173
inside curved seam, 259
interfaced hem, 229
interfacing, 295
interlining, 296
interlocking buckle, 184, 323
interlocking of pattern pieces, 102
intersecting seam, 260
inverted pleat, 7
invisible thread, 126
   twisted, 127
invisible zipper, 214, 324
iron
   electric puff, 314

portable steam presser, 315
pressure tank, 315
steam, 315
temperature regulated, 316
iron rest, 317
iron shoe, 317
iron stand, 317
iron-on seam binding, 141, 231
ironing, 322
ironing board
home or small shop, 316
industrial, 316
pressing form, 317
irregular curve, 16
irregular design fabric
pattern layout, 79

Jeans seam, 240
jet clip, 202

keyhole buttonhole, 209
kick pleat, 8
knife. *See also* cutter
band, 86
circular, 89
portable rotary, 89
razor, 93
round, 89
knife edge shears, 97
knife pleat, 8
knit fabric structure, 62
pattern layout, 79
knit-ribbed band, 292, 323

L square, 18
adjustable, 18
tailor's square, 18
lace fabric structure, 63
lace seam, 245
lace seam binding, 142, 231
lacing, 192
laminated fabric structure, 60
lap zipper insertion, 218
lapped seam, 242
large head pin, 149, 323
large print fabric
pattern layout, 79
lay, 104
layering, 306
layout of pattern pieces, 102
layup, 104
lead disc weights, 159, 324
lead pellet weights, 159, 324
leather point needle, 115
Machine Needle/Fabric Selection Guide, 115
lengthgrain, 69
lettuce edging, 274
light-reflecting fabric
pattern layout, 80
lingerie
bra hook, 189, 323
elastic, 178, 323
strap holder, 296, 323
lingerie hem, 269
lining, 297
backing, 296
interlining, 296
partial, 297
underlining, 296
lockstitch zigzag machine stitch, 275

loop
chain-thread, 206
cord, 206
crochet, 206
fabric, 206
rouleau, 206
soutache braid, 206
thread, 207
worked-thread, 207
loop turner, 158, 323

machine basting, 161
machine-fused buttonhole, 207
Machine Needle Blade Size Designations for Various Machines, 120
Machine Needle/Fabric Selection Guide, 113-14, 115, 116-18
Machine Needle Size Chart, 119
machine shell stitch, 278
machine smocking, 12
machine-stitched hem, 229
machine-stitched zipper application, 216
machine stitches, 272-80. *See also* hand stitches
bline, 273
chain, 273
double-locked, 272
double-needle machine, 274
elasticized shirring, 279
Federal standard classifications, 272
flat seam, 272
gathering, 278
hemstitch, 274
lettuce edging, 274
lockstitch zigzag, 275
Merrow®, 275
machine shell, 278
mock safety, 277
multi-thread chainstitch, 272
New stitch 801, 279
overedge, 275
overlock, 275
picot edging, 276
pull-out overedge, 276
purl edging, 276
safety, 277
scallop edging, 277
scallop overedge, 277
serging overcast, 275
shirring, 278
simulated hand, 279
single-needle lockstitch, 280
smocking, 280
three-stitch zigzag, 275
two-stitch zigzag, 275
machine understitching, 311
machine-worked buttonhole, 207
with cord, 208
magnet, 148, 323
manual cloth notcher, 88
manual spreader, 99
marker, 103
marking, 40, 51-53
marking pencil, 148
master pattern, 25
mending thread, 124
mercerization, 121
mercerized cotton thread, 123
heavy duty, 124
Merrow®, 272
metallic thread, 125
milliners needle, 109
mitered hem, 229
mitering, 302

mock flat-felled seam, 249
mock safety stitch, 277
model form, 19
    verifying, 50
model arm form, 19
modified back stitch, 263
moiré
    pattern layout, 80
monocord nylon thread, 126
monofilament thread, 126
motif design fabric
    pattern layout, 79
motor-driven scissors, 94
mucilage, 140, 323
multi-plies, 104
multi-ply layout, 73
muslin, 19
    balancing, 38
    grainlines, 42
    guide lines, 42
muslin proof, 56

napery stitch, 267
napped fabric structure, 64
    pattern layout, 80
neckline curve, 16
neckline zipper, skirt or, 213, 324
needle
    ball point
        hand sewing, 107
        sewing machine, 113-14
    betweens, 107
    calyx-eyed, 107
    chenilles, 108
    cotton darners, 108
    crewel, 109
    curved, 108
    embroidery, 109
    glovers, 109
    hand sewing, 106-10, 323
    leather point, 115
    milliners, 109
    parts of, 111
    round point, 116-18
    sailmakers, 110
    set point, 116-18
    sewing machine, 111-20, 323
    sharps, 109
    straws, 109
    Suggested Needle Sizes for Industrial Thread, 138
    tapestry, 110
    tufting, 110
    twin, 119
    yarn darners, 108
needle board, 318
needle threader, 148, 323
net binding, 225
net-bound seam finish, 251
net fabric structure, 64
New stitch 801, 279
non-roll ribbed elastic, 176, 323
non-slip-belting, 141, 323
    backed straight waistband, 288
nonwoven fabric structure, 61
no-sew snap, 194, 323
    parts of, 194
no-sew snap setter, 153
no-sew tape, 195, 323
notcher, 20. See also cloth notcher
notches, 47
notching, 103, 306
notions and findings, 323-25

nylon snap, 323
nylon thread, 126
    Thread/Fabric Selection Guide, 137

Oak Tag, 20
off grain, 69
on grain, 70
100% polyester thread, 128
one-piece facing, 181
one-way design fabric
    pattern layout, 78
one-way spreader, 99
opening in skins, 208
openings. See buttonhole
open-ply spread layout, 74
open slit buttonhole, 208
open welt seam, 248
outside applied casing, 173
outside curved seam, 259
outside facing, 180
overall buckle, 185, 323
overcast seam finish
    double-ply, 255
    single-ply, 254
    whipped, 255
overcasting stitch, 266
overedge machine stitch, 275
overedged hem, 230
overedged seam, 243
overhanding stitch, 267

padded hem, 230
padded seam, 243
padding stitch, 267
paired rings, 193, 323
pajama webbing, 177
panels, 43
paper shears, 96
paper strips, 318
parallel rule, 23
patch
    applied, 297
    reinforcing, 298
patch slit, 205
pattern
    balancing patternmaking lines, 31
    basic, 25
    block, 25
    break point line, 31
    commercial, 55
    compromise, 33
    cutting guide line, 32
    draft, 32
    drafted, 55
    draped, 55
    equalize, 33
    final, 33
    foundation, 25
    graded, 56
    grainline indicator, 33
    identification, 34
    interlocking of pieces, 102
    layout. See pattern layout
    master, 25
    muslin proof, 56
    perimeter, 103
    pivoting, 34
    production, 56
    right angle line, 36
    roll line, 35
    sloper, 25, 35

squared line, 36
standard block, 57
test muslin, 56
trade block, 57
types of, 54-57
pattern hook, 21
pattern identification, 34
pattern layout, 75-83, 102
   animal skin, 76
   border design fabric, 76
   border fabric, 76
   check fabric, 77
   diagonal design fabric, 77
   diagonal weave fabric, 77
   directional design fabric, 78
   irregular design fabric, 79
   knit fabric, 79
   one-way design fabric, 78
   large print fabric, 79
   light-reflecting fabric, 80
   motif design fabric, 79
   napped design fabric, 80
   pile fabric, 81
   plaid fabric, 81, 82
   plastic fabric, 82
   striped fabric, 82, 83
   twill type fabric, 78
pattern perforator, 92
pattern punch, 21
pattern string, 21
patternmaking paper, 21
patternmaking shears, 96
pencil, 22
   chalking, 148
   marking, 148
perimeter of pattern, 103
pick stitch, 268
picking stitch, 268
picot edging, 276
pile fabric structure, 65
   pattern layout, 81
pin
   ball point, 149, 323
   large head, 149, 323
   push pin, 22
   straight, 22, 150, 323
   T-head, 151, 323
   "T" Pin, 151
pin basting, 162
pin cushion, 151, 323
pin markings, 53
pin tack, 309
pin tucks, 13
pinked flat hem, 227
pinked seam finish, 255
   double-stitched, 257
   stitched, 256
pinking shears, 96
pinning, 40
piped seam, 244
piping, 168
   corded, 166
   French, 167
   welt, 168
pivot point, 34
pivoting, 34, 306
placket, 234-37
   band, 235
   bound, 235
   continuous lap, 235, 236
   dress, 236
   faced-slashed, 236

   hemmed-edge, 237
   seam, 236
   shirtsleeve, 237
   tab, 235
   tailored, 237
plaid
   pattern layout
      balanced plaid, 81
      even plaid, 81
      unbalanced plaid, 81
      uneven plaid, 82
plain hem, 227
plain seam, 243
plain weave, 66
plastic fabric structure, 66
   pattern layout, 82
pleat, 6
   accordion, 6
   box, 7
   crystal, 7
   dimensional, 1
   flat, 1
   inverted, 7
   kick, 8
   knife, 8
   side, 8-9
   sunburst, 9
plies, 104
ply, 104
point and tube turner, 158, 324
point paper, 20
point presser, 318
polyester thread, 127-28
   Thread/Fabric Selection Guide, 137
poodle cloth, 65
portable steam presser, 315
pounding block, 319
powdered chalk, 152, 323
press
   click, 86
   die cutting, 86
   foot, 314
   point presser, 318
   steam, 314
press basting, 162
press mitt, 319
press-on tape, 141
pressing, 322
   tools and equipment, 312-21
pressing buck, 314
pressing cloth, 319
pressing form, 317
pressing pad, 320
prick stitch, 263
production eased seam, 240
production pattern, 56
prong, 189
puff iron, 314
pull-out overedge machine stitch, 276
punch
   eyelet setter, 152, 323
   hole punch, 153, 323
   no-sew snap setter, 153, 323
purl edging, 276
push pins, 22

quilting thread, 128

ratchet buckle, 185, 323
raw edge, 306
razor blade, 93
razor knife, 93

regulation zipper, 213
reinforced button, 202
reinforcing, 306
reinforcing patch, 298
released tucks, 13
reversible zipper, 214, 324
rib knit, 62
rib-type braid, 175
ribbed elastic, 323
ribbing band, 292, 323
ribbon-backed straight waistband, 288
ribbon braid, 175
ribbon, elastic, 176
ribbon-faced waistline, 284
ribbon seam binding, 142, 232
ribbon waistband, 286
right angle line, 36
roll, 307
roll line, 35
rolled hem
    hand, 230
    machine, 231
rolled seam edge, 261
rolled seam finish, 251
rolling, 307
rouleau, 206
round point needle, 116-18
    Machine Needle/Fabric Selection Guide, 116-18
rubberized belting, 141, 323
rubberized-belting-backed straight waistband, 288
ruler, 23
    adjustable L-square, 18
    center finding rule, 23
    centimeter stick, 24
    clear plastic, 24
    combination ruler and curve, 15
    L square, 18
    parallel rule, 23
    see through T square, 26
    six-inch, 24
    T square, 25
    tailor's square, 18
    transparent, 24
    vertical rule, 24
    yardstick, 24
running stitch, 268

saddle stitch, 268
safety stitch, 277
    mock, 277
safety-stitched seam, 244
sailmakers needle, 110
satin weave, 66
scallop edging, 277
scallop gauge, 146
scallop overedge, 277
scalloping shears, 97
scissors, 84-85. *See also* shears
    blade tips, 85
    buttonhole, 93
    embroidery, 94
    motor-driven, 94
    sewing, 94
    weaver's, 100
seam, 9, 238-49, 258-61
    abutted, 239
    animal skins, 245
    butted, 239
    corded piped, 239
    crossed, 260
    eased, 239
    enclosed, 259

    exposed, 260
    extended seam edge, 260
    false French, 241
    finish. *See* seam finishes
    flat-felled, 246
    French, 240
    fur, 244
    fused, 241
    glued, 241
    hairline, 242
    inside curved, 259
    intersecting, 260
    Jeans, 240
    lace, 245
    lapped, 242
    mock flat-felled, 249
    open welt, 248
    outside curved, 259
    overedged, 243
    padded, 243
    piped, 244
    plain, 243
    production eased, 240
    rolled seam edge, 261
    safety-stitched, 244
    simulated French, 241
    skins, 245
    slot, 245
    stayed, 246
    strapped, 246
    taped, 247
    tissue-stitched, 247
    top-stitched, 248
    tucked, 248
    welt, 248, 249
    zigzagged, 249
seam allowance, 48
    extended, 260
seam binding, 142, 232
seam with ease, 239, 240
seam finish, 250-57
    book, 251
    bound, 251, 252
    double-stitched, 252, 253
    edge-stitched, 253
    glued, 254
    net-bound, 251
    overcast, 254
    pinked, 255, 256
    plain, 256
    rolled, 251
    serging, 256
    turned under edge, 253
    untreated, 256
    whipped, 255
seam line, 48
    directional, 48
seam placket, 236
seam ripper, 153
seam stick, 320
seamed waistline, 285
see-through T square, 26
self casing, 173
self facing, 181
self-filled bias tubing, 167
self-stick tape, 156
selvage, 70
selvedge, 70
separating zipper, 215, 324
serging, 256
serrated blade shears, 97
set, 322

set point needle, 116-18
   Machine Needle/Fabric Selection Guide, 116-18
sew-through button, 201, 323
   two-hole, 201
   four-hole, 201
sewing gauge, 146
sewing machine stitches. *See* machine stitches
sewing scissors, 94
shank button, 201, 323
   cloth, 201
   metal, 201
   plastic, 201
   self-mold, 201
   thread, 201
shape and design control, 1-13
shaped facing, 181
sharps needle, 109
shears. *See also* scissors
   ball-tipped, 95
   bent handle dressmaker's, 95
   bent trimmers, 95
   dressmaker's, 95
   knife edge, 97
   paper, 96
   patternmaking, 96
   pinking, 96
   scalloping, 97
   serrated blade, 97
   straight trimmers, 95
   synthetic fabric, 97
   tailor's, 97
shell stitch
   hand sewing, 269
   sewing machine, 278
shirring, 10
   elasticized, 10
   French, 11
   waffle, 11
shirring stitch, 278
shirtsleeve placket, 237
shoulder pads, 154, 323
shrink, 322
side pleat
   multiple, 9
   single, 8
silk thread, 129
   Thread/Fabric Selection Guide, 132
simulated French seam, 241
simulated hand stitch, 279
single-fold bias binding, 224
single-needle lockstitch, 280
single-ply overedged seam finish, 256
single-ply spread layout, 74
six-cord cotton thread, 129
   Thread/Fabric Selection Guide, 134
skin. *See* animal skin
skin, seams, 245
skirt marker, 154
skirt or neckline zipper, 213, 324
slash, 43, 308
   for design detail, 43
slash and spread, 35
slashing, 32, 40, 308
sleeve board, 320
sleeve gauge, 146
sleeve guide, 146
sleeve roll, 321
sleigh curve, 17
slip basting, 162
slip stitch, 269
sloper, 25, 35
slot buttonhole, 209
slot seam, 245

slot zipper insertion, 218
smocking
   hand, 12
   machine, 12
smocking stitch, 280
soutache braid loop, 206
snap, 193, 323
   covered, 194
   hammer-on, 194
   no-sew, 194
snap setter, no-sew, 153, 323
snap tape, 195, 323
   hammer-on, 195
   no-sew, 195
snipping, 302
soutache braid loop, 206
sponging, 322
squared line, 36
spanker, 319
sponge, 321
spreading, 105. *See also* fold layout
spring-and-hook type buckle, 185, 323
spun nylon thread, 127
spun polyester thread, 128
stand, 36
standard block pattern, 57
stay
   collar-pocket, 298, 323
   fabric, 299, 323
stay stitching, 308
stay strip, 155
stayed seam, 246
stayed waistline
   with ribbon, 285
   with tape or binding, 285
steam, 322
steam iron, 315
steam iron pressure tank, 315
steam press, 314
stiletto, 140, 323
stitched and pinked flat hem, 228
stitches. *See* hand stitches and machine stitches
straight pin, 22, 150, 323
   Straight Pin Specifications, 150
straight trimmers, 95
straight waistband, 287
   reinforced with commercial backing, 287
straightening, 70
strapped seam, 246
strapping, 299
straws needle, 109
stretch waistband, 288
stripe
   pattern layout
      balanced stripe, 82
      even stripe, 83
      unbalanced stripe, 83
      uneven stripe, 83
style line, 49
style tape, 25
sunburst pleat, 9
support
   boning, 155
   collar-pocket stay, 298
   feather boning, 155
   stay strip, 155
suspender clip, 195, 323
sweep of the hem, 49
swimwear
   elastic, 178
   hook, 189
synthetic fabric shears, 97

T-head pin, 151, 323
  T-Head Pin Specifications, 151
"T" Pin, 25
T-square, 25
  see-through, 26
tab, 196
tab placket, 235
table
  cutting table, 90
  work table, 129
tack
  back, 309
  bar, 270, 309
  pin, 309
tack marker, tailor's, 26
tack stitch
  arrowhead, 270
  bar, 270, 309
  French, 270
  triangular, 270
tacks, tailor's, 53
tailor basting, 161
tailored buttonhole, 209
tailored placket, 237
tailor's chalk, 26
tailor's ham, 321
tailor's shears, 97
tailor's square, 18
tailor's tack marker, 26
tailor's tacks, 53
tailor's thimble, 157, 323
tailor's wax, 27
tape
  double-faced, 155, 323
  hook and eye, 191, 323
  hook and loop, 192, 323
  iron-on seam binding, 141, 231, 323
  lace seam binding, 142, 231, 323
  press-on, 141, 231, 323
  ribbon seam tape, 142, 232, 323
  seam binding, 142, 232, 323
  self-stick, 156, 323
  snap, 195
  tissue, 156, 323
  transparent, 28, 323
  twill, 156, 323
  Velcro®, 192
tape measure, 27
taped seam, 247
tapestry needle, 110
temperature regulated iron, 316
temporary dart, 36
test muslin pattern, 56
thimble, 157, 323
  tailor's, 157, 323
thread, 121-38
  bonded invisible (Nymo®), 126
  button and carpet, 123
  cotton, 123
    Thread/Fabric Selection Guide, 133
  dacron
    Thread/Fabric Selection Guide, 137
  darning, 124
  elastic, 177
  embroidery, 124
  glazing, 121
  hank, 130
  industrial, 125
    needle sizes, 138
    physical properties, 138
    ticket numbers, 138
  invisible, 126, 127
  mending, 124

  mercerized, 121, 123, 124
  metallic, 125
  monocord nylon, 126
  monofilament, 126
  nylon, 126, 127
  nylon and dacron
    Thread/Fabric Selection Guide, 137
  polyester, 127, 128
    Thread/Fabric Selection Guide, 137
  quilting thread, 128
  silk, 129
    Thread/Fabric Selection Guide, 132
  six-cord cotton, 129
    Thread/Fabric Selection Guide, 134
  spun nylon, 127
  spun polyester, 128
  twisted invisible, 127
  waxed, 121, 130-31
    Thread/Fabric Selection Guide, 135
  yarn, 131
thread clippers, 100
thread eye, 196
thread hank, 130
thread loop, 207
thread marker, cutting room, 90
thread snips, 100
thread tracing, 53
tie belt, 282
ties, 196
tissue-stitched seam, 247
tissue tape, 156
toggle, 197, 323
top-stitched seam, 248
  double, 248
top stitching, 310
tracing, 51-53
tracing board, 27
tracing paper, 28
tracing wheel, 28
trade block pattern, 57
transferring, 49
transparent tape, 28
triangle, 29
  cutting table, 91
triangular tack stitch, 270
trimmers
  bent, 95
  straight, 95
trimming, 310
trouser fly zipper insertion, 219
trouser waistband, 289, 323
trouser zipper, 215
true bias, 68
trueing, 50
tubing
  cord-filled bias, 167
  self-filled bias, 167
tubular cording, 323
tubular knit, 62
tubular knit spreader, 99
tucked seam, 248
tucks
  dart, 5
  pin, 13
  released, 13
tufting needle, 110
turned flat hem, 227
turned under edge seam finish, 253
turner, 157-58, 323
  crease, 157
  loop, 158
  point and tube 158
twill tape, 156, 323

twill-type fabric
    pattern layout, 78
twill weave, 66
twin needle, 119
twisted invisible thread, 127
two-way zipper, 216, 324

underlay, 50, 300
    zipper with, 219
underlining, 296
underpress, 322
understitching
    hand, 311
    machine, 311
uneven basting, 163
unseamed waistline, 286
untreated seam finish, 256

vary form curve, 16
Velcro® fastener, 191, 323
Velcro® tape, 192, 323
velour
    pattern layout, 81
velvet board, 318
velveteen, 65
Venise lace, 63
verifying the form, 50

waffle shirring, 11
waistband. *See* waistline
waistband belting, 323
waistline, 281-89. *See also* belt
    bias-faced, 284
    built-up, 283
    casing, waistline with, 289
    contoured, 286
    curtain, 289
    elasticized, 283
    faced, 283
    insert, 284
    inset, 284
    non-slip-belting-backed straight waistband, 288
    ribbon, 286
    ribbon-backed straight waistband, 288
    ribbon-faced waistline, 284
    rubberized-belting-backed straight waistband, 288
    seamed, 285
    stayed, 285
    straight, 287
        reinforced with commercial backing, 287
    stretch, 288
    trouser, 289
    unseamed, 286
waistline with casing, 289
warp knitting, 62
wax, tailor's, 27
waxed thread, 130-31
    Thread/Fabric Selection Guide, 135
waxing, 121
weave
    plain, 66
    satin, 66
    twill, 66
weaver's scissors, 100
webbing
    elastic, 177
    pajama, 177
weft knitting, 62
weighted hem, 232-33
weights, 100, 324
    chain, 158, 233, 324
    in garments, 300
    lead disc, 159, 232, 324
    lead pellet, 159, 232, 324

welt bound buttonhole, 204
welt piping, 168
welt seam, 249
    double, 249
whip stitch, 271
whipped seam finish, 255
wired hem, 233
work table, 29
    portable, 29
worked-thread loop, 207
working dart, 36
woven fabric structure, 66
yardstick, 24
yarn, 131
yarn darners needle, 108

zigzag seam finish
    double-ply, 257
    single-ply, 257
zigzagged seam, 249
zipper, 211-21
    application, 217
    centered zipper insertion, 218
    chain-constructed, 211
    closed end, 213
    coil-constructed, 211
    conventional, 211, 213
    decorative, 213, 324
    dress, 213, 324
    dress placket insertion, 217
    dual opening, 216, 324
    exposed zipper, 217
    fly-front concealed, 218
    industrial, 213
    insertion, 217
    invisible, 211, 214, 324
    lap zipper insertion, 218
    parts of, 212
    regulation, 211, 213
    reversible, 214, 324
    separating, 211, 215, 324
    side seam zipper insertion, 217
    skirt or neckline, 213, 324
    slot zipper insertion, 218
    trouser, 215
    trouser fly zipper insertion, 219
    two-way, 216, 324
    underlay, zipper with, 219
zipper application
    hand-stitched, 217
    machine-stitched, 217
zipper foot attachments
    adjustable (left or right), 219
    cording foot, 221
    grooved (invisible zipper), 220
    one-sided, 221
    roller (invisible zipper), 220
    single-toed, 221
    slit, 221
    two-toed, 221
zipper insertion
    centered, 218
    dress placket, 217
    exposed decorative, 217
    exposed industrial, 217
    exposed zipper in a slash, 217
    fly-front concealed, 218
    lap zipper, 218
    side seam, 217
    slot zipper, 218
    trouser fly, 219
    zipper with underlay, 219
zipper lubricant, 324
zipper with underlay, 219